AF845029

ECONOMIC HISTORY

A SHORT HISTORY OF THE WORLD'S SHIPPING INDUSTRY

BUSINESS HISTORY

A SHORT HISTORY OF THE WORLD'S SHIPPING INDUSTRY

C. ERNEST FAYLE

Routledge
Taylor & Francis Group
LONDON AND NEW YORK

First published in 1933

Published in 2006 by
Routledge
2 Park Square, Milton Park, Abingdon, Oxfordshire OX14 4RN
711 Third Avenue, New York, NY 10017

First issued in paperback 2015

Routledge is an imprint of the Taylor and Francis Group, an informa business

© 1933 C. Ernest Fayle

All rights reserved. No part of this book may be reprinted or reproduced or utilized in any form or by any electronic, mechanical, or other means, now known or hereafter invented, including photocopying and recording, or in any information storage or retrieval system, without permission in writing from the publishers.

The publishers have made every effort to contact authors and copyright holders of the works reprinted in the *Economic History* series. This has not been possible in every case, however, and we would welcome correspondence from those individuals or organisations we have been unable to trace.

These reprints are taken from original copies of each book. In many cases the condition of these originals is not perfect. The publisher has gone to great lengths to ensure the quality of these reprints, but wishes to point out that certain characteristics of the original copies will, of necessity, be apparent in reprints thereof.

British Library Cataloguing in Publication Data
A CIP catalogue record for this book
is available from the British Library

A Short History of the World's Shipping Industry
ISBN 0-415-28619-0 (set)
ISBN13: 978-0-415-61291-3 (pbk)
ISBN13: 978-0-415-38163-5 (hbk)

Routledge Library Editions: Economic History

A SHORT HISTORY OF THE WORLD'S SHIPPING INDUSTRY

By the same Author

SEABORNE TRADE
Official History of the Great War

THE WAR AND THE SHIPPING INDUSTRY

With Charles Wright
A HISTORY OF LLOYD'S

A SHORT HISTORY OF THE
WORLD'S SHIPPING INDUSTRY

by

C. ERNEST FAYLE

With a Foreword by

SIR ALAN G. ANDERSON, K.B.E.
Past-President of the Chamber of Shipping of the U.K.

LONDON
GEORGE ALLEN & UNWIN LTD
MUSEUM STREET

FIRST PUBLISHED IN 1933

All rights reserved

To My Wife

My helper in this Book

as in all things

FOREWORD

THERE may be a few neutrals but most of us either hate or love the sea. In these days of steadier and well-ventilated ships the number of sea lovers grows from year to year, and I am one of them.

In work and play, at sea and ashore, seamen and ships big and little, have made up much of my life, and just because I love the sea, and seamen, and ships, I open sea books with a qualm. Some authors, when they put to sea, wear yachting caps, hitch up their slacks, cut a hornpipe caper, and generally indulge in what R. L. S. calls "tushery."

If any prospective reader shares my dislike for grimaces I assure him he will find none in this book. The author ranges through time and space and tells his tale with the dignity that his great subject deserves.

Moreover, although he compresses much into this book, he gives a surprising amount of the detail which is the sauce of any story, and in homely facts and plain figures he lights up those old rough voyages so that we can almost smell and suffer them; how rough they were; and how hard and brave the men; and, between ourselves, how business-like and matter of fact.

These mariners and shipowners and merchants of all nations and all ages would feel at home in the Baltic or the Chamber of Shipping to-day, and they knew just as well as we do who serve the sea to-day that to voyage safely and to succeed one must face facts: ships are always in fierce competition with waves and rocks and fogs and with other ships. No make-believe was good enough for those old mariners, no subsidies could command success then—nor can to-day.

ALAN G. ANDERSON

PREFACE

THE idea of this book arose in conversation with some very good friends of the British merchant seaman who were regretting their inability to put into his hands any comprehensive one-volume history of the shipping industry. What they wanted was something which would give him a picture of the way in which the business of carrying goods and passengers by sea had been carried on, from the earliest times to the present day, and of what it had stood for in the life of the world. Others besides seamen and those directly interested in shipping must have felt the lack of such a book. There are a great number of books, many of them very good, describing the development of the ship itself, from coracle to Cunarder, or telling the story of particular phases or particular periods of sea-trading; but the reader who wants to form a broad general picture of the development of the shipping industry and its contribution to human progress, must either fall back on the four ponderous volumes of Lindsay's *History of Merchant Shipping*, published more than half a century ago, or go to a large number of different authors and combine their information.

This volume is an attempt to fill the gap. Its object is to tell, in very broad outline, the story of shipping as a business; to describe the way in which, at each period of the world's history, merchant ships were owned and operated; to say something of the routes they followed and the cargoes they carried, the relations between shipowners and governments, and the conditions of life and work afloat. Above all, it attempts to bring out, as clearly as possible, the contribution which this greatest of key industries has made in each period to the development of the world's resources, the peopling of its open spaces, and the gradual building up of the civilization we see around us to-day.

Preface

In order to bring the story within the compass of a single volume, it has been necessary to leave out much on which it would have been pleasant to dwell. Improvements in ship design and construction have been referred to only when they arose from or brought about some fundamental change in the scope and methods of the shipowner's business, and the voyages of great explorers and navigators, with all their wealth of adventure, have been compressed into a sentence, to make room for a fuller account of the more prosaic commercial developments which those voyages made possible. The growth of the shipping industry itself is illustrated, at each stage, mainly from the history of those peoples who were then predominant at sea, and whose methods and achievements could be taken as most typical of the period.

Even within these limitations, nothing more than an outline picture could be given, and those who are specially interested in some particular aspect of the industry—social or economic—may sometimes feel that it has received too little attention. I can only plead that in striving to tell, as a continuous story, the history of the shipping industry as a whole, it has been necessary to jettison much that might properly be required in a separate treatment of any of its phases.

To those who wish to go a little further into the matter, the notes on books at the end of each chapter may afford some assistance. It need hardly be said that these notes do not pretend to form anything like a bibliography of the subject. They have been confined to books which I have found specially helpful, and as far as possible, to books which are fairly easily accessible.

I am indebted, as always, to the London Library and its staff, especially my friend, Mr. G. E. Mainwaring, for assistance and advice in the collection of material.

C. E. F.

CONTENTS

Contents

Contents

Contents

PROLOGUE

THE SEA AS BARRIER AND HIGHWAY

The unplumb'd, salt, estranging sea. MATTHEW ARNOLD

And seas but join the regions they divide. POPE

WHEN Mr. Rudyard Kipling coined the phrase "Transportation is Civilization," as a motto for his imaginary "Aerial Board of Control," he gave expression to about as much truth as can conveniently be packed into three words. It is possible, of course, to have doubts as to the precise value of the kind of civilization we see around us to-day. One thing is quite certain; it could not have been worked out by any single nation for itself. In order that the people of any country may live what we regard as a civilized life, they must be supplied with a wide variety of products which they have learned to regard as necessaries but which they could not possibly produce for themselves. We hear so much to-day about the desirability of nations being "self-sufficient" that we are apt to forget that the term can be used only in a very limited sense. It is possible, no doubt, to stimulate the production of those agricultural products which the soil of a country is capable of bearing, and to "encourage home industries" in so far as the raw materials for those industries are available; but no form of economic policy will enable us to raise coal, or iron, or copper, or tin, or manganese where nature has not chosen to put them, or to grow cotton, or tea, or rubber where the conditions of soil and climate are unsuitable.

It is often said that the originator of all the world's wealth is the actual producer: the person who grows or makes something, or grows or raises the materials from which things are made. That is true in a sense; transportation and marketing could not even exist if there were nothing to transport or sell. Nevertheless, a very large proportion of the world's production would be utterly useless if there were no means of transporting it far beyond the limits of the producing area. One district produces iron ore in abundance, but has hardly any coal wherewith to smelt it. Another, with rich coal seams, is poor in other materials. A third, destitute of coal or iron, has a tropical or semi-tropical climate which enables it to produce rubber or cotton. Each of them can produce far more than enough of its characteristic product for the immediate needs of its own inhabitants; but it is only when the iron ore can be carried to the coal, or the coal to the iron, and the products of the blast furnaces and iron foundries exchanged for rubber and cotton, that the full productive power of each region can be utilized, and a full and varied life made possible for their inhabitants. The growth of civilization, on its material side, is bound up with the process by which the resources of the world have been pooled, and the specialized products of every land made available to humanity as a whole. This is the work of transport.

Alongside with this exchange of goods has gone on the interchange of ideas. Each nation has developed, in accordance with its racial characteristics and circumstances, its own institutions, its own schools of art and literature, and its own way of looking at social, religious, and political problems. But behind all these things is a common stock of fundamental ideas and traditions, built up from the contributions of thinkers, and artists, and philosophers in many lands. The ideas of Roman lawyers, and English legislators, and French philosophers, and German scientists are reflected in the institutions and the thoughts of every nation that we can call civilized. Our theories of life, our fashions in dress and manners and amusements are continually being affected by the ideas and habits of peoples living hundreds and even thousands of miles away from us.

This interchange of ideas has been very closely connected with the development of commerce. Even the wandering missionary, or teacher, or student, has usually been glad, like St. Paul, to follow the routes opened up by traders, and to take his passage in a merchant ship. Merchants themselves, travelling with their goods, and the crews of ships "trading foreign" played a very large part in the development of social and intellectual intercourse between the peoples of widely-sundered lands, and when once the traders had shown the way, tourists and emigrants soon followed, to satisfy the curiosity aroused by travellers' tales, or to seek a new opening in new countries. Wherever they went, they took with them not merely the products but the thoughts and fashions and habits of their own country, and when they returned they brought new ideas as well as rare and strange commodities.

Some nations, in the course of history, have had isolation imposed upon them by circumstances; others have made it deliberately an object of policy. Such nations have not necessarily remained savage or barbarous (though many have done so, like the Red Indians or the Australian aborigines); but not only have the benefits of their national development been lost to the rest of the world; that development itself has become stunted and sterile through the in-breeding of ideas. The civilization discovered by the Spaniards in Peru, and the civilizations evolved by the Chinese and Japanese during the long centuries when they refused all intercourse with the outside world, had many wonderful and beautiful features; in some respects they were much finer than the contemporary civilization of any European country. But they were not, like the European civilizations, stimulated by daily contact with fresh ideas and alien ways of life, and for all their beauty they had become narrow and unprogressive. They had ceased to grow, and whatever has ceased to grow has already begun to decay.

Civilization therefore must expand—must establish contacts with other civilizations—or perish of inanition. Nor, as we have seen, can civilization be carried very far on the material side, without the means of bringing together products seldom or never found side by side. The Bronze Age, for instance, came early in the history of man's development; but for bronze you need copper and tin, and the sources of both, of tin especially, were widely scattered. Even where local supplies existed they often were soon exhausted, and it was necessary to look far afield for their replacement.

Yet while Nature herself, by the capricious distribution of her gifts, urged man to travel, Nature had set boundaries and obstacles to his progress. Long chains of mountains, waterless deserts, wide and impassable swamps, and the impenetrable tangle of the primaeval forests, hemmed in on every side the settlements in which primitive man took his first step on the long upward journey. The great tribal migrations by which the inhabited area of the earth was gradually extended, must often have been checked by these barriers, or passed them only at fearful cost of life and suffering. Even when one convulsive effort had carried a migrating tribe across a belt of sandy wastes or densely wooded highlands, these remained as a practically insuperable obstacle to any regular intercourse, and above all, to any regular exchange of bulky commodities with people living on the other side. We must not underrate the engineering skill of such peoples as those who brought the gigantic monoliths of Stonehenge to Salisbury Plain and erected them there in accordance with a regular design, and we know that remarkable work in clearing and drainage and road-making was done in prehistoric times; but the majority of ancient communities were shut off from each other in an isolation which it is difficult to picture to ourselves to-day.

It was natural, therefore, that men should make as much use as possible of the great highways that Nature herself had provided: the broad rivers whose smooth surface presented no obstacles (except where interrupted by cataracts), and could be utilized without any expenditure of labour in felling trees or beating out a pathway. Even where good roads existed, or could be made with comparative ease, water-transport was always easier and cheaper than land-transport for the carriage of bulky commodities over long distances. That is true even to-day, and that is why, for instance, millions of tons of coal, exported from Germany to Italy, go down the Rhine to the Dutch ports and follow the long sea route down the English Channel, and across the Bay of Biscay, along the coast of Portugal, through the Straits of Gibraltar, and up the Mediterranean to Genoa or Naples, instead of following a much shorter route by land. To-day, however, the choice between rail and water transport, when both are available, turns mainly on the question of comparative cost. In the dawn of civilization, it must often have been decided by the sheer inability of ox-carts and camel-train to carry the loads required.

It was convenience of transport, as well as the supply of water for irrigation, that led to the growth of the earliest civilizations on the banks of navigable rivers. The Nile was not only the source of the fertility of Egypt; it was the link that bound the whole country together, and even in the earliest days practically the whole traffic of the country flowed up and down its stream.

Down the rivers, or by the land tracks through forest and marsh and desert, men came at last to the sea—the ultimate barrier, as it seemed, to all further progress. What, if anything, lay beyond it they could not tell, and gradually the legend grew up in many countries of the "ocean flood," the great waste of waters, with no further shore, which encircled the inhabited world.

Even when, greatly daring, men began to put to sea on rafts, or in dug-out canoes, for the purpose of fishing, of reaching some island visible from the shore, or of visiting the next bay on the coast without the trouble of hacking a way through the forest or climbing a rocky headland, the idea of putting out into the open sea was too strange to occur to any but the mad, the desperate, or the heroic. The ships of ancient times were too frail to stand heavy weather; too small to be provisioned for long voyages. Their crews had no means of directing their course, once the familiar landmarks were out of sight, save by observation of the sun by day and the stars by night. At the end of the voyage there might be—nothing, or anything. If the unknown coasts existed at all, they might be peopled with man-eaters, or demons. The way to them was beset with nameless terrors; for down to times we think of as comparatively modern, the sea was the place where anything was possible. So late as the sixteenth century after Christ it was thought necessary to warn an explorer setting out to discover a north-east passage to Asia

> to beware of the artifices of certain creatures, which with heads of men and tails of fish swim about with bows and arrows in the fiords and bays and live on human flesh.

When we think of the superstitious terrors with which our forefathers peopled the unknown, of the cockleshells in which they went to sea, and of their almost complete lack of geographical knowledge and scientific aids to navigation, we cannot wonder that for many centuries after a busy trade had grown up in the Mediterranean and along the coasts of northern Europe, the open ocean still remained as a final bar to men's activities, and America and Australia lay unknown and unsuspected.

Pioneers of the Sea Routes

The pioneers who opened up the sea routes were, in many instances, pirates seeking loot along the coasts, fugitives fleeing from an invader, emigrants driven out of their own land by the pressure of hard times, or explorers animated by curiosity and love of adventure. But the work of the explorers would have been thrown away, and the colonies founded by emigrants or fugitives would have perished, if they had not been followed by the sea-carriers, the people who made their living out of providing a reliable, regular means of communication by sea between countries whose products could not readily, or could not possibly, be exchanged by land.

It is with these people that we have to deal. At first they were mostly merchants, who had ships built to carry their own goods to distant markets, or to seek out new ones. Yet even in very early days a merchant who had no ship might have goods that would command a ready sale oversea, and the owner of a ship might be short of goods to fill her, and ready, at a price, to carry other people's goods as well as his own. As the volume of commerce increased, this side of the business became a paying game, and the experienced skipper, who could save or borrow money enough to build a ship, found that there were plenty of merchants eager to charter her. Still later came the monied man who did not go to sea himself, but laid out part of his money in having ships built to his orders, and engaging skilled navigators to command and skilled business men to manage them. All three types are with us to-day. The oil, or coal, or fruit company which owns (perhaps through a subsidiary) its own tankers or freighters, corresponds to the old merchant shipowner. The enterprising Greek skipper whose ships could be hired by all and sundry has his counterpart in the tramp ship-master who is owner or part owner of his vessel. The Roman capitalist with a ship or two in the Alexandrine corn trade was the forerunner of hundreds of shipping firms and companies of to-day.

These are the people who, during the course of many centuries, have gradually converted the sea from the ultimate barrier to human progress into the great highway which has made the whole world one. It is their story which this book will try to tell, in very broad outline, and with many omissions, for it will only be possible to deal with the outstanding features in each stage of the development of the shipping industry.

First of all we shall see how the sea-traders of Egypt, Phoenicia, and Greece linked together Europe and Asia, and gradually spread commerce, and with commerce civilization, over the whole of the Mediterranean Sea. The work began in times which are almost prehistoric; it received its crown during the first two centuries of the Christian era, the golden age of the Roman Empire, when the whole Western world was united under a single rule, and a period of unexampled peace and prosperity led to an immense increase in the volume of trade, and a rapid development in the technique of shipowning (Chapter I).

This golden age was succeeded by a long period of stagnation and decay, during the decline and break-up of the Roman Empire, and the Dark Ages which followed. Then, with the rise of the Italian City States, there came a second Mediterranean epoch, which we may roughly identify with the period of Venetian greatness, from the eleventh to the fifteenth century. The Mediterranean itself was still the centre of trade and civilization; but the Venetian merchant-galleasses and the Genoese carracks were stretching far afield, and pouring Mediterranean produce and the riches of the East into the ports of northern Europe. The methods of carrying on the shipping industry will strike us at first as crude and primitive compared with those of the Romans; but latterly the development of commercial organization was rapid; banking and insurance came to the aid of shipping, and we shall come across elaborate Charter-parties, careful regulation of wages and conditions afloat, and the first foreshadowing of the Plimsoll mark and the classification of shipping (Chapter II).

Overlapping this second Mediterranean epoch came the development of the shipping industry in Northern Europe, based mainly on the distribution of the herring catch and of English wool. It was dominated throughout by the Hansa, the League of German merchant cities, who built up immense wealth and great political power on their predominance in the carrying trade; but we shall see English seamen learning their job in the Bordeaux wine trade, and the pilgrim traffic (Chapter III).

Meanwhile, the arts of shipbuilding and of navigation had made a great advance, and at the end of the fifteenth century the voyages of explorers like Vasco da Gama, Columbus, and Magellan, altered the whole balance of the world. The opening of a direct sea route to India cut at the very roots of the prosperity of the Mediterranean States. Across the Atlantic there was a new world to be peopled and exploited. Throughout the sixteenth and seventeenth centuries, oceanic expansion was rapid, and the influx of precious metals from Mexico and Peru changed the whole basis of Europe's economic life and gave an unprecedented impetus to the accumulation of capital. The Spanish and Portuguese led the way, but they were conquerors rather than traders, and the real development of ocean trade was left mainly to the English and Dutch, who developed it chiefly by means of great Chartered Companies. The lead, at first, was taken by the Dutch, who, succeeding also to the position of the Hansa as masters of the Northern fisheries, proved themselves the most efficient shipowners the world had ever seen, and got a great part of the world's carrying trade into their hands (Chapters IV, V, and VI).

As the colonies planted in the sixteenth and early seventeenth centuries grew up, ocean trade became more and more important. Every country was bent on planting new colonies, or conquering other peoples', and monopolizing their commerce, and especially their carrying trade. In the course of the long struggle, lasting roughly from 1650 to 1815, Great Britain gradually pushed her way to the front, as the first of naval, commercial, and shipowning Powers, and the United States became a nation. Throughout this period the shipping industry was being gradually modernized. Except in the East Indies trade, the Chartered Companies gave way to the individual merchant and shipowner, and though many, perhaps most, shipowners were also engaged in trade, the "shipping interest"—the people who looked mainly to the freight market for their profit—began to emerge as distinct from the general body of commercial men (Chapters VII and VIII).

The close of the struggle for maritime supremacy coincided with the beginnings of the Industrial Revolution in Great Britain, and it was followed by a period of rapid growth in industry and population, which was further stimulated, about the middle of the nineteenth century, by gold discoveries in California and Australia. The increased demand for carrying-power, both for trade and for emigration, was met by the culmination of the sailing vessel in the Clipper Ship and by the simultaneous development of the steamer as the rival and destined supplanter of the sailing vessel herself. Under the combined pressure of new conditions and new economic ideas, the restrictions imposed by national jealousies on the carrying trade were finally broken down, and Governments began to turn their attention from the protection of the shipping industry to measures for increasing its efficiency, for ensuring the safety of life and property afloat, and for improving the conditions of employment, which had sadly deteriorated since the Middle Ages.

Despite the withdrawal of protection, British shipping continued to maintain its predominance—at one time seriously challenged by the Americans—and British shipowners led the way in the change-over from wood and sail to iron (or steel) and steam, on which our modern industrial civilization is based. It was the rapid multiplication of carrying-power by steam which transformed oversea commerce, during the nineteenth century, from a means for the enrichment of life into a necessity of life itself (Chapter IX).

Side by side with this revolution in the carrying trade there took place a revolution in the technique of shipowning; in which the speeding-up of communications by the electric cable, and the facilities for the employment of capital provided by the limited liability company, played as important a part as that of steam itself. The regular trades fell more and more into the hands of big liner companies, while the growth of tramp tonnage facilitated the adjustment of supply to demand, and assisted in the development of a world pool of tonnage, composed of ships under many flags, on which all nations could draw as need required (Chapter X).

The closing years of the nineteenth century and the opening years of the twentieth were marked by increasingly severe competition in the shipping industry, largely international in character. This affected particularly the management of the liner trades, in which it led to the establishment of the "Conference" System and a growing tendency to amalgamation and the formation of huge "Combines." The shipping industry as a whole became more closely organized, and better organization, as well as an increased stringency of Government regulations, played its part in a notable improvement of conditions afloat. The Great War of 1914–1918, while it led to a revival of economic nationalism which has cursed the world with a heavy burden of surplus tonnage and threatened it with a revival of obsolete restrictions on the carrying trade, led also to a new realization of the necessity for international co-operation in the attainment of common interests. It is the growing recognition of such common interests in the welfare of the world's key industry that affords the best hope for the future prosperity either of those who own or those who man the ships by which all countries are linked together in one great economic organism (Chapters XI and XII).

CHAPTER I

"SHIPS OF TARSHISH"

THE SEA-TRADERS OF ANTIQUITY

And say unto Tyrus, O thou that art situate at the entry of the sea, which art a merchant of the people for many isles . . . all the ships of the sea with their mariners were in thee to occupy thy merchandise. . . . The ships of Tarshish did sing of thee in thy market. EZEKIEL xxvii. 3, 9, 25

So many are the merchant vessels that arrive here that Rome has practically become a common workshop for the whole world. . . . There are always ships putting into or sailing out of the harbour. ARISTIDES

IT is a very good rule, in telling a story, to begin at the beginning; but it is not at all an easy rule to follow in telling the story of any of the main branches of human activity. Primitive man had taken the most important steps on his progress to civilization long before he was able to leave any permanent, connected record of his doings: he had found out, for instance, how to make fire, to sow grain and to reap it, to shape tools, and to weave fabrics. We can learn a great deal about the way he went to work from the implements and fragments of pottery dug up by archeologists and from a study of the backward races of to-day, but our knowledge is far too scrappy for the writing of a detailed, consecutive narrative. The earliest peoples of whom we have any clear, connected account, were already civilized peoples, living in settled, orderly communities, and skilful in arts and industries.

Shipping is no exception to the general rule. We can, if we like, make a picture in our minds of our remote ancestors being carried down stream in flood-time on a fallen tree-trunk or a mass of floating brushwood, and we can go on to imagine the stages by which, in the course of centuries, they learned how to hollow out the tree trunk so as to form a clumsy canoe or to tie a bundle of reeds together to serve as a raft. We can guess how the punt pole or paddle developed from a mere aimless splashing in the water with a bit of wood, and the sail from a piece of bark held up to catch the wind. There is a great fascination in all this, but it is not history, and it belongs to the story of the ship rather than to the story of shipping as a business.

At first, no doubt, the dug-out and reed-raft were used only for crossing rivers, for moving from one hunting ground to another, for fishing close inshore along the coast, or perhaps for carrying the warriors of the tribe on a raid. At a later stage, the members of little settlements, strung out along the banks of a great river or dotted along the seashore, would find room in their canoes for a few skins, or weapons, or earthen pots, to be bartered for similar primitive products with the people of other tiny communities. This stage, too, was prehistoric. Long before the point is reached at which we can begin to base our knowledge of the past on written, painted, or sculptured records, the dug-out and reed-raft had developed into the sea-going ship, capable of carrying passengers and an appreciable quantity of cargo between port and port with a reasonable degree of certainty. The shipping industry goes much further back than any history we can write of it.

Some great scholars believe that there is evidence of direct intercourse by sea between Babylonia and India three thousand years before the birth of Christ, and this would imply previous centuries of trading and exploration along the coasts of Asia. It is practically certain that a people living in Crete had sufficiently regular communication with Greece and Egypt to exchange goods and ideas some time between 4000 and 3000 B.C. All this, however, rests on inferences from such scraps of evidence as the finding in one place of a type of pottery known to have been produced in another. Our first definite record of sea-borne trade on a large scale comes, as might be expected, from Egypt.

From the earliest times the Nile was the highway of Egypt, and by 3500 B.C., if not before, the original reed-rafts used on the great river had developed into ships, propelled by oars and sails, of substantial carrying capacity. Once possessed of such ships, it could be only a question of time before the Egyptians used them for voyages beyond the Nile Delta, especially for the purpose of avoiding the difficult overland route through Palestine and Syria. Egypt itself produced almost all that was required, in those early days, for the needs of its inhabitants; but there was always a shortage of big timber, and we learn from the Egyptian records that somewhere about 3000 B.C. King Snefru sent out a fleet of forty ships to Phoenicia, to bring back great baulks of cedar, cut in the forests of Lebanon. This is really the starting point of our history; for the number of the ships, the length of the voyage, and the bulky nature of the return cargo, all go to prove that this was no pioneering expedition, but an indication of steady, established trade between Egypt and the Phoenician ports.

For the next fifteen hundred or two thousand years our knowledge of what was happening on the sea is very scanty. There are abundant traces of intercourse between Egypt, Syria, Crete, Cyprus, and Greece, but we cannot speak confidently as to its character. In the absence of decipherable written records it is often impossible to say whether goods of foreign origin, found when excavating some lost city, were acquired by trade, or carried there by emigrants, or sent as tribute by conquered peoples, or simply brought back as loot by pirates. We know that Crete was the centre not merely of a highly cultured civilization but of a great sea-power, with colonies or trading stations on the mainland of Greece and the islands of the Aegean; but it is extremely doubtful how far the goods which filled the storehouses of Knossos were the fruits of commerce, piracy, or conquest.

The Egyptians, at least, were definitely a trading people. Under the great kings Thutmose III and Ramses II (roughly from 1300 to 1225 B.C.), Egypt became a great naval power, with a fleet which exercised some measure of control over the whole of the Levant and the Aegean; but this fleet was used not merely for conquest but for the protection of an extensive sea-borne commerce. An efficient marine police patrolled the Delta, to give security against pirates. Custom Houses at all the ports provided for the supervision of the trade and the collection of dues. The King himself kept a large part of the traffic in his own hands; but the importance attached to the Customs shows that much of it was carried on by private merchants, and it was quite a common thing for a wealthy landowner to keep his own ship for the import of Asiatic luxuries from the Palestinian and Syrian ports.

From Phoenicia and Syria the Egyptians imported timber, dyed fabrics woven on Phoenician looms, gold and silver vessels chased by Phoenician craftsmen, and spices and aromatic woods brought by the caravans from Arabia and the East. Weapons, gold-mounted chariots, furniture of carved ivory or ebony, rare plants and animals, and delicacies for the table flowed in from Syria, Asia Minor, Cyprus, and the Aegean. Gold and silver, made up for commercial purposes in rings of fixed weight, were received mainly as tribute from vassal states.

Another route ran down the Red Sea to Punt (Somaliland). It was used for warlike and trading expeditions at least as early as 2500 B.C., and long before the time of Thutmose III, its superiority to the overland route had led to the creation of trading and victualling stations at intervals along the African coast. A ship canal led from the most easterly branch of the Nile, through the Bitter Lakes, to the Red Sea, thus enabling the vessels from Punt to bring their cargoes to the Nile ports, and anticipating by at least three thousand years one of the landmarks in the history of modern transport.

The principal imports from Punt were gold, ivory, ebony, and other woods valuable to the cabinet-maker, incense, cinammon, skins, and eye-cosmetic—this last a very modern touch! Small cattle were also imported, and wild animals, such as baboons and monkeys for the amusement of the kings, priests, and nobles.

A considerable proportion of the imports, both by the Mediterranean and the Red Sea routes, were probably paid for in gold and silver, originally received as tribute; but Egypt had also her own products to export; grain, fine linen, papyrus, cordage, pottery, glazed tiles, and oxhides. Probably, too, some of the imported products of Asia and Africa were exchanged against each other. Altogether, we get from the records the picture of an extensive and varied sea-borne commerce, quite apart from the trade carried on by the land routes.

The goods which poured down the Nile into Egypt were not all carried in Egyptian ships. Arabs, Cretans, and various peoples of Asia Minor took a share of the traffic; but of all the foreign merchants and shipowners who thronged the foreign quarter at Memphis, the most numerous and the most enterprising were the Phoenicians, and as the might of Egypt decayed, her trade fell largely into Phoenician hands.

The Phoenicians—the men of Tyre and Sidon, Berytus (Beyrut), and half a dozen other towns on what is now the Syrian coast—were undoubtedly the greatest seafarers and greatest merchants of remote antiquity. They were not merely traders but manufacturers, celebrated for the excellence of their textiles and embroideries, their metal-work, and their glassware. From a shellfish called the murex they obtained a very beautiful dye, and garments or hangings dipped in Tyrian purple were amongst the most treasured possessions of kings and rich men in every land. Nevertheless it was as traders and shipowners that the Phoenicians left their deepest mark.

It was their good fortune to be seated at the central focal point of the trade routes of the ancient world. Their cities were the western terminals of great caravan routes, bringing down to them the merchandise of Armenia, and Assyria, and Babylonia, and Persia, and even of the more remote East. Other routes led up from ports in Southern Arabia or on the Persian Gulf. The Phoenicians themselves were dwellers in seaports, with natural harbours, carefully improved by art. The forests of Lebanon provided them with abundant shipbuilding material. The sea gave them access to Egypt, Cyprus, Crete, and the shores of Asia Minor, and to the newer Mediterranean civilizations which were springing up in Greece and Italy, and they sent to Egypt not only timber and their own manufactures, but re-exports of Eastern produce, bronze vessels from Asia Minor, and works of art from Greece. In return they imported sail-cloth and cordage, papyrus, ivory and ebony, for all of which they could find a ready market not only at home but amongst the peoples of the Levant and Aegean. They shipped Egyptian grain also, not so much for their own use as to make good the shortage of corn in Southern Greece, and erected great storehouses on the island of Cythera (Cerigo) as a centre for its distribution.

At a very early date they began to establish trading stations and settlements for working local mines and exploiting local produce in the Levant and Aegean. As their skill in navigation increased and their population expanded, they pushed steadily westward, establishing a chain of colonies along the North African coast, in Sicily, and in Spain. The first of the African colonies seems to have been Utica on the Gulf of Tunis (about 1100 B.C.); Carthage, a few miles south-west of Utica, was incomparably the most famous. Not long after the founding of Utica they even ventured to pass beyond the "Pillars of Hercules" (Gibraltar) into the unknown ocean, the boundary of the world, where the sun every night plunged into the sea with a hissing terrible to hear, on its journey through the underworld to the East. Here, outside the straits, they planted their colony of Gades, the modern Cadiz, long the farthest outpost of civilization.

Each of these colonies, with its "sphere of influence" in the hinterland, represented an enlargement of the borders of the civilized world, and a new market not only for Phoenician wares but for the rich hangings, and carpets, and garments of Mesopotamia, and the gems and spices of Arabia and India. Each could send in return raw materials for the Phoenician manufactures and products readily saleable in the East or the Levant. From Carthage and the other African colonies came gold, ebony, ivory, leather, and all manner of animal products; from Spain, silver, iron, tin, lead, salt-fish, and sword-blades.

Thus the Phoenicians developed more and more into the middlemen and general carriers of the ancient world, and their cities into entrepôts and markets where the products of all lands were gathered together, and from which they were distributed. Ezekiel's description of Tyre, allowing for the poetical language, gives an astonishingly clear and vivid picture of a state whose greatness and prosperity depended mainly on the carrying trade, "situate at the entry of the sea . . . a merchant of the people for many isles."

Nobody, in a world organized on a basis of slave labour, would have made it a reproach to the Phoenician merchants that a large part of their profits came from the traffic in war-captives, insolvent debtors, and other raw material of the slave-market. Nor need any modern ideas on the morality of the slave-trade prevent us from recognizing, as Ezekiel recognized, even in his denunciation of Tyrian pride and luxury, that in covering the known world with their network of trade routes, the Phoenicians were doing more than any of their contemporaries to raise the general level of material prosperity.

> When thy wares went forth out of the seas, thou filledst many people; thou didst enrich the kings of the earth with the multitude of thy riches and of thy merchandise.

As the chief shipowners and most skilful navigators of their day, the Phoenicians were freely employed by the rulers of other nations when they required tonnage. It was not only that they had the cleverest shipbuilders and caulkers, and crews expert in handling oar and sail. Even more important were their jealously guarded navigational secrets, the knowledge they had picked up of ports and landfalls, stars and winds and tides and currents; for in days when there were no charts or navigational instruments, the observations handed down from one generation to another by experienced mariners were the foundation of all navigational science. ("Thy wise men, O Tyrus, that were in thee, were thy pilots!") We cannot, perhaps, rely on all the details of the story which tells how Solomon hired Phoenician pilots and sailors, and chartered Phoenician ships to tow rafts of timber from Lebanon for the temple, and to bring him gold from Ophir (probably in Arabia) and gold and silver, ivory and apes and peacocks, from Tarshish (Tartessus in Spain); but there is little doubt that it is true in essence. Later, it is said that a company of Phoenician seamen in the service of Necho of Egypt actually circumnavigated Africa, starting from a Red Sea port and returning by way of the Mediterranean.

For the successful conduct of a world-wide carrying trade, however, something more was required than daring and skilful seamanship, and in the pages of Xenophon we get a glimpse of the Phoenicians' ability in the technique of ship-owning, which shows, incidentally, that the qualities which made them great as sea-traders survived for centuries the fall of Tyre and Sidon as independent states. "I think," says one of his characters, "that the best and most perfect arrangement of things which I ever saw was when I went to look at the great Phoenician sailing vessel"; and he goes on to describe the excellence of the stowage, how the tackle, and the weapons and utensils of the crew, and the "merchandise, which the owner carried with him for his own profit," were all stowed in the smallest possible space, and in such a way that everything could be got at the moment it was wanted. He tells, too, how he found the captain's assistant going over the ship, as she lay in port, to see that everything was ship-shape and properly arranged, so that there should be no defect in gear or stowage to hamper her working when she put to sea.

It will be noted that this big Phoenician merchantman was a sailing vessel. In days when ramming was the chief method of attack in naval warfare, it was necessary that a warship should be, above everything else, fast and handy. The long, narrow galley, crowded with rowers, very fast for a short burst, and easily manoeuvred, could make rings round any sailing vessel of the time, or of many hundred years later. She used her sails whenever possible for cruising, so as to conserve the energy of her rowers for battle or chase; but she was fundamentally an oared vessel. For the merchant, on the contrary, carrying capacity was more important than speed, and carrying capacity implied a deep, broad, heavy ship. Moreover, a big crew of rowers, with their food and kit, would occupy space needed for cargo, and their food and pay (or their cost if they were slaves) would soon eat up the profits of a voyage. Hence the merchantman gradually developed into a tub-shaped sailing vessel, carrying big oars or sweeps for use in calms or in working against the wind, but dependent mainly on her single big sail for her motive power. Details of the types and of their subsequent development must be looked for elsewhere; but for many centuries—so long indeed as the Mediterranean was the chief theatre of maritime activity—this fundamental distinction between the "long ship" used in war and the "round ship" of commerce continued. Commercially, this very sharp distinction between the types had important effects. It compelled every state aiming at naval power to build a fleet solely for war; merchant ships could not be used, as they were in later times, to take a place in the line. This was all to the good, for it avoided the necessity of taking up merchantmen to form scratch fleets whenever hostilities were expected; but another effect of the distinction was that the slow, clumsy, trading vessel was quite unable either to resist or to fly from the nimble war galley or pirate. In such conditions the development of trade was inevitably limited, in ages when wars were almost incessant, and piracy was a popular and respectable profession.

So firmly was the commercial greatness of the Phoenicians based upon their geographical position and natural aptitude for the sea that it survived centuries of destructive conflict and of successive domination by Assyrians, Babylonians, Persians, and Macedonians. To each successive conqueror they furnished powerful fleets of warships; under each successive conqueror they continued to carry a great part of the trade of the civilized world.

They had to reckon, however, from about 450 B.C. onwards, with the competition of the Greeks. Living on groups of tiny islands and a mainland that was nearly all coastline, the Greeks were drawn instinctively to the sea; but for some hundreds of years they had launched their ships for the purposes of piracy, conquest, or emigration, more often than for commerce. The little City States, each with its strip of agricultural land, were largely self-sufficing in the simple necessities of their life, and were too poor to afford many luxuries. Their natural resources gave them little to export beyond wine and olive oil, and no well-trodden caravan routes brought down to them, as to Tyre and Sidon, the wealth of great inland Empires; nor was trade encouraged by political conditions in which every ship not belonging to your own city was assumed to be "good prize," unless protected by a special treaty.

Yet even in the early days of Athens and Corinth there was trade to be done. The armourers wanted iron and bronze. There were well-to-do citizens who would put down good money for luxuries, such as perfumes and spices, or purple cloth from Tyre, or table-delicacies (vegetable-relish from Cyrene in Northern Africa, for instance), or for curiosities such as monkeys and negro slaves. At first the traffic would be mainly with Egypt and Phoenicia, and the Greek colonies on the western coast of Asia Minor; but the Greeks, like the Phoenicians, were openers-up of new lands and many of their colonies in Sicily and Southern Italy grew into great commercial centres. It was probably through these Italian settlements that they opened up an export trade in pottery to the Etruscans—a mysterious people who took kindly to the sea, but seem to have devoted their chief attention to piracy rather than to commerce. They traded with Carthage too, and even found their way to Tartessus. Indeed it was probably the Greeks of Massilia (Marseilles), and not the Phoenicians of Gades, who first coasted along the shores of the Atlantic and brought back tin from the Scillies or Cornwall. This was a discovery of immense importance, as the demand for tin was very great in an age when bronze was indispensable for weapons, armour, and household utensils; but its very importance was the undoing of the Massilians, for the powerful Carthaginians soon got on their tracks, and having ousted them from the traffic, long preserved jealously the secrets of the route.

Most of this early trade seems to have been in the hands of the merchant-skipper, the lucky man who owned a ship or could persuade a small syndicate of friends and neighbours to subscribe the cost of one. With any spare cash he could raise or borrow, he would purchase a cargo of pottery, or wine, or olive-oil (which was everywhere in demand for cooking, for lighting, and for the bath). Putting out in the spring, he would follow the well-known routes along the coasts to a string of ports in Italy and Sicily, or the Levant, where he could dispose of his wares, and pick up, in exchange, any local products for which he could hear of a market. So he would spend the summer, sticking to no fixed itinerary and no fixed line of trade, but careful to wind up at some place whose products were readily saleable in his home-town, to which he must return before the winter gales were due. It was all very like the work done by a modern tramp steamer, except that one man combined the functions of Master, and shipowner, and skipper.

There were other owners, especially dwellers on islands which did not produce much for export, who did not lade their vessels with their own goods, but acted as tramps in the true sense of the word, carrying merchants and their wares wherever they wished to go, for no other consideration than the payment of freight. The proportion of these shipowners pure and simple seems steadily to have increased as trade expanded.

Luxuries like perfumes and spices do not take up much room aboard ship, but as time went on the need for bulkier and more essential cargoes swelled the demand for tonnage. The great war navies kept up by Athens and Corinth needed to be continually renewed, for the losses of galley fleets were very heavy, both by battle and by shipwreck. So it became necessary to import timber and pitch in large quantities from Macedonia and Thrace, and sails, or flax for sail-making, and cordage from Egypt. Still more vital was the question of the food supply. Even in the early days of Greece there were some cities whose territories did not produce enough corn for the support of their inhabitants. Others, like Corinth, which were normally self-sufficing, were obliged to import corn after every bad harvest. Athens, at first, could feed her people from the produce of Attica, but as her population increased she became as dependent upon the import of grain as Imperial Rome, or Great Britain to-day. At first she procured it mainly from Cyprus and Egypt; but when the growth of Persian domination rendered these sources of supply uncertain, her enterprising statesmen and seamen established commercial relations with the tribes of Southern Russia where, as Herodotus wonderingly remarks, men actually grew corn "not to eat but to sell."

The necessity of importing two-thirds of her corn supply gave Athens a new outlook on trade. Her rulers began to attach more and more importance to sea-power and to the conclusion of commercial treaties providing for free intercourse; they began also to regulate the trade itself. No one was allowed to lend money on the security of ship or goods, unless the ship was commissioned to carry a cargo of corn or other specified necessaries to Athens on her return voyage. No Athenian ship was allowed to carry corn direct to any other harbour than Piraeus, the port of Athens, and a special Board, the Wardens of the Hellespont, was established to supervise the traffic passing through the Dardanelles. Arrived at Piraeus, the grain cargoes had to be placed in an official warehouse, under the eye of inspectors, who saw to it that two-thirds of the cargo should be sent to the Athenian corn-market. The remaining one-third it was permissible to re-export.

As the export trade of Athens was never very large, the imports of corn and timber must have been paid for largely in silver derived from the mines at Laurium, or from the tribute paid by her subordinate allies, or by the proceeds of cargoes purchased for silver in foreign ports. We can get a good idea of the way in which trade was carried on from the speeches of Demosthenes, who was not only the greatest of Greek orators but a practising lawyer, frequently retained in mercantile actions, which were tried before special Courts during the winter months when the ships were laid up in harbour.

By this time, the shipowner, who was usually his own skipper, seems generally to have been a separate person from the merchant who chartered the ship. Both were generally dependent upon the monied man with capital to invest. The shipowner borrowed, on the security of ship and freight, money for the expenses of the voyage. The merchant borrowed the money for freight advances and the purchase of cargo. "Neither ship, nor shipowner, nor passenger," says Demosthenes, "can put to sea without the assistance of the lenders." ("Passenger" probably means the merchant travelling with his goods.) Of the estate which Demosthenes himself inherited, about one-twelfth was money lent "on a maritime adventure."

The rule with regard to all such loans was that if the ship or cargo was lost, the loss was borne by the lender; but if they arrived safely, he received his money back with a substantial premium; the laws limiting the rate of interest being relaxed, in consideration of the risks accepted. In order to diminish these risks, especially the risk of fraud, the lender often sent his own agent in the vessel, to see that the agreement was duly carried out.

Here are the essential facts of a typical transaction:

A and B lend 3,000 drachmas in silver to C and D, on a written agreement that C and D will proceed to one of two named ports, and there load 3,000 jars of wine, "in the twenty-oared vessel of which E is the owner." They shall then proceed to the Bosphorus, with liberty to continue the voyage into the Black Sea (within specified limits), and there sell the wine and load a return cargo for Athens. On safe arrival at Athens, the return cargo is to be delivered to the lenders as security for repayment of the loan within twenty days after arrival, together with a premium of 22½ per cent (or 30 per cent if a return passage from the Black Sea is begun after a certain date). Payment is to be made without any deduction except for jettison made "by common resolution" or "payments made to enemies." In default of payment, the lenders may sell the cargo, and if there is any deficiency, they may distrain for the balance on any other property of the charterers. The charterers give a guarantee that they have not borrowed and will not borrow any other money on the same security.

As between the charterer and the shipowner, it would appear that the shipowner was usually paid a lump sum freight; that the merchant provided victualling for himself and any servants of his who went with the ship, and that stevedoring charges were for charterer's account.

The high rates of premium on maritime loans were fully justified not only by the risks of war and piracy but by the risks of fraud in those days of restricted jurisdictions, long voyages, and uncertain communications. The shipping world has always had its seamy side, and it may console sufferers by more recent misdeeds of the countrymen of Demosthenes to read his outburst against Zenothemis:

"What can have encouraged the plaintiff to come here and commence his action? I will tell you men of the jury: it gives me pain to do so, I solemnly assure you, but I am compelled. There are gangs of rascally fellows leagued together in Piraeus; you've only to see them to know who they are."

These rascally fellows were up to all sorts of tricks: borrowing twice on the same security; imperilling a venture by taking an improper deckload; conspiring with the shipowner to carry the cargo into a port not allowed by the agreement; making false depositions of shipwreck in order to evade repayment of a loan. In one particularly unsavoury case, the owner of a vessel chartered to carry wheat from Syracuse to Athens entered into an elaborate conspiracy with a passenger which speaks well for his ingenuity if not for his honesty. The two rogues went about Syracuse holding themselves out as the actual owners of the cargo and borrowed a substantial sum on that security. They then sent off the money by another vessel to Massilia (their home-town), and when their own ship was three days out from port, Hegestratus, the owner, proceeded to bore a hole in its bottom at night, intending to escape with his confederate in the boat, and evade return of the loan on the plea of a marine casualty. Unfortunately for him, the other passengers discovered him at his work, whereon he threw himself overboard and was drowned.

These scamps, whose evil reputation the fame of Demosthenes has preserved, were no doubt in a minority, and the political decay of Athens and Corinth, worn out by incessant wars, did not put an end to the commercial activities of the Greeks. Greek traders followed in the wake of Alexander of Macedon and his successors, and when the Ptolemies founded a Macedonian kingdom in Egypt, the Greek settlers in Alexandria took rank with the greatest merchants and shipowners of the world. In the Western Mediterranean, Greek colonies like Syracuse, and Tarentum (Taranto) continued to compete for commercial and political supremacy with Carthage—the Tyre of the West—

which had swallowed up all the other Phoenician colonies in Africa and Spain. Even the Greeks of Syracuse, however, had to take second place to the great Carthaginian merchant-shipowners, who not only covered the Mediterranean with their commerce, but pushed out far beyond the Straits, northwards to Britain and southwards to the Gold Coast.

Finally Carthage, like the Greek colonies and Greece itself, went down before the overmastering power of Rome, and in the long run, it was the establishment of the Roman Empire on the ruins of a hundred warring states that gave to the business of the shipowner the greatest impetus it had ever yet received, or was to receive for many centuries after Rome itself fell.

We are much too apt to think of the Roman Empire only in terms of what was lost. No doubt there were moralists and philosophers, even in the best days of the Empire, who looked back with regret to the rugged virtues of the Republic and the eager, colourful life of the Greek City States. But for the trader and shipowner, and for the multitudes of quiet, ordinary folk whom they served, the earlier Empire, at any rate, was a golden age, for it brought them freedom to go about their daily work without the ever-present dread of war, brigandage, and piracy. From the shores of the Atlantic to the Arabian desert and the Red Sea, the Caesars exercised undisputed sway. Throughout the whole of this vast area the Roman laws and the Roman legions protected the husbandman and artisan at their labours and gave to the capitalist the security he needed for large-scale industry and commerce. The Roman roads, well constructed and well policed, bore an ever increasing stream of products to the ports for shipment. The Roman fleets, free from pre-occupation with external enemies, stamped out piracy in the Mediterranean and curbed it in the Black Sea and Indian Ocean. Shipowners, merchants, and manufacturers, rejoicing in this new-found security, were not likely to trouble themselves about the decay of political institutions or the blotting out of old national boundaries. Their point of view, we may be sure, was well expressed by the orator, addressing Marcus Aurelius, who summed up the whole matter in the question, "What could be better or more profitable than the present state of affairs?" and answered himself with the simple statement, "Now any man can go where he pleases with absolute confidence; the harbours all over the Empire are full of business."

Not only were the seas made safe for shipping as they had never been before except for short periods and within narrow limits, but the demand for tonnage was also far in excess of anything hitherto known. Imperial Rome itself depended upon sea-borne trade not only for its wealth and magnificence but for dear life. The crowded urban population of the world's metropolis would have starved in a few weeks but for the corn fleets which brought annually 20,000,000 bushels of grain from Egypt. Even these supplies were insufficient and had to be supplemented by shipments from Africa (or as we should say from Tunis). Later, when the Egyptian export had diminished, the shipments from Africa are said to have reached nearly 10,000,000 bushels a year.

The corn trade it was that employed both the largest individual ships and the biggest aggregate block of tonnage. Building and road-making materials may have come next in volume. But the extent and variety of sea-borne commerce can best be shown by giving a short list of the most important exports of each province. These, it must be remembered, were not only sent to Rome itself but exchanged for the products of other provinces, where the foundation of Roman cities and the extension of Roman culture was continually increasing the demand for the comforts of civilized life, even among people hitherto outside the pale of commercial intercourse. Here, then, is a brief epitome of the index to an *Annual Statement of the Trade of the Roman Empire*:

> EGYPT: Corn, dates, beans, papyrus (for paper making), porphyry, granite and building-stone, soda, alum (for dyeing and tanning), flax, linen, and clothing, glassware; gold and iron from Aetheopia; ivory from the interior of Africa; copper from Sinai; gems and spices from Arabia; re-exports of Indian products.
> SYRIA.—Limestone and basalt for road-making, timber, fruit (fresh and dried), wine, silk and linen manufactures, dyes and dyed cloths, glassware.
> ASIA MINOR.—Olive oil, wine, truffles, fish, medical herbs, dried fruits, wax, resins, flax, sulphide of lead, arsenic, red lead, mica, marble, whetstones, goat's-hair garments, tents.
> GREECE.—Olive oil, wine, honey, marble, stones, pottery.
> AFRICA.—Corn, fruit, olives, oil, truffles, cucumbers, fish, pickles, ebony, citrus wood, marble, mica, leather, furs, wild animals (for the games), slaves.
> NUMIDIA.—Marbles, wild animals.
> MAURETANIA.—Ebony and citrus woods, purple dye, woollen goods, big game and wild animals, lamps from the great factory at Iol Caesarea, hunting dogs from the Canaries.
> SPAIN.—Gold, silver, lead, iron, copper, fish, pickles and sauces, oil, honey, wine, fruit, flax, esparto grass, wool, cloth, nets.
> GAUL (by sea).—Corn, oil, wine, iron, woollen goods, pottery, glassware.
> BRITAIN.—Tin, lead, hides and fleeces, oysters, geese, hunting dogs.

By far the most important trade with countries outside the Empire was that with India and China. Chinese silk and silk manufactures reached Rome mainly by the long overland route to the Syrian ports, but the Indian trade gave employment to a large volume of shipping. For at least six centuries before the birth of Christ Indian goods had reached the West by means of coasting routes to ports on the Persian Gulf and the southern coast of Arabia, whence caravan routes led to the great Syrian entrepôts. Under the Ptolemies, Greek merchants from Egypt succeeded, by hugging the Arabian coast, in reaching India from Red Sea ports, and there is an old farce representing some Greek sailors, who have been shipwrecked on the Indian coast, being entertained by the local monarch. As the king addresses them in Canarese they cannot understand a word he says, but they prudently translate every sentence as "Have another drink"—an invitation which is always politely accepted.

Under the Romans this traffic greatly increased. The demand for Indian perfumes, spices, pepper, drugs, gems, pearls, ivory, silk, cotton, muslins, hides, and teak increased with the Empire's growth in wealth and luxury, and the Emperors were anxious to divert as much of the trade as possible to the sea-route, which enabled them to keep in their own hands dues which would otherwise be collected by the Parthians, who controlled the passes on the overland route. They kept Arabian pirates in check, cleared out the canal from the Nile to Arsinoe on the Red Sea, which had silted up, and constructed a good road from Coptos on the Nile to Myos Hermos, a more southerly Red Sea port with a better harbour than Arsinoe. Strabo was told that no fewer than one hundred and twenty vessels left Myos Hermos alone every year, with wine, metals, manufactured goods, and gold, to exchange for Indian products. About A.D. 50, an immense impetus to the trade was given by the discovery, by one Hippalus, of the periodicity of the monsoons, which enabled a direct sea passage to be made to India from Aden. A merchant could now leave Egypt in July, reach the Indian ports about the end of September, and, returning about the end of November, be back in Alexandria by February. He avoided, moreover, not only the dangers from brigands and civil disturbances on the overland route through Parthia, but the risks of piracy and the extortions of local rulers at the Arabian ports. From this time onward the sea route was increasingly followed, and by about A.D. 160 it extended even as far as China.

Alongside with this great expansion in sea-borne commerce went a great increase in the passenger traffic. Roman officials and army officers going to take up appointments in distant provinces or returning from them, drafts for the legions and time-expired soldiers, merchants and capitalists anxious to examine for themselves the possibilities of new markets, deputations bearing petitions to the Emperor, and State prisoners who, like St. Paul, had "appealed unto Caesar," provided a very useful sideline for the shipowners of the Empire. Emigration, too, was common, for the growing tendency of the Empire towards unity in law, in speech, in coinage, and in habits and taste, made things easy for the professional man or artisan who was moved to try his fortune abroad. Moreover, the new security given to the sea-routes, coupled with the growth of a rich, leisured class, made travel popular. Educated Romans were fond of history and antiquities, and many of them had been educated in Greece, and imbibed a love of Greek culture. Hence, there grew up a regular tourist traffic to the islands of the Aegean and the coast towns of Greece and Asia Minor, and this was swelled at intervals by sightseers going to the great festivals such as the Olympic Games. Many of those who had done the round of Athens, Delphi, Troy, Ephesus, and Rhodes, would continue the journey to Egypt, and after seeing the sights of Egypt, return to Rome with the corn fleet.

The corn ships, indeed, and other cargo-vessels carried great numbers of people travelling for business or pleasure (the ship in which St. Paul travelled carried 276 persons inclusive of the crew); but there were also ships built specially for the passenger traffic. Some of these were light, swift packet boats, such as those on the Brindisi–Durazzo ferry service. Others were larger vessels fitted for longer voyages; but the ships of which we read in some ancient authors, with baths and libraries in their deck-houses, and covered walks decorated with flowers in pots, seem to have been house-boats for use on lakes and rivers, rather than ancestors of the luxury liners of to-day.

The merchant ships themselves differed little in essentials from the round-ships of the Phoenicians, but the demands of commerce led to a great increase in size. We cannot trust Lucian when he describes a corn ship in the Egyptian trade as 180 feet long, with an extreme breadth of 46 feet, and 43½ feet in depth from the upper deck to the bottom of the hold; but it is known that the cargo capacity of ships in this trade frequently rose to 250 tons, so that they were decidedly bigger than many ships used in the seventeenth and eighteenth centuries in long-distance trades. Occasionally much larger ships must have been built, for the Vatican obelisk, brought to Rome about A.D. 40, weighed nearly 500 tons, and the vessel which carried it is said to have shipped as dunnage nearly 800 tons of lentils.

There were improvements in rig also, some Roman vessels having even a second mast, but no fore-and-aft sails were carried, and oars were still used in working against the wind as well as in calms. With such unhandy ships and with no instruments of navigation—for seamen still trusted to seamarks and the sun by day and to the stars by night—shipowners and sailing-masters were naturally reluctant to face the risk of winter voyages, or to venture far from the coast. Except in grave emergency, as when the stocks in the granaries at Ostia (the port of Rome) had fallen below the safety margin, and the Emperors offered bounties for a winter voyage to Egypt, sea-borne commerce was practically at a standstill between the middle of November and the middle of March. Even in summer, the majority of voyages were made by coasting from port to port and from landfall to landfall. The corn ships from Alexandria steered a direct course for Ostia or Puteoli (near Naples) during the early part of the summer, but about mid-July, the Etesians, a strong north-westerly wind, stopped the direct west-bound traffic for about six weeks and drove the corn fleets to adopt the inshore tracks along the coasts of Syria and Asia Minor, and for other vessels this seems always to have been the most popular route. It was by coasting along the shores of the Bay of Biscay that the Phoenicians had reached Britain, and in Roman times the British trade seems mostly to have crossed by a short sea passage from the Isle of Wight to the mouth of the Seine or Boulogne, whence it proceeded down the Seine and Rhone for transhipment at Marseilles. The direct sea route to India was an exception, rendered possible by the steadiness of the monsoon. In general, the voyages of St. Paul (Acts xxvii and xxviii) are thoroughly typical of the time in their short sea passages from one port of call to another, as well as in their search for a safe harbour in which to winter.

Of the time occupied by the voyages we have little certain knowledge. The record passage from Rome to Alexandria was nine days, but this was probably exceptional, and accomplished by a fast sailing ship with the help of the Etesians. The average passage, Ostia to Alexandria, was probably about eighteen or nineteen days. The corn ships, sailing in company, probably took about twenty-five days when following the direct west-bound route. By the inshore routes, the voyage might well run to double that time. From Ostia to Tarrasco (Tarragona) in Spain, was four days' sail; to Gades, seven days was a good, and ten days might be an average passage. From Carthage to Gades was reckoned as seven days' sail.

Despite the lack of navigational instruments, navigation was much easier than in the days of Phoenician predominance, for the routes were better known. Maps were coming into use and men like Marinus of Tyre and Strabo were laying the foundations of scientific geography. Even so many hundred years before the invention of printing, useful and popular books had quite a substantial circulation, thanks to the labours of the copyists, and a prudent merchant or shipowner could procure "Itineraries" of most of the main trade routes. The *Periplus of the Erythræan Sea* is a good example—a combination of Sailing Directions and Commercial Gazetteer for the Indian Ocean, packed with hints as to harbours and anchorages, tides and prevailing winds, markets, suitable cargoes, and character sketches of the local inhabitants.

> Beyond this place, the coast trending toward the south, there is the Market and Cape of Spices, an abrupt promontory, at the very end of the Berber coast toward the east. The anchorage is dangerous at times from the ground-swell, because the place is exposed to the north. A sign of an approaching storm which is peculiar to the place, is that the deep water becomes more turgid and changes its colour. When this happens they all run to a large promontory called Tabae, which offers safe shelter.
>
> . . . three settlements of Fish-eaters, a villainous lot, who use the Arabian language and wear girdles of palm-leaves.
>
> There are imported into this market-town [In India] wine, Italian preferred, also Laodicean and Arabian; copper, tin, and lead . . . thin clothing and inferior sorts of all kinds; bright-coloured girdles a cubit wide . . . gold and silver coin, on which there is a profit when exchanged for the money of the country; and ointment, but not very costly and not much.[1]

Other aids to safe navigation were the erection of lighthouses or beacons (as, for instance, at Alexandria, Ostia, Boulogne, and Dover) and the multiplication of safe harbours. As might be expected of such remarkable builders, the Romans were great hands at port development. The

[1] From the translation by Wilfred H. Schoff, New York and London, 1912.

Emperors themselves were active in the construction of new, and the improvement of old, harbours, and in building roads by which exports could be collected for shipment and imports distributed from the ports. At the larger ports, like Ostia and Puteoli, the quays, granaries, and warehouses were of vast extent, and merchants and shipowners from all over the Empire had their offices and agencies. There was, for instance, a special agent at Ostia, whose business it was to give assistance to all Carthaginian shipmasters in their dealings with the local merchants and port officials.

The trade of the Roman Empire in fact, was not only extensive but highly organized. A well-developed system of commercial law defined the rights and obligations of the parties to commercial and maritime contracts, and embodied whatever the Romans found useful in Greek law and practice. Among the doctrines thus borrowed from the Greeks and extended to the trade of the whole world was that of jettison, which the Romans themselves attributed to the Rhodians, who for a brief period in the fourth and third centuries B.C. had succeeded to the position of Athens as the chief maritime power in the Eastern Mediterranean:

> The Rhodian law provides [says a Roman jurist] that, if goods are thrown overboard in order to lighten the ship, what is sacrificed for the common benefit should be made good by a common contribution.

Neither the shipowners nor the cargo owners who were concerned in the shipwreck which cast St. Paul ashore on Malta, could profit by this rule; for, under Roman law, no claim to contribution arose unless the ship was saved. The principle of General Average by which all interests concerned contribute rateably to make good any loss caused by a marine casualty was an invention of a later date.

The shipowners themselves were all officially enrolled in corporations (*navicularii marini*), of which there seems to have been one for each considerable port. These were Shipowners' Associations or guilds, rather than chartered companies, for the members traded each on his own account, and not in common. During the decline of the Empire the corporations were brought more strictly under the control of the State, and merchant shipping became in effect an hereditary State service; but for the first two centuries at least the shipping industry was carried on by private enterprise. This was true even in the corn trade, although the import of the corn itself was a Government monopoly, and owners who employed their ships regularly in the traffic were rewarded or subsidized by receiving certain privileges, such as the exclusion of their ships from the property assessment for taxation.

Many owners were capitalists pure and simple, who took no part in the management of their ships but let them out on hire, either for a definite period or for the whole life of the ship, to people with more knowledge of the business. The time charterer under such a contract could employ the ship as he pleased, and received all freights for his own benefit; his responsibility to the original owner being limited to payment of the agreed rate of hire. He was, therefore, treated in law as owner of the vessel, and was eligible for membership of a Shipowners' corporation.

Other owners ran their ships on their own account. Many of them were merchants and loaded the ships with cargoes of their own goods; but it seems to have been more usual for the shipowner and the cargo-owner to be distinct persons in fact, as they were in law. The owner usually appointed two principal officers for each ship: the *gubernator* or sailing-master, who was responsible for the navigation; and the *magister*, or business manager, whose duties were to contract for cargo or passengers, to collect freights and passage monies, to see to repairs and the provision of tackle, and to buy and sell goods for the owner's account if it proved impossible to obtain a charter. Some owners, however, acted as their own business managers, and, more rarely, as their own sailing-masters. When a ship was owned in partnership it was customary for the partners to appoint one of their number as managing owner, who might either act himself as *magister* or engage one on behalf of the firm. The sailors, except when an owner manned the ship with his slaves, were paid fixed wages as in modern times and were not, as they often were in the Middle Ages, parties to the adventure.

All contracts for freight were now recorded in a written Charter-Party. One such document, made in A.D. 236, will serve as an example. It begins by setting out the names of the captain and merchant, and states that the captain is also owner of the ship, the cargo-capacity of which is specified. The merchant charters the whole vessel for a specified voyage and agrees to pay a lump sum freight of 100 drachmas of silver, of which 40 are to be paid on conclusion of the charter-party and the rest on delivery of the cargo. The shipowner binds himself to provide adequate equipment and a proper crew, to load the goods in two days, and to deliver them safe and undamaged by seawater. If unloading at the port of discharge is not completed within four days, the owner is to receive 16 drachmas *per diem* as demurrage.

This is a short and simple document compared with—let us say—a liner bill of lading, with its elaborate list of all the matters for which the shipowner will *not* take responsibility—but it is clear, business-like, and covers the main points in the contract. It shows, at any rate, that the shipping industry—the business of running ships for profit and not merely for carriage of the owner's own goods, was well-established on quite modern lines. It seems to have been a profitable business—Lucian asserts that the *Isis*, the big corn ship he describes, was worth at least twelve talents a year to her owners—say £2,925, with, of course, a vastly greater purchasing power than that sum would have to-day. But the development of the shipping industry under the Roman Empire was not important solely, or chiefly, for the profit it brought to individuals. The Roman shipowners, whether they were Italians, or Alexandrine Greeks, or Phoenicians from Tyre, or natives of Gaul or Africa, were in the business, like their Greek and Phoenician predecessors, for what they could get out of it; but in pursuing their own interests they were doing more than had been possible for their predecessors, or was to be possible for many generations of their successors, to make the products of the whole world available to the people of all nations.

SOME BOOKS ON THE PERIOD

For the Egyptians and Phoenicians and for very early trade generally, see *The Cambridge Ancient History.* Rawlinson's *Phoenicia* ("Story of the Nations" Series), London, 1889, is still useful. For the Greek and Roman periods I have made unbridled use of two invaluable books: *The Greek Commonwealth*, by A. E. Zimmern, Oxford, 1911, and *The Trade Routes of the Roman Empire*, by M. P. Charlesworth, Cambridge, 1924. There are some interesting details in the *Companion to Latin Studies*, ed. J. E. Sandys, 3rd edition, Cambridge, 1921, and *Ancient Ships*, by Cecil Torr, Cambridge, 1894, while mainly technical, gives useful particulars as to capacity, etc. The *Orations of Demosthenes* are quoted from the Bohn translation, ed. Kennedy, 1861. The chief "shipping cases" are those against Phormio, Lacritus, and Zenothemis.

CHAPTER II

"BRIDES OF THE ADRIATIC"

THE MEDITERRANEAN EPOCH

Once did she hold the gorgeous East in Fee. . . .
And, when she took unto herself a mate,
She must espouse the everlasting Sea.
WORDSWORTH, "On the Extinction of the Venetian Republic"

Here begin the good institutions and the good customs relating to maritime commerce which skilful men who have made voyages all over the world taught to our ancestors. . . . In what follows you may find the obligations of the captain of a ship, great or small, towards the merchants, the sailors, and the passengers, and the obligations of the merchant, the sailor, and the passengers towards the captain. *Consulat de la Mer*

THE "Peace of the Augustans" which produced such a wonderful expansion in the volume of sea-borne commerce, and such remarkable developments in the organization of the shipping industry itself, lasted for no more than a couple of centuries. As the strength of the Empire gradually declined under the combined effects of civil wars and external assaults, the volume of commerce contracted, and when the Empire finally broke up and province after province was plunged back into barbarism, shipping, as a large-scale industry, simply disappeared from the greater part of Europe. The Frankish, Gothic, and Vandal kingdoms which arose on the ruins of the Empire were too poor, too uncivilized, and too subject to internal disturbances, to carry on a big oversea trade, and now that the Roman fleets no longer maintained the police of the seas, the trade routes were too unsafe for many people to care to risk their lives and property upon them.

One great centre of trade and shipping alone stood out from the general chaos. In A.D. 328 Constantine the Great had refounded, as Constantinople, the city of Byzantium, and transferred the seat of Imperial Government from the banks of the Tiber to the shores of the Bosphorus, and when the Empire finally split, it was the Eastern, the Byzantine Empire, which alone retained something of the old Roman vitality and genius for administration. Within little space, Constantinople became the commercial as well as the political centre of the civilized world.

Even in Greek, and still more in Roman times, Byzantium had been an important centre of trade and shipping. It commanded the entrance to the Black Sea, and was separated only by a narrow strait from the terminals of the great highways of Asia Minor. When Syria and Egypt went down, first before the Persian, and later before the Saracen invaders, the caravan routes through Asia Minor became the only means of communication with the East, and Constantinople succeeded to the position of Tyre and Sidon as the bottle-neck of the whole traffic between Europe and Asia. The Saracen invasion in the seventh century, turned back only with difficulty from the walls of Constantinople, completed the Byzantine monopoly of sea-borne commerce. For the Saracens, if not sea-traders, were expert sea-rovers, and their piratical fleets swept from the seas practically all commerce other than that of the Byzantines themselves. It was only in Byzantine ships, protected by the powerful East Roman navy, that the products of the East could find their way, through the great entrepôt on the Bosphorus, to the countries of Western Europe.

When shipping began to revive in the Mediterranean proper, it was not through the agency of any great single Power, but through the gradual rise or revival of a score of scattered seaports: notably, Venice, Genoa, Pisa, and Amalfi in Italy; Zara, Ragusa, and the other Latin colonies on the Dalmatian coast; Marseilles in France, and Barcelona in Spain. Some of these were independent Republics, like the old Greek City States; others, though not independent, enjoyed a measure of autonomy in all that related to their trade and shipping; and it is from the laws and archives of these ports that we get the best picture of how the shipowner's business was carried on in the Mediterranean in mediaeval times.

At first the volume of their commerce must have been very small; but as the civilization of Central and Western Europe revived, their trade and wealth rapidly expanded. They built war fleets of galleys to protect their merchantmen; they engaged in wars, and acquired colonies. By the eleventh century, Venice and Genoa were strong enough to be welcome allies or formidable enemies to the Eastern Empire itself, which was falling to pieces under the strain of its ceaseless wars with Persian, Saracen, Slav, and Turkish invaders. In 1081, Venice secured, as the price of her assistance against the Normans of Sicily, a commercial treaty which gave her merchants a privileged position in Constantinople, and made Venetian merchantmen the distributors of Eastern products to the West. But it was the great adventure of the Crusades—that strange blend of religious fervour, the spirit of adventure, and the greed of plunder—which finally shifted back to Italy the centre of commercial activity. The Crusaders needed ships for transport and supply; they needed warships and expert sea-fighters to meet the Saracen fleets in battle. The Eastern Empire, so long the bulwark of Christendom against the Moslem, had by this time fallen into decay; but Venice, Genoa, and Pisa were ready enough to supply transport and convoy—for a consideration. The reward of their services to the cause of true religion was not money alone, but exclusive commercial privileges in the Syrian ports recaptured by the Crusaders from the Saracen. By thus opening up direct communication between Italy and the East, the flank of the Byzantine position was turned, and Sir Charles Oman has estimated that during the fifty years that followed the first Crusade, from one-third to one-half the trade of Constantinople was diverted to the Italian ports. Finally, in 1203–1204, the old blind Venetian Doge, Henry Dandolo, persuaded the leaders of the Fourth Crusade to divert their efforts from the delivery of the Holy Sepulchre to the conquest of Constantinople, and the historic link between East and West sank into a mere halfway house for Venetian trade with the Black Sea.

The people of the Italian Republics, with Venice at their head, had thus succeeded the Phoenicians and Byzantines as the distributors of Eastern products to the West, and like their predecessors, they derived from their position as carriers and middlemen for Eastern products an almost unbounded prosperity. This was not, of course, the only employment of their shipping; for as the civilization of the West revived there was again an abundance of trade to be carried between the ports of the Mediterranean itself, and the countries of Northern Europe required Mediterranean products as well as re-exports of Eastern goods; but it was primarily their command of the trade with the Syrian and Egyptian ports that gave to the merchants and shipowners of Venice and Genoa, down to the end of the fifteenth century, a position to which no others could aspire.

It is true that the shipping industry was no longer confined to the Mediterranean. Even in Roman times there had been a busy traffic between England and the Continent. The Norsemen, who played so large a part in breaking up the remains of the Roman Empire in the West, were keen traders as well as fighters and explorers. They owned trading vessels as well as the dreaded longships, and they were perhaps the most daring seamen the world has ever seen. Even in the Dark Ages, there was considerable traffic between England, Iceland, and Scandinavia, and for some centuries communication was kept up between Iceland or Norway and the Icelandic colony of Greenland. From the twelfth century onward English shipping steadily increased. The Flemings were still more active traders, and the people of the great Confederation of the Hanse towns, headed by Lubeck, Hamburg, and Bremen, attained a position as general carriers in Northern waters comparable to that of the Venetians themselves in the Mediterranean. We shall have to take account in the next chapter of this early development of the shipping industry in the North; but for the moment we may set it aside. So long as Venice "held the gorgeous East in Fee," the primacy in wealth, in civilization, and in shipping remained with the Mediterranean states. Indeed, the Northern nations themselves, making as they did a much later start in the race, went to school to the Italians in the business of shipowning. The Third Crusade, which brought English ships and sailors to the Mediterranean in 1190, taught many lessons to the Northern shipbuilders and navigators, and the maritime laws and customs of England, and France, and even the Hansa itself, were modelled to a great extent on those of the Mediterranean seaports.

With the Mediterranean trade itself, the northerners had no power, and hardly even the ambition to meddle. Venice and Genoa were too rich and powerful to be affronted, and so long as the war-galley retained her old supremacy as a fighting ship—at any rate in Mediterranean waters—no northern vessel dared to intrude unauthorized into the Italian preserves. It was by the Venetian "merchant-galleasses" and the Genoese carracks, that the silks and spices of the East, and the oil, wine, and dyestuffs of the Mediterranean found their way to England and Flanders, and through Flanders to all northern Europe.

We have to think then of the ships owned and operated

under the Statutes of the various Mediterranean ports as plying an extensive and ever increasing trade. There were the great trade routes to the East—to Egypt, to Syria and Palestine, and to Byzantium—which supplied the shipowners of Venice and Genoa with their most precious cargoes; there were the Western trade routes by which these rare and costly freights were distributed to Spain and France and England and Flanders; there were innumerable cross-tracks between Italian and Spanish and North African ports, for the exchange of local products such as Venetian salt and glassware, and African gold and hides, and there was a busy coasting and short sea trade which occupied, profitably enough, a great number of smaller vessels.

The starting-point of all the local Statutes by which this traffic was regulated was probably the so-called "Sea Law of the Rhodians," a Byzantine code, or rather a compilation of maritime laws and customs, which seems to have been put together, sometime between A.D. 600 and 800, as a sort of commercial text-book. It contains materials from sources of different date and varying authority, and its evidence can only be used with caution, but it is sufficient to show that the change from Roman to mediaeval methods of shipowning had begun in Byzantine times. As might be expected from the scattered origins of the revival of Mediterranean shipping, the new methods developed along divergent lines, and the Statutes and commercial documents of the mediaeval ports show a great variety of local usage. Both law and usage too were in a continual state of development, and no general statement as to the way in which the Mediterranean shipping industry was carried on from, say, A.D. 1000 to 1500, can be true for all times and all places. Nevertheless, we can form a fairly reliable picture of the general conditions in which the shipowner went about his work.

The most striking features of mediaeval shipowning are

the great variety of methods by which a ship might be owned and freighted and the frequent confusion of functions between the various parties to the transaction. In Roman Law the distinction between the parties to a maritime adventure was perfectly clear and quite in accordance with modern practice. The shipowner owned the vessel, engaged a crew to navigate her, and contracted with the charterer to carry his goods for a fixed freight. In the Middle Ages it was a common thing for the members of a single syndicate to own the ship, lade her with their own goods, and sail in her as mariners, so that the same persons acted as shipowners, cargo-owners, and crew. Even when ship and cargo were separately owned, the goods were often carried and the mariners remunerated on a profit-sharing basis.

One of the oldest of these joint adventure systems is described in the "Table of Amalfi," the earliest parts of which probably date back to the eleventh century. By the "custom of the coast," the shipowners, merchants, and seamen all constituted a single partnership. The owners appointed one of their number as manager (*patronus*) with a general control of the adventure. Other owners probably served as mariners, as did any merchants who went to sea with their goods.

In the accounts, the shipowners were credited with a certain number of shares in the adventure, according to the size or value of the ship; each merchant received shares according to the value of his money or goods adventured; each mariner was credited with one share in reward of his services (in addition to any interest in the voyage he might have as part-owner or merchant). The managing-owner might grant an additional share or shares to the sailing-master and clerk, but only with the consent of his co-owners.

The clerk or supercargo (*scribanus*) was a very important personage. It was his duty to keep a sort of combined share-register, cargo-manifest, and ledger, in which were entered the ship, with the number of shares belonging to the shipowners; the goods belonging to each merchant and the shares they carried; the names of the mariners, and the receipts and expenses of the adventure. All profits made by trading with the cargo went into partnership account, together with any stray freights and passage monies received from persons outside the syndicate. On completion of the round voyage, the accounts were audited in Court, and the net profits divided among shipowners, merchants, and mariners, in accordance with their respective shares.

A different and peculiar form of partnership is referred to by the Statutes of Ragusa, 1272, among other systems of shipowning and trading then in use. By this system, a number of merchants each entrusted to the captain and crew either a sum of money to be employed in trade, or goods to a fixed amount. Either an owner or a mariner could make such contribution on his private account. Freight on the goods so adventured (or on goods purchased with the money entrusted to the ship) was allowed in the accounts, and the profits made by the ship (including those arising from casual freights and passage monies) were brought into one common fund with the profits arising from trafficking in the goods. At the end of the round voyage, the ship and mariners took one half of this common fund and the merchant adventurers divided the other half in proportion to the value of their contributions.

Side by side with these joint-adventure systems there went on the ordinary business of shipowning and chartering. There were some ports at which the joint-adventure system was never in force, and at others it seems to have been gradually superseded, at any rate in the more important trades, by the normal relations between owner and charterer. The single owner, managing his own ship or sending an agent in her to look after the business of the voyage, seems always to have been rather rare. Business in the Middle Ages was carried on mainly by syndicates, and the majority of the ships were owned by partnerships, one member of which acted as managing owner, while the others, or some of them, frequently went to sea as members of the crew. By the fifteenth century most ships seem to have been owned in twenty-fourths, though a single partner might, of course, hold two or more of such shares.

The owners might or might not also be merchants able to fill the holds with their own goods. If they were not, the usual course was to arrange a charter with a syndicate of merchants, who were not necessarily trading in partnership, but clubbed together to hire and fill the vessel, each merchant being responsible for the freight on his own goods. The commonest form of chartering seems to have been for a round voyage, for the merchants usually accompanied their goods, and having sold them in the foreign port, purchased a return cargo with the proceeds. Time-chartering was also in vogue, and it was often possible for merchants who did not require a whole ship, to engage space for a specific quantity of goods, as on a modern liner.

Under all the various forms of the joint-adventure system, the crew, or some of them, were partners in the adventure, and received the reward of their services in the form of profits, not wages. Even under the joint-adventure system, however, it was sometimes necessary to complete a crew with men who were unwilling to take the risks of partnership, and served simply for hire. Where the joint-adventure system was not in use, crews were engaged in the ordinary way, and part-owners who went to sea as mariners seem usually to have received wages as seamen in addition to their share of profits on the voyage.

Wages were paid either by the month, or by the voyage, or by the season, and provision is frequently made in the Statute for wage advances, and for the payments to be made in the event of death or illness. A typical form of engagement is that common at Zara and Spalato (Split) in the early part of the fourteenth century. The seaman signed on for the whole period of open navigation, March 1st to November 30th, for which he received a fixed lump sum, payable in three instalments, on March 1st, June 1st, and September 1st, respectively, with a proportional increase if the ship remained out after November 30th. If he died during the first three months, his representatives were entitled to receive his wages for the whole of that period. If he died after May 31st, they could only claim his actual earnings, apportioned up to the day of his death. If, however, his death was due to injuries received in the course of his work, or in defending the ship against enemies or pirates, they were entitled to his wages for the full season, without regard to the date of his death.

As a rule, a sailor who fell ill and had to be put ashore was only entitled to pay up to the date of his leaving the ship, but some Statutes provided for a small maintenance allowance to be paid him for a month thereafter. In this they were a little behind the Judgments of Oléron, a code drawn up in or about the year 1194, which became the foundation of the customary maritime law of northern Europe. The Judgments provide that if a sailor should fall ill while in the ship's service, and have to be put ashore, the captain must provide him with lodging and light, and rations. He was not obliged to supply anything more delicate than the ship's ordinary dietary; but he had to put one of the ship's servants ashore to attend to the invalid, or to engage a nurse for him. If the sailor recovered he could claim his full wages for the voyage; if he died they were to be paid to his heirs.

In the Mediterranean there was another danger to provide for—capture by the Moslem pirates and condemnation to slavery. If a seaman was captured during the voyage, his wages continued to run, under many of the Statutes, during the term of his captivity, and the shipowners or partnership whom he served were under an obligation to provide his ransom.

In addition to his wages, the seaman was generally entitled to carry a small quantity of goods, free of freight, with which to trade on his own account. This was a valuable privilege, for a shrewd man might easily pick up in Byzantium, or Beyrut, or Tunis, light novelties or curiosities which would fetch a good price at home.

When he served for pay, he also received his victuals from the shipowner. If he went on shares, the cost of provisioning was deducted from the gross receipts before profits were divided. A typical victualling scale is that laid down in the Barcelona Ordinance of 1258. It includes salt meat, bread, vegetables, oil, wine, and water. The *Consulat de la Mer*, a late fourteenth-century Catalan compilation of sea laws and customs, states that the seaman is entitled to meat on Sundays, Tuesdays, and Thursdays, and soup on other days; together with bread and cheese, onions, or fish, every evening. Wine is to be provided if it can be procured at a reasonable price, and on solemn feast-days double rations are to be issued. As voyages were still made mostly by hugging the coast, with frequent stoppages at ports where fresh vegetables and other supplies could be obtained, the mediaeval seaman in the Mediterranean was probably better fed, and was certainly less exposed to the ravages of scurvy, than an English sailor on a typical trading voyage of the eighteenth century.

The seaman was not, as a rule, obliged to take any part in the loading and discharge of the cargo; for at most ports there were guilds of stevedores who attended to this work. He was generally bound to stand by the ship for a stated period in the event of a casualty other than a total loss, and to take part in the work of salvage. At Venice, the seamen received a fixed commission of three per cent on everything that was saved.

Discipline was very lax. Neither the captain (*patronus*) nor the sailing-master had anything like the autocratic authority of later times. The mariner himself, as we have seen, was often a part-owner of ship or cargo, equal in social status to anyone on board. The passengers were often merchants who had made many voyages, and knew at least as much about the topography of the coasts, the soundings, and the dangers of navigation as the ship's officers, and as navigation, in the absence of scientific instruments or scientific knowledge, was conducted on rule-of-thumb lines, the hired sailor was likely to know as much about the job as his captain. By the Judgments of Oléron the captain is actually bound to consult the ship's company before setting sail:

> When a ship is in harbour and awaiting a favourable moment to leave, the captain must not sail without consulting the ship's company,[1] and should say to them: "Gentlemen, what do you think of the weather?" If some of them answer, "The weather is bad," and others, on the contrary, say, "The weather is fine and favourable," the captain ought to be guided by the opinion of the greater number; for if he does otherwise, and the ship is lost, he is liable to indemnify the owners of the ship and cargo as far as he has the wherewithal.

None of the Mediterranean statutes go as far as this; but it was clearly customary for the captain to consult with everyone on board in times of difficulty or danger, and the confusion arising therefrom must have led to many disasters. A Venetian Statute of 1240 made some attempt to regulate it by placing the entire control of the navigation in the hands of the captain, sailing-master, and three merchants; but, while navigation by committee may have been an

[1] The words used seem to mean everyone on board, merchants, passengers, and mariners.

improvement on navigation by popular assembly, we should not care to-day to go to sea in a ship so commanded.

The captain was, in fact, only a leader among equals, and his relations with the crew were paternal rather than autocratic. The Judgments of Oléron make it his duty "to keep peace among the sailors and compose their differences." If one of them gives the lie to another at table he must pay a fine of fourpence; for a similar offence committed either by or against the captain, a double fine is to be paid.

> If the captain strikes a sailor, the latter must put up with the first blow; and if the captain strikes him again, he may defend himself. Whoever strikes the captain first must pay a hundred sous,[1] or lose his hand, at the sailor's own choice.
>
> That is the judgment in this case.

Another curious provision relates to quarrels arising at the common mess. If a sailor who has made himself offensive offers amends to the satisfaction of the mess, but the captain is "so hard-hearted that he will content himself with nothing less than putting him ashore," the sailor may follow the vessel to her port of discharge in another ship, and claim his full wages for the whole voyage, less his fine to the mess. If the ship should be lost because the captain was unable to replace him with an equally able seaman, then the captain is liable up to the full extent of his property.

According to the Mediterranean statutes, theft, brawling, and other offences were punishable by dismissal; but they make very little other provision for enforcing discipline. Even when they permit whipping, it is sometimes provided that blood must not be drawn, so that it was a very different thing from a naval flogging in the eighteenth century.

[1] About half the wages given for a voyage between England and Bordeaux.

Desertion would seem to have given rise simply to a claim for damages, and some of the Statutes provide that a seaman should be entitled to quit, without any penalty, if he were offered a position as an officer in another vessel. The fact that it was necessary to insert such a stipulation, shows, at any rate, that the hired seaman had a reasonable chance of bettering himself in his profession. More alien to modern ideas is the clause allowing him to break his contract if he should have made a vow during the voyage to go on a pilgrimage to the Holy Sepulchre, or to Rome, or to St. James of Compostella. But the shipowners of the Middle Ages could afford to look kindly on the fashion for pilgrimage, for it gave them something like an equivalent of the modern emigrant traffic, and must have employed a great number of vessels. The extent of the traffic is shown by the fact that it brought into existence a number of agencies who made themselves responsible for the chartering of ships and the supply of provisions for the pilgrims during the voyage.

Upon the whole, the Statutes of these mediaeval Mediterranean States show an amount of care in defining the seaman's rights and providing for contingencies such as illness or death which is distinctly in advance of the conditions prevailing in ships of the eighteenth or even the first half of the nineteenth century. The explanation is that, as we have already seen, the crews contained a large proportion of men who could regard themselves as socially equal to anyone on board, and would not put up with harsh discipline or bad conditions. This is brought out very clearly in the *Consulat de la Mer*, in a clause to the effect that if a *Senyor de nau* (captain or managing owner), having engaged a crew for a series of voyages, charters the ship to a third party of whom the sailors, on experience, do not approve, they may quit the ship at the end of the first voyage.

> This is why this provision was made: many men who are merchants or people of good position hire themselves out as sailors: and there may come along (as Charterer) some one who is a low fellow, though rich, with whom such decent people would not care to sail.

In the Sea-Laws of Wisby, a fourteenth century Baltic code, there is another very striking illustration of the status of the mediaeval sailor. The code contains a clause providing that if a sailor, after signing on, shall buy a ship of his own, he shall be free from his engagement on repayment of any wage advances he has received.

The presence of men in the crews who were equal in social status to the captain, and rich enough to buy him out, helps to explain a great deal that seems odd to us in the mediaeval arrangements for navigation and discipline; but it did ensure proper attention to the seaman's pay and comfort—comfort, that is to say, according to the ideas of the time; for no sailor of to-day would willingly sign articles containing the clause in the *Consulat de la Mer* "Of the sailor who undresses."

> Further, a sailor must not undress except in a port of wintering; if he does so, let him be ducked three times in the sea from the yard-arm on each occasion; and after a third repetition of the offence, he is to forfeit his wages and all his property on board.

The idea, presumably, was that he should always be ready for duty, and the men of the Middle Ages thought it no hardship to sleep in their clothes. They would not have been at all startled by the discovery, at an elementary school medical examination, some years ago, of a small child who had been sewn in for the winter.

Not only were the seaman's pay and conditions relatively better in the Middle Ages than in some more modern times, but the regulations of the Italian City States, at any rate, for ensuring the safety of life and property at sea were distinctly in advance of anything known to English Law a hundred years ago. The Venetian Statutes, for instance, laid down prescribed limits of length, breadth, etc., for ships of various sizes, and compliance with these regulations must clearly have entailed an official inspection while the ship was still on the stocks. Other, less detailed laws, simply prescribe that the hull must be well-caulked and water-tight. The internal arrangements, at least in the Venetian Statutes, were also subject to legal regulation; the places where cabins and store-rooms might be placed, and the uses to which they could be put, being carefully prescribed. It must be remembered that, at this period, cabins were only temporary structures, formed by putting up light partitions as required for each voyage.

With regard to the equipment, very elaborate regulations were laid down. Many Statutes set out the precise number of sails which vessels of various classes must carry, and the materials of which they must be made, together with the number of anchors and cables, and the provision to be made of other tackle. Most of the Statutes specify that a long-boat is to be towed, and some of them, notably those of Venice, require a second, smaller boat to be provided. For better assurance, or in order to secure an equipment in excess of the requirements of the local Statutes, the equipment to be provided by the shipowners was often set out in great detail in the Charter-party itself.

Ballasting and stowage were also carefully regulated. At Venice, ballasting had to be carried out under the supervision of a committee composed of the sailing-master and representatives of the owners and charterers. Deck cargoes were usually confined by law to very light articles such as silk manufactures or goods that could be carried in chests. Carriage of goods in the 'tween-decks was also restricted; at Venice to light goods only; at Pisa to one-fourth of the total cargo. Exceptions were sometimes made for ships loaded with provisions, pilgrim-ships, and vessels used in specialized trades, such as timber-ships and horse-ships.

The stowage of cargo in the hold was usually left to the discretion of the Master and stevedores; but careful provision was made against overloading. At Venice, an official mark was placed on the outside of the hull, and the ship was inspected before she sailed. If the mark was found to be more than a specified depth below the water-line, the excess cargo was removed by the authorities and the owners heavily fined. The permitted depth varied with the age of the ship, all vessels being divided for this purpose into three classes—under five years old, from five to seven years old, and over seven years old. Thus, we have here a foreshadowing not only of Plimsoll's Mark but of the classification of shipping.

Finally, the Venetian Statutes laid down a definite manning-scale for merchantmen. Every ship of 200 *milliaria*[1] was to have 20 mariners, exclusive of soldiers and cooks, and for every 10 *milliaria* above that size, an additional sailor was to be engaged. At other ports, where the strength of the crew was not defined by law, it was usually specified in the Charter-parties.

The same care that was exercised in ensuring that ships should be seaworthy (by the standard of the times), well equipped, and properly manned, was extended to the business aspect of the voyage. Where the merchants are the governing class, as they were in Venice, Genoa, and the other Mediterranean City States, the legislature is not likely to leave the merchants' interests to chance, and the obligations of shipowners and charterers are laid down in many of the Statutes with a precision unknown in classical times.

This new pre-occupation with commercial interests is

[1] Mediaeval measurements are so confused that it is impossible to give an equivalent in modern tonnage.

illustrated by the position and duties of the Scribe or Clerk (*Scribanus*), an officer of whom there is no trace before the Middle Ages. Many Statutes, including those of Venice, made it compulsory for every ship to carry a Scribe, and his very important duties were defined with great precision. He was provided with a book or register in which he had to insert (*a*) the Charter-party and all other agreements entered into between shipowners and charterers; (*b*) the names of the crew and the terms of their engagements; (*c*) a list of all goods comprised in the cargo, with their identifying marks, if any, and their owners. The scribe's book was thus a sort of combination of Official Log and Cargo Manifest. Moreover, he was obliged to hand to every shipper, on demand, a copy of the entry relating to his goods. This copy had the force of a receipt for the goods and the Charter-party generally provided that goods should be delivered *per apurtum scriptum*, or as we should say, "as signed for." The copy, in effect, acted as something between a mate's receipt and a Bill of Lading.

The scribe himself was sworn before the authorities to a faithful discharge of his duties, sometimes after an examination into his qualifications, and all documents made by him, whether entries in his register or on separate sheets of paper, had the authority of public instruments. He was, in fact, something more than a clerical assistant to the captain; he was to some extent a public official, with a duty to the shippers and seamen as well as to the shipowners. Venetian law even imposed upon him the duty—shipowners' servant as he was—of reporting any case of overloading.

Provisions relating to demurrage, short freight, and the limitation of shipowners' liability are common in mediaeval law. By Venetian law, for instance, the shipowner was not responsible for damage to silk goods carried as deck-load with the consent of the shipper. In general, he was liable for all damage arising through negligence (such as leakiness of the ship due to bad caulking), but not for the consequence of Acts of God (such as tempest). These were covered, though partially and uncertainly, by a new principle which had apparently been developed during the Byzantine period, and now found its way, to some extent, into mediaeval law and practice. By Roman law the only maritime losses made good by contribution from all parties interested in the adventure were sacrifices—such as jettison of cargo—voluntarily incurred for the common safety. By the new principle of general average, any loss of ship or cargo, for which no one was responsible by default or negligence, was to be made good by the contributions of shipowners and cargo-owners in proportion to the value of their respective interests in the adventure.

This idea of spreading the risks, so that many men should suffer slight loss rather than that one man should be ruined, was carried still further in the principle of insurance, by which the risks were shared, for a consideration, by persons with no part in the adventure. There is definite evidence that marine insurance, in the full modern sense of the term, was practised at Genoa, Pisa, and Florence so early as the first half of the fourteenth century. The western Italian States seem to have been rather ahead of the Venetians in this respect; perhaps because of the early development of banking by the Lombards and the growth of a class of monied men who were capitalists and financiers rather than merchants.

Mediterranean commerce in the later Middle Ages presents, indeed, a queer blend of ancient and modern. Formal Charter-parties of quite an elaborate character, an elaborate code of laws relating to such matters as general average and jettison, a highly developed banking system, and the beginnings of marine insurance, are found side by side with survivals of the old joint-adventure system of shipowning, an almost complete absence of anything we should consider as discipline aboard ship, and a curiously clumsy method of computing freights.

The great difficulty in arriving at fair freights arose from the uncertainty of mediaeval ship-measurement. The capacity of the ship was always stated in terms of weight; but goods of the same weight might take up very different space in stowage. To get round this difficulty, two methods were adopted. Goods of high value in relation to bulk were often charged a percentage of their value. For other goods, an elaborate table of equivalents was drawn up. The ship's capacity was estimated in tons (or their mediaeval and local equivalent) of the staple export from her home port, and on this a freight per ton was fixed. Other commodities were charged an equivalent based on the estimated space occupied. Thus at Gerba, a port in Tunis, freight was calculated on the basis of a "cantaro" of skins; but alum, also an export of the port, only took up half as much space on board as its equivalent weight in skins; hence two "cantaria" of alum only counted as one in calculating freight. Sugar, on the other hand, was lighter than skins, and a "cantaro" of sugar paid freight on two "cantaria" of ship-space. These tables of equivalents were often embodied in local Statutes as a guide to the custom of the trade and an aid to arithmetic; but shipowners and charterers were always free to over-ride them by a special bargain.

A Charter-party made in 1263 for a voyage between Porto Pisano (the Port of Pisa) and Bugea, gives a very clear and full picture of how the shipowner's business was carried on, in the Mediterranean, in the thirteenth century. It is a much more elaborate document than the classical example quoted in Chapter I, and much of it has an astonishingly modern ring. It is made between A, B, and C, shipowners (apparently acting for a more numerous partnership) and D, E, F, and G, on behalf of themselves and other merchants, and its principal provisions are as follows:

The shipowners undertake to provide the ship in good condition and furnished with tackle and equipment as specified, together with a crew of thirty-six skilful seamen (including the Master and Clerk or Supercargo) and six servants. Master and mariners are to be properly armed.

The shipowners will provide lighters at their own expense for bringing down the cargo from Pisa to the ship; will take the cargo on board, and sail from Porto Pisano within ten days from the date of the contract. Before sailing they will cause their partners, the master, sailors, and stevedore, to take an oath to observe all the terms of the contract.

The cargo is to be carried at the customary freight. No charge is to be made for the carriage of the charterers and their partners, or their personal effects.

On arrival at Bugea, the shipowners will discharge the cargo, and hand it over to the merchants as signed for.

The shipowners will begin to load the return cargo within ten days after arrival at Bugea, and will complete within a month the loading of a specified quantity. The amount to be loaded for each merchant is specified. The return cargo is to be brought to the ship at the merchants' expense, but the shipowners will load and stow it properly. A weigher, appointed by the parties, will weigh the cargo at the shipowners' expense, and the weights are to be entered by the clerk in the ship's register.

The third deck and the upper poop are to remain free for the use of the merchants and their personal effects.

Freight on the return cargo is fixed at a specified rate *per cantarium.* If wool or sheepskins are compressed beyond a certain amount in stowage, the freight is to be proportionately reduced. No freight is to be claimed except on goods duly delivered at Porto Pisano, where the return cargo is to be discharged at the shipowners' expense. The shipowners will keep the master and three-quarters of the mariners standing by the ship until discharge is completed.

The voyage is to be made direct from Porto Pisano to Bugea and back. The shipowners will accept no cargo from anyone other than the Charterers and their partners, unless the latter fail to fill the ship. The shipowners will not demand average for any tackle lost or injured on the voyage out or back. If a mariner is missing, they will recover him without average.

Freight is to be paid in currency, or in gold and silver, within eight days of delivery of the return cargo at Porto Pisano. If cargo is actually delivered before freight is paid, a banker's guarantee is to be given.

The shipowners swear to observe all the terms of the contract unless prevented by tempest or other Act of God. The penalty for any default is to be double damages. Any breach of contract by the charterers renders them liable to pay double damages and freight in addition.

It will be noted that the Charter-party expressly provides for the crew to be properly armed. This was a very necessary provision. With the break-up of the Roman Empire, the plague of piracy had again broken out in the Mediterranean, and it was rampant all through the Middle Ages. Although States like Venice, Genoa, and Pisa developed into great naval Powers, no one of them was strong enough, or exercised a sufficiently wide jurisdiction, to put down piracy by its own strength, and their wars and jealousies prevented them from combining effectively for that purpose. When actually at war, all the maritime States issued freely the equivalent of letters of marque, and the line between the privateer and the pirate was always fine and wavering. Even the most pious and respectable corsair—such as the one who borrowed money to go on a pilgrimage, and charged the debt on the profits he hoped to make (D.V.) from his next cruise—was apt to extend his depredations from enemies to all foreigners and from war time to times of peace; considering that his conscience was clear if he refrained from plundering his own countrymen. Nor was he nice in his methods. "Where are you going?" some Pisans asked a distinguished Genoese corsair in 1165, and received the uncompromising answer, "I am going to capture you and your goods and persons and to cut off your noses."

Equally liable to abuse was the system of "reprisals" which sprang up in the Middle Ages and endured until the seventeenth century. International law was in its infancy: diplomatic representation was imperfect and communications were very slow. Hence it was often extremely difficult for a citizen of State A to obtain satisfaction of a claim against a citizen of State B. His only remedy was to obtain a license from his own Government to capture goods belonging to any citizen of State B up to the amount of his claim, leaving the aggrieved parties to seek a remedy from their own Government. It is to be feared he was not always careful to take only the exact amount of his original claim from the third parties who thus, involuntarily, satisfied it.

Enemy fleets, corsairs, pirates, and merchants exercising the right of reprisals, made shipowning an adventurous business. Its risks were enormously increased by the advent of the Turk, with whom the Christian States were almost perpetually at war, and the establishment of a group of Moslem States, having piracy for their chief national industry, all along the North African Coast.

In these circumstances it was natural enough that both Statutes and Charter-parties frequently provided that ship and crew should be armed for defence. Many Charter-parties further provided that professional men-at-arms and crossbow-men should be carried. Very often, ships would arrange to sail in groups of two or three, under an obligation to afford each other mutual support; the shipowners and merchants agreeing to bear jointly any loss caused by pirates and to divide the proceeds of any capture they themselves made. The more important and lucrative long-distance trades were carried on only in organized fleets of well-armed ships, sailing in company, at fixed periods, under strict Government regulations, and often with an escort of men-of-war.

This system of regulated sailings was carried to its highest perfection by the Venetians. From the thirteenth to the fifteenth century, at least, Venice was one of the Great Powers of Europe. Her fleets swept the seas; her alliance was sought, and her enmity was feared by States with a hundred times her population and many hundred times her territory. But the power of Venice depended solely on her wealth, and her wealth depended solely on her commerce. The annual ceremony by which the Doge solemnly celebrated the marriage of the Republic and the Adriatic was a true symbol of the dependence of Venetian prosperity on the sea. Under Doge after Doge, Venetian policy was directed to the one object of fostering the growth of Venetian trade and shipping, with a persistence possible only in a City State in which the trading class and the ruling class were absolutely identical. Every weapon in the armoury of protection was used with ruthless efficiency; every form of retaliation and pressure was employed to extort privileges for Venetian ships and Venetian goods in foreign ports. Discriminatory tariffs, discriminatory shipping dues, navigation laws restricting the employment of ships under foreign flags, embargoes on exports and on imports were the commonplaces of Venetian diplomacy. Trade and shipping themselves were controlled by the State at every stage and at every turn. Special dues were imposed on goods imported by land, in order to encourage the use of the sea-routes and thus increase the demand for tonnage; the masters of privately-owned ships were licensed by the State, and were liable to receive instructions from the Government as to the cargoes to be loaded and the freights to be charged. The pick of the long-distance traffic was reserved for ships owned by the State itself.

These ships developed in course of time into the celebrated merchant-galleasses; vessels which combined the characteristics of the war-galley and the ordinary merchantman, having a low freeboard amidships, and oar as well as sail power. They were very big ships for their day, and as their cargoes were mostly goods of high value but small bulk, there were not very many of them. The "Flanders Galleys" which carried the pick of the trade with England and northern Europe were never more than five in number.

At least as early as the twelfth century, the sailing of these State-owned ships had been organized in a regular series of annual convoys. Twice a year, a squadron sailed for Egyptian and Syrian ports. One convoy, sailing in the spring, returned in September; the other sailed in August, wintered abroad and returned in May of the following year. There were three annual sailings for "Romania"—Constantinople and the Balkans; one in the spring, one at the end of June, and the third (to winter abroad) in August. Later, the Syrian and Egyptian sailings were divided; two convoys sailing every year for Alexandria and one for Beyrut.

At the height of Venetian prosperity, in the fourteenth and fifteenth centuries, the State-owned merchantmen ran six distinct services. The Galleys of Egypt, Syria, and "Romania" brought to Venice the high-priced Eastern products from the re-export of which her wealth was mainly derived. The Galleys of Barbary made a long annual voyage, touching at Syracuse, at Tripoli and other North African ports, and at Malaga and Almeria in Spain, with a call at Tunis on the homeward passage. They must have carried a great deal of local Mediterranean trade, in addition to taking part in the distribution of the rich cargoes brought by the Eastern services. Two other squadrons carried a costly freightage of Eastern luxuries, together with Mediterranean produce and Venetian manufactures, to the nations of northern Europe. The Galleys of Acquemorte served the ports of northern Spain and France. The Flanders Galleys, dating from at least as early as 1317, after calling at various Mediterranean ports, passed through the Straits and made for the English Channel, where they separated into two groups; one proceeding to London, Sandwich, or latterly Southampton, where the proceeds of the cargoes were invested in English wool, while the other went on to Antwerp and the Flanders ports. The return passage was made in company, and the round voyage occupied, usually, at least the full twelve months.

The method of engaging freight in these State fleets was peculiar; the cargo-space being disposed of by public auction. Private competition was not forbidden, but if the State ships had any difficulty in completing their cargoes, all merchants loading goods in privately owned vessels were obliged to pay a fine equal to a quarter, or even half of the freight.

Strange as it may seem to us to-day, when so many hundreds of British ships pass yearly through the Straits, the Flanders Galleys and the Genoese carracks—very broad, deep, sailing vessels—were, for some centuries, practically the only link by sea between northern Europe and the Mediterranean. Yet even in those centuries there were shipbuilders, shipowners, merchants, and statesmen in northern Europe, capable of profiting by the lessons which the Italians had to teach in marine architecture, in maritime enterprise, and in commercial organization. To these we must now turn and trace the development of the shipping industry in the North down to the time when the discovery of a new sea-route to India and of a hitherto unknown Continent in the West shifted the centre of naval power and commercial activity from the Mediterranean to the Atlantic.

The "Flanders Galleys"

SOME BOOKS FOR FURTHER READING

Mr. David Hannay's *The Sea Trader*, London, 1912, gives a short account of mediaeval shipping in the Mediterranean, and *The Navy of Venice* by Alethea Weil, London, 1910, is well worth reading for its account of Venetian trade and shipping. Most of the details as to methods of ownership, etc., can be found in the Introduction to Ashburner's edition of *The Rhodian Sea Law*, Oxford, 1909, an invaluable book to the student, but not one that can be recommended for general reading. For the text of the mediaeval codes, both in the Mediterranean and elsewhere, see the great *Collection des Lois Maritimes* by J. M. Pardessus, (6 vols., Paris, 1828–1845), and *The Black Book of the Admiralty*, ed. Sir Travers Twiss, Rolls Series, 4 vols., 1871–1876.

CHAPTER III

KING HERRING AND GOLDEN FLEECE

THE EARLY SHIPPING INDUSTRY OF NORTHERN EUROPE

The apostolic occupation of trafficking in fish. SIDNEY SMITH

The generous wool-sacks of England became her title of entry into the ranks of the progressing nations of the world.
J. A. WILLIAMSON, *Maritime Enterprise*

GREAT and varied as was the commerce carried by the Venetians and their Italian rivals, the real foundation of their wealth was their command of the trade with the Levant, through which they became the distributors to all Europe of the silks, gems, and spices of the East. The Venetian merchant-galleasses and the Genoese carracks were brought into being by the general demand for a more luxurious life than the native resources of European countries could provide. Very different, much more prosaic, but not less important, were the factors which chiefly influenced the growth of shipping in the North.

So long as the main trade route to India led through the Mediterranean and the Mediterranean States were powerful enough to control it, the nations of northern Europe were debarred from any direct share in the traffic. They drew their supplies of Eastern luxuries through Venice and Genoa, either in Italian bottoms or overland. There was another great trade route, however, which was all their own—that by which the furs, wax, and timber of Russia and the Baltic were brought to western Europe, together with the Persian and Chinese silks with which long trains of caravans had toiled across the deserts of Central Asia to the great mart at Novgorod.

Both the spices and silks of the East and the furs and

wax of Moscovy had to be paid for; and they were paid for mainly by manufactured goods, of which woollen cloth was the most important. The manufacture of cloth was carried on in Venice itself and in other Italian cities, but its chief centre was in Flanders, in the cities of the Rhine delta. Italians and Flemings both derived from England the bulk of their raw material.

English wool then was one of the chief factors in the demand for tonnage. Some of it went to Italy, as return cargoes, in the merchant-galleasses and the carracks; but there was also an overland route through Calais, and the shipments to Calais were not in Italian hands. Even more important was the export of raw wool, or of rough half-made cloth, to the great manufacturing centres of Flanders, and this, too, was carried wholly in northern ships. Yet, though the traffic in English wool was lucrative enough to merchants and shipowners to recall the fable of "The Golden Fleece," it is doubtful whether it gave employment to as much tonnage as was set afloat, directly or indirectly, by the fish which swarmed in the Northern seas, of which "King Herring" was the chief.

It requires a very considerable effort of the imagination to realize the importance of the fisheries to the people of the Middle Ages. Most of us think of fish simply as an agreeable means of giving variety to our diet. A kipper for breakfast makes a pleasant change from eggs and bacon. A fish course is a great help in the construction of a nicely balanced menu, and a bit of fish before the joint, turning "supper" into "dinner," has marked for thousands of middle-class households a definite stage in the achievement of prosperity and social advancement. We should miss our fish if we could no longer procure it; but very few of us look on it as one of the absolute necessities of life, and the fishing fleets seem a very small thing in comparison with the enormous volume of modern commerce.

In order to understand what fish meant in the Middle Ages, we must remember first that all Europe was then Catholic or Orthodox, and the many fast days rigidly and universally observed—especially the Lenten fast—would have been unendurable, in cold climates at any rate, if fish had not been available to take the place of meat. Moreover, meat itself was comparatively scarce and dear, and the poorer classes got very little of it at the best of times. In winter, supplies were short all round, for the scanty hay harvest barely sufficed to keep a few lean beasts alive, and apart from the curing of hams and the salting of a certain amount of pork, preserved meats were confined to costly luxuries like spiced beef.

In these circumstances, large supplies of dried or salted fish were absolutely indispensable as a supplement to the local fisheries on fast days, as winter store, and for the provisioning of towns expecting to stand a siege and of armies in the field. It was no doubt some camp humorist who gave its name to the "Battle of the Herrings"; but for the besiegers of Orleans, the safe arrival of Sir John Fastolf's convoy of salted fish was a very serious matter.

The effect of all this was threefold. In the first place, the actual fisheries employed a much larger number of people, in proportion to the population, than they do to-day. In the second place, the centres to which the fishermen brought their catch became busy marts, importing large quantities of salt for curing the fish, and of provisions and other necessaries for those engaged in the trade. Finally, the masters of the fisheries, especially the great herring fisheries of the North Sea and Baltic, found themselves in possession of a bulky product in great demand all over northern and western Europe, for which they could obtain in exchange whatever they themselves lacked, so that they were led to build big ships, capable of long voyages, in order to dispose of the catch.

The Scania Herring Fishery

Coastal fishing had, of course, been carried on all over Europe from prehistoric times, and from the sixth century A.D. onwards there are records shewing that Englishmen, French, and Flemings, were actively engaged in the Channel and North Sea fisheries and in the distribution of the catches, but the first appearance of King Herring as a dominant factor in the development of commerce was the rise of the great Scania Fishery at the entrance to the Baltic in the twelfth and thirteenth centuries. For ten months in the year the little Scania Peninsula at the south-west corner of Sweden, with its tiny towns of Scanor and Falsterbo, slept peacefully behind its sand dunes. For two months, from July 25th to September 29th, it was one of the busiest marts in Europe. Fishermen came in their thousands from near and far to share in the richest harvest of the northern seas; workmen in thousands came to salt and pack the catch; merchants came in hundreds to deal in the herrings themselves or to supply the needs of the fishermen and packers. Their huts and booths and stalls formed a great town of wood and canvas, where men chaffered, and sang, and quarrelled in every tongue of northern and western Europe. But from tne first it was the merchants of the Hanseatic towns who took the leading place, and it was not long before they attained such a predominance that their rivals were gradually edged out, or compelled to trade on sufferance, and within restricted limits.

The Hanseatic League, which dominated for three centuries, at least, the sea routes of northern Europe, was a confederation of German trading towns, owning allegiance to the Emperor, but self-governing in all that concerned their commerce and internal affairs. Its origins are obscure, for its organization was built up gradually and secretly; but by the middle of the thirteenth century, it was already well-established. The Treaty of Stralsund which concluded, in 1370, the League's victorious war with Denmark, revealed it as one of the Great Powers of Europe.

Lubeck, Bremen, Hamburg, and the other Hanseatic towns had long been important centres of trade, but the greatness of the Hansa was based, to a very large extent, on the command which the League obtained of the Scania fishery, and of the allied herring fishery carried on off the Baltic island of Rügen. The Germans did not themselves engage in fishing, for Scania was Danish territory and the actual fishermen were mostly Danes and Swedes. Moreover, the Hanseatics, who were always more interested in trade than in industry, were ready enough to leave to others the most toilsome and least remunerative part of the business. They found their profit in purchasing, salting, packing, and distributing the greater part of the catch, and in the supply of salt and barrels for the work, and of provisions and beer—above all beer, for fish-curing is thirsty work—for the temporary population of the Peninsula. This population was so large that 20,000 men are said to have been engaged in a free fight between Danes and Germans which broke out in 1463, so that the business of ministering to their needs must have been a profitable sideline. But it was the distribution of the catch that was the real gold-mine. In Germany itself, in Russia, Poland, and all the Baltic States, in Flanders, in France, in Spain and Portugal, Scania herrings found ready buyers and the Hanseatic merchants reaped large profits.

Thus the disposal of the herrings entailed long voyages and the use of big sea-going ships; and the proceeds of the herrings were used to procure return cargoes of the characteristic local products. These products could be disposed of, not only at home, but in every country where they were not produced, thus opening up fresh avenues of trade. With plenty of money and plenty of tonnage at their command, the Hanseatic merchants were always restlessly striving to extend the scope of their activities, and in no long time they became the great middlemen and carriers for the whole of northern Europe.

Wherever they traded, the Hanseatics set up their "Kontors" or factories, where the merchants lived in common, sworn to a definite period of residence, to celibacy during the term of their stay, and to strict obedience to the Aldermen and Council. And wherever they traded they worked ceaselessly and ruthlessly, by peaceful penetration, by diplomacy, and if needs be by war, to secure for the Kontor a monopoly of the external trade of the country in which it was situated. In cities like Bruges, already the seat of great manufactures and of a thriving international trade, they had, perforce, to content themselves with the grant of such privileges as would secure to them a fair share of the traffic. In less civilized centres, where commercial organization was undeveloped, and the Government weak, they often succeeded in making their monopoly absolute. In particular, they passed on from control of the Scania fishery to an almost complete command of the Baltic and Scandinavian trade, and through their settlement at Novgorod they monopolized the trade with Russia.

This gave them an immensely strong position. In addition to hides, skins, and tallow, Russia provided an inexhaustible supply of furs, which fetched high prices from the proud nobles and wealthy burghers of the west; honey—which took, in the Middle Ages, the place of sugar—and wax, for which there was an immense demand all over Europe for the manufacture of the hundreds of thousands of votive candles annually offered by the piety of worshippers and pilgrims. Through Novgorod, too, the silks of Persia and Cathay passed, by Hanseatic hands, into the markets of Western Europe. The Baltic and Scandinavian trade was even more important. Iron, copper, and building stone came from Scandinavia. Treaties with the Danish

Kings secured for the Germans a big share in distributing the products of the Norwegian and Icelandic cod-fisheries. Grain in large quantities was shipped from Poland and Russia to the Netherlands and Flanders, and even, when the local harvest was short, to England. Above all, the Baltic and Scandinavian countries were the main source of supply for all the chief materials of shipbuilding—timber for planking, tall fir-trees for masts, tar and pitch for caulking, flax and hemp for sails and cordage. It was this monopoly of the supply of shipbuilding materials, even more than their own naval force, which rendered the goodwill of the League cities indispensable to Powers bent on naval and maritime expansion.

It must not, of course, be imagined that the Hanseatic merchants monopolized the whole of the carrying trade outside the Mediterranean. Even the Hansa viewed with respect, and jealousy, the fat Flemish hulks which carried heavy cargoes of English wool to the Flanders ports, and distributed to England and elsewhere the products of the craftsmen and artisans of Bruges and Ghent. In Western waters, too, there was a considerable amount of traffic in which the Hansa played little part, and which was carried mainly by English, French, and Spanish ships. There was, for instance, the export of salt from Rochelle and other Bay of Biscay ports. The Hanseatics bought occasional cargoes, but they preferred Luneberg salt, which was cheaper, for the curing of their herrings; whereas England, until her own deposits of rock-salt began to be worked in the seventeenth century, depended largely on "Bay Salt," which was also in good demand in Spain and Portugal.

By far the most notable of the Biscay trades, however, was the export of wine from Bordeaux. Fortunately for the growth of English shipping, the Germans were chiefly beer-drinkers, and had their own supply of wine, when they wanted it, in the vineyards of the Rhineland. The trade was thus left to the English and French, and it must be remembered that, down to the middle of the fifteenth century, the winefields of Gascony and Guienne, with the port of Bordeaux itself, formed part of the English possessions in France.

It was mainly for the regulation of this traffic that the Judgments of Oléron were drawn up. This celebrated code takes its name from the island of Oléron, off the French coast, where a maritime Court is said to have been held. According to one rather doubtful story it was compiled, or at least edited for English use, by the orders of King Richard Cœur de Lion, who had acquired an interest in shipping as the result of his experiences on the Third Crusade. Be this as it may, the Judgments are, in effect, a series of pronouncements on maritime law and practice, based on long custom and on the decisions arrived at by local Courts in cases of difficulty. They followed, to a great extent, Mediterranean usage, and they were themselves very widely copied or adapted; notably in the Sea Laws of Wisby, and the codes adopted by Lubeck, Amsterdam, and other German, Dutch, and Flemish ports. For it cannot be too often emphasized that shipping is an international industry, and it is very inconvenient to both shipowner and merchant if the laws and customs by which it is regulated are not approximately the same at all ports. The unification of the law under the Roman Empire had a great deal to do with the great development of commerce under the Augustans, and, now that the Empire was gone, something had to be found to take its place. As there was no League of Nations or Hague Court to do the work for them, the merchants and shipowners had to do it for themselves (as indeed they have often done it in recent years, through such bodies as the International Shipowners' Conference and the International Maritime Committee), and the result was the building up of a great body of customary law, widely adopted, and only varied in detail to suit local conditions.

In their general provisions, the Judgments of Oléron reflect—as we have already seen—a state of things very similar to that prevailing in the Mediterranean in the early Middle Ages. Master and crew form one family, messing together, and having very much the same status. The Captain has to consult the ship's company before effecting jettison or borrowing money for necessaries on the security of the ship's gear. The sailors are entitled, in addition to their wages, to the carriage of a certain quantity of goods freight free, or, if they prefer it, to a percentage on the total freight of the ship. In the event of shipwreck, they are required to help in the work of salvage, but in return are entitled not only to a reward, but to the receipt of conduct money for their return to their own country. If the captain is short of cash for this purpose, he may raise the necessary sum on the security of the salved goods.

Other clauses are more strictly local. Brittany seamen are entitled to only one cooked meal a day, because they get wine on both the outward and the homeward passage. The seamen of Normandy, which is not a wine country, are entitled to two meals, because they get only water when going out; but they may demand wine when they come to a country where it is grown.

If a Charter-party contains a clause to the effect that the charterers are to bear the expenses of towing (or warping) and coasting pilotage, the pilots whose charges the ship is entitled to recover are those taken for passing the island of Batz (off the coast of Brittany), and those taken for passing Guernsey, Calais, and Yarmouth.

It is in relation to the treatment of pilots that the Judgments break out for once into true mediaeval savagery. Suppose a local pilot, who has sworn "by his head" to take a ship safely into port should lose her or run her into peril, then:

> If the captain or any of the sailors or any of the merchants should cut off his head, they are not liable to any penalty; but before killing him it is always well to find out whether he has the means of making amends. And that is the judgment in this case.

"Never kill a man from whom you could recover damages," is an excellently business-like injunction.

Many clauses relate specifically to the wine-trade, such as those which make the captain and mariners responsible for damage caused through negligent stowage of the casks, or through using ropes or a windlass of insufficient strength when discharging cargo. Another clause added at a later date, and found only in the British Admiralty's manuscript of the Judgments, provides that if the consignee of wine or other goods has not taken delivery within 21 days after the ship's arrival, the captain may put the cargo ashore on a quay, and place an agent in charge of it, to see that it is not given up until freight has been paid.

This provision for a fixed term of "lay days" was common in the Middle Ages. The Dutch version of the sea laws, for instance, provides that ships from Hamburg and other near ports must be discharged, and the freight paid, within eight days of arrival, and ships from more distant ports within fourteen days. It fixes also the payment to be made to the ship for the discharge of various kinds of cargo, including grain, planks, staves, ashes, herrings, resin, tar, flax, cloth, and wine. The three last-named are classed as "heavy goods," on which a higher rate must be paid, as they can only be unloaded by fixing a tackle on the ship's mast.

To return to the Judgments of Oléron, another of the additional clauses shows that there was plenty of human nature in the seaman of the twelfth century. It sets out that although sailors on a wine ship often expect the charterer to give them on fête days or at each port of call a "pot of wine, or two, or three;" they are not really entitled to it, and if the merchant agrees to their demand, it is purely an act of grace.

These local or specialized provisions give us, in fact, some of our most intimate glimpses into life aboard a mediaeval trading vessel; but in actual historical importance, they yield to the more general provisions which, in various adaptations, regulated trade from the Bay to the Baltic throughout the earlier Middle Ages. As the trade of the Hanseatic cities developed, however, they, like the Venetians and their competitors in the Mediterranean, found it necessary to supplement the earlier codes, and Hanseatic trade in the fifteenth century was governed mainly by special decrees issued by the Council of the League.

One of the chief objects of the Council was, of course, to preserve that predominance in the carrying trade to which the Hansa owed its prosperity even more than to the enterprise of its merchants in the buying and selling of goods. A long series of decrees is directed to keeping Northern waters, so far as possible, as a Hanseatic preserve. Thus, a decree of 1412 sets out that:

> Many foreigners belonging to various countries which have no part in the League, have done serious injuries to the Hanseatic merchants, by loading merchandize, navigating and trade. . . .

and proceeds to prohibit the sale to foreigners of any ship or of any part-interest in a ship. In 1434, the Council contented itself with prohibiting shipbuilding for Lombards, Englishmen, Frenchmen, Dutch or other foreigners, or the sale to them of any ship which had not been engaged in trade for at least a year; but in 1441 the sale of any ship to a foreigner was again absolutely prohibited, and it was even forbidden for foreigners to charter a Hanseatic vessel.

Nor was any foreigner allowed to build, own, or act as captain of a ship within the jurisdiction of the League. Six years later all Hanseatic merchants were definitely forbidden to load any goods in a foreign-owned ship.

It appears from the decrees that most Hanseatic ships were owned by syndicates, of which the captain was usually, though not always, a member. Whether he was a shareholder in the ship or not, he was responsible to the owners as a body; he had to render them voyage accounts, and he was not allowed to engage freight against their wishes or without their knowledge; nor had he authority to borrow money on the security of ship or goods.

The ship would probably be loaded, in part, with the owners' goods; but the League embraced inland as well as coastal towns, and even the merchants of the seaports were not all shipowners; so that the chartering of ships or ship-space, in the modern style, was carried on on a very large scale and the Captain appears, to a much greater extent than in the earlier sea laws, as a mere servant of his owners and charterers. The captain's responsibilities to the charterers were fixed not only by the general body of mediaeval sea law, but by special decrees of the Council, some of them very drastic. It was provided, for instance, by a law of 1447 that, if a captain should take the ship to any other port than that to which she was freighted, or should sell goods belonging to the charterers without their consent, he should be punishable with death.

As was natural in a mercantile community, every care was taken to secure safe carriage of goods by sea. The ships had to be built under the supervision of experts appointed by the towns. A law of 1412 provides that no ship should be built with a greater capacity than 100 last (1,400 barrels) of herrings, or with a loaded draught of water exceeding six Lubeck ells, and the surveyors were instructed to mark the ship with the arms of the town, before she left the stocks, as a token that she had been built in compliance with the law.[1]

By the same law the Councils of the towns and the heads of the factories abroad were charged with the duty of seeing that ships were not overloaded. If overloading occurred the captain was responsible for any consequent damage, and even if the ship arrived safely, he was liable to a fine equal to the freight on the excess cargo. A later law (1447) absolutely prohibited the carriage of a deck-cargo or the stowage of goods in the cabin.

If the ship was loaded with wheat, it was the captain's duty to see that the cargo was shifted so often as might be necessary, and he was empowered to pay the crew a fixed bonus for the work.

Winter voyages were strenuously discouraged. No ship was allowed to put to sea between Martinmas (November 11th) and Candlemas (February 2nd) except those loaded with herrings, cod, or beer, who were allowed a later date in order to take advantage of the winter market.

The usual method of paying the crews seems to have been a lump sum for the round voyage, payable one-third on setting sail, one-third on arrival at the port of discharge, and one-third on the return to the ship's home port. In addition to their wages, the men were entitled to extra pay for ballasting the ship, or for shifting grain cargoes, and like the captain, they were entitled to the carriage of a certain amount of goods free on their private account.

The earliest victualling regulations date from 1530, but probably embody long-established usage. They provide for the issue of beef or bacon, peas and "boiled dishes" on meat days, and salt fish, gruel, beans and peas on other days, but do not specify quantities. The Hansa were hard masters and the victualling was probably not lavish.

[1] These dimensions were largely exceeded in later times, when the art of shipbuilding had advanced.

Discipline was very severe for, by the fourteenth century, at any rate, the crews of the Hanseatic ships were simply hired seamen, with no interest in the voyage, except their small allowance of free space. By a law of 1380, desertion after receipt of a wage advance, was a capital offence. Later, the punishment was reduced to restitution of the wages and three months' imprisonment on bread and water. A sailor who disobeyed the lawful commands of his captain was liable to forfeit his wages, to be put ashore at the first port of call, and declared incapable of employment in any Hanseatic ship.

These drastic laws do not seem to have been very effective, for in 1441 the Council complained movingly that:

> Sailors are daily found disobedient to their captains, which has caused great damage to the merchants' goods and may be to their prejudice in the future unless something is done about it.

They decided, therefore, that any complaints by captains against their sailors should be strictly investigated, and if they were found to be just, the guilty men should be "punished as the circumstances may require in order to serve as an example to others." These words have an ominous ring; for German justice in the fifteenth century worked largely by means of the rack, the wheel, and the whipping post.

Harsh as the decrees may have been, the stricter discipline, and clearer fixing of responsibility which they reflect, as compared with such codes as the Judgment of Oléron, were part cause and part result of the ruthless commercial efficiency which brought so great a share of the trade of Northern Europe into Hanseatic hands. Nowhere, outside the Baltic, was the Hansa seated in the saddle more firmly than in England. Its merchants were drawn there, like all other alien traders, mainly by the lure of the golden fleece.

England had not, in those days, many commodities to send abroad; indeed wool, tin, and hides comprised the staple exports of the country. But of these, tin was valuable, being scarce elsewhere, and English wool was the basis of the great continental cloth industries in Italy and Flanders. Export duties on wool formed a large proportion of the Crown revenues, and with the object of checking smuggling, the export of the three staples was confined (apart from direct shipments to Italy in Italian bottoms) to a single channel. They could be shipped only to the "Staple" town abroad, where their discharge was carefully supervised. At first this was fixed in Flanders, but after the capture of Calais in 1347 it was removed to that port, which was now under English jurisdiction, and which was accessible and convenient to Flemish, German, and French buyers, and could easily be made the starting point of the overland route to Italy. The whole trade was at first in foreign hands (chiefly Italian), English subjects being actually prohibited from engaging in it; but in 1362 Englishmen were admitted to the trade, and the "Merchants of the Staple" gradually became a close corporation of English traders.

It was not then, in the export of raw wool, that the Hansa—at any rate after the establishment of the Staple—found their advantage. But, by this time the English had begun to manufacture on their own account a rough coarse cloth, of which large quantities were exported, especially to Flanders, where the Flemings put it through the finishing processes of rowing, shearing, and dyeing, and were thus able to sell dear what they had bought cheap. The export of this half-made cloth to Flanders grew rapidly and both English and Flemish merchants engaged in the trade. But the Hanseatics, already firmly settled both in London and in Bruges, got a grip upon it at an early date, and when England began to export cloth direct to other parts of Europe, the Hanse merchants took the lion's share of the traffic.

It may seem strange that the export of England's chief product—the one thing that made her an indispensable factor in the commercial system of Europe—should have been allowed to pass so largely into foreign hands. It must be remembered, however, that feudal England was a poor, and in material civilization, a backward country. The English people were making great advances in the development of social and political institutions, and they were great in arms, thanks to their adoption of the long-bow; but in the accumulation of capital, in arts and industries, and in appreciation of the comforts and amenities of life, they lagged far behind the burghers of the great trading cities of Italy, Germany, and Flanders.

Broadly speaking, the commercial policy of the English kings, from the thirteenth to the fifteenth century, had two main objects; first, to increase the royal revenues by encouraging the growth of imports and exports on which dues could be levied; secondly, to raise the standard of life and civilization by ensuring a cheap and plentiful supply of goods. With these objects in view, they deliberately encouraged the settlement of alien citizens who could bring new industries into the country, and they sought to promote intercourse with the great trading centres of the Continent, by granting commercial privileges to foreign merchants, such as the Hanseatics and Lombards.

This policy brought them into frequent collision with the craft and merchant guilds, and particularly the citizens of London, but it was generally supported by Parliament, which represented mainly the interests of consumers—nobles and landowners. Indeed, although the favour shown to foreign merchants was often carried to unfair extremes (especially when the King had borrowed money from them to defray the expenses of the French wars), it probably did more to promote the growth of wealth and enterprise in England itself than any protective measures could have done. It was not, however, favourable to the growth of English shipping; for the German and Italian merchants, who obtained so firm a grip on the trade, carried the goods in their own ships or in those of their countrymen.

English ships found their chief employment in the fisheries, in the coasting trade, and in the trade with the English possessions in France. The coasting trade was considerable, for the cost of water transport was only about one-sixth the cost of carriage by land. The trade with France received a great impetus from the capture of Calais and its substitution for Bruges as the "Staple" town; but from the point of view of shipping, by far the most important branch of this trade was the import of wine from Bordeaux, which became one of the chief schools of ocean navigation for English seamen, and one of the chief incentives to the building of large ships. Its commercial importance may be gathered from the fact that the capacity of all ships was measured by the number of tuns of Bordeaux wine they could carry.

Although the Third Crusade had carried English ships to the Mediterranean so early as 1190, and contact with Mediterranean shipping had, probably, some influence on naval architecture in England, no trading voyages to that sea are recorded earlier than the fifteenth century. The monopoly of the Venetians and Genoese was too strong to be challenged. There were voyages to Spain, however, for oil and wine, and a flourishing passenger traffic sprang up, during the twelfth century, with the growing popularity of the pilgrimage to the shrine of St. James of Compostella in northern Spain. Many English ships went to Iceland, to take part in the fisheries or to trade with the Icelanders for stockfish, and there was some intercourse with Scandinavia and the Baltic, though it was always restricted, owing to the jealousy and power of the Hansa. Chaucer's "Shipman"—a master-mariner who owned his own ship, the *Maudelayne*, and was learned in the stars, and tides, and all the lore of pilotage—was a much travelled fellow who had been in every port from Gothland in Sweden to Finisterre, and knew every creek in Spain and Brittany.

He was also, it must be confessed, a bit of a scamp. "Of nicë conscience took he no keepe," and, when in the Bordeaux trade, he helped himself to many a good draught of wine while the merchants were sleeping. There is a hint, too, of darker misdeeds in the lines which follow:

> If that he faught, and hadde the hyer hond;
> By water he sente hem hoom to every lond.

He may have been in the King's service when he disposed of his prisoners so summarily, by throwing them overboard; but it is just as likely that he was not, for the English seaman was an incorrigible pirate. He was not under the thumb of the State or of great merchant princes, like the Venetians and Hanseatics (not that their hands were clean), and the French wars gave him plenty of opportunity for privateering and "reprisals" which easily degenerated into down-right piracy. There was not enough steady, remunerative trade available for English shipping to make piracy unattractive, and the English seaman took to it like a duck to water. He raided the French coasts both in war and in peace; he plundered many a fat Flemish merchant ship; he carried away Icelanders into slavery. When things were quiet he was always ready to fill in time by a little private warfare over some question of trading or fishing rights—the ships of the Cinque ports against those of Yarmouth, for example. It was all great fun, and it bred a hardy, dare-devil race of seamen, who were later to find a wider and more legitimate outlet for their energies; but it was not helpful to the growth of an orderly, prosperous shipping industry.

This tendency to prefer piracy to trade was accentuated by the identity between the trading and fighting fleets, which was, in itself a serious hindrance to the development of commerce. Unlike the great naval powers of the Mediterranean, England possessed no strong, permanent naval force. The mediaeval Englishman (and the French outside the Mediterranean) had little use for the galley. Its unsuitability for the stormy, northern seas may have had something to do with it, though the Norseman had shown what the oared long-ship was capable of doing in northern waters. Probably the chief reason was that the kings were too poor to keep up a big navy of ships built exclusively for war. The Plantagenets maintained a few galleys for police purposes; but in the main, when the Englishman wanted a fighting ship, he simply erected platforms for archers and men-at-arms at the bow and stern of his deep, heavy sailing vessel, and endeavoured to run alongside and board his enemy. The king might have a few ships of his own, which were often chartered to merchants for trading voyages in time of peace. The Cinque Ports were bound, in return for their privileges, to furnish fifty-seven vessels for fifteen days at their own expense, and for any longer period on receipt of hire; but the bulk of the fleets were composed of ordinary merchantmen, requisitioned under the royal prerogative.

The results of this were very bad for trade. While only too many merchant seamen acquired a strong taste for fighting and plunder, these scratch fleets of armed merchantmen were not very effective in the protection of commerce against enemies in time of war, or against pirates in time of peace. Moreover, war, or even the threat of war involved, under these conditions, the withdrawal of a large part of the available shipping from commercial employment.

So far as the shipowner himself was concerned, this was not, taking a short view, necessarily a bad thing. The king's right to requisition ships and impress men was modified by an obligation to pay compensation. Masters and mariners received their wages, and the shipowner was paid hire for the use of his vessel, on a time-tonnage basis. In the fourteenth and fifteenth centuries the usual rate "duly and loyally paid from time immemorial," seems to have been three shillings and fourpence a quarter "per tun tyght." Coupled with the prospect of plunder and prize-money, this probably made war-service at least as profitable as peaceful trading, so long as these "Blue Book Rates" were "duly and loyally" paid. Unfortunately, this could not be relied upon, and as the resources of the Crown became more and more exhausted by the long drain of the French wars, there were frequent complaints of intolerable delays in payment. Further, ships were often taken up long before they were actually wanted, and as hire only began to run from the actual entry into service, they lay idle for weeks, or even months, at their owners' charges. So early as 1340, the year of the great victory at Sluys, it became necessary to prohibit the sale of ships to foreigners in order to evade the burden of requisition (it all sounds very much like the Great War!), and by the death of Edward III, when the tide of war at sea had turned against England, the combined effect of war losses, requisitioning, and foreign competition had brought English shipping into a sad state of decay.

By this time the trading and mercantile classes had become wealthy enough and strong enough to put effective pressure on the Government, and in 1381 they persuaded the Parliament of Richard II to pass the first English Navigation Act, in order to "Increase the Navy of England, which is now greatly diminished." It will be noted that then, and for two centuries afterwards, "the Navy of England" meant not merely the Royal, but all English ships. By this Act all subjects of the Crown were forbidden to ship any merchandise into or out of England, except in vessels "of the king's liegance." This left the Italian and German merchants free to employ their own ships, but apparently there was not enough English shipping even for the needs of English traders, for in the following year it was enacted that foreign ships might be chartered if English ships were not readily available. Eight years later another Act was passed, which compelled all English merchants to export their goods in English ships, provided their owners were willing to "take reasonable gains for the freight of the same." Very prudently, Parliament shrank from the task of defining "reasonable gains."

Whether these Acts had any real effect is very doubtful. They were certainly powerless to offset the continued losses from enemies and pirates and the irregularities in payment of hire for requisitioned ships. A petition addressed to Henry IV makes bitter complaint that many owners are laying up their vessels, in sheer despair of running them at a profit. It is certainly noteworthy that Henry V, under whom the shipping industry experienced the first boom it had known for many years, seems to have allowed the Acts to fall into disuse. What that energetic ruler gave to shipping was something much more important—the protection of a strong fleet.

A man of military genius, Henry appears to have grasped the essential weakness of the usual scratch mediaeval fleet, and to have set himself steadily to the building up of a force capable of carrying out the normal police of the seas, and of bearing the main brunt of the fighting in time of war. A complete "Navy List" of his reign shows a total of thirty-eight vessels, of which twelve were prizes captured from the French and retained in the Royal service. Most of these latter were big Genoese and Spanish carracks serving with the French, and these provided English shipbuilders with excellent models for the building of larger ships than they had yet produced. When not required for war, the King's ships were sometimes made to earn their keep by being chartered to merchants for commerce, and as they were well suited to long voyages and big cargoes, this, too, acted as a stimulus to English enterprise.

Thanks to Royal encouragement, adequate naval protection, the growth of the cloth manufacture, and the general revival of the national spirit which marked Henry's short reign, the opening years of the fifteenth century witnessed a remarkable increase of activity in shipping circles. The trade with Iceland for stockfish (salt cod) became important; voyages were undertaken to Portugal and Morocco, and in the year of the King's death, English traders appeared for the first time in the Mediterranean itself.

With Henry's death his navy disappeared. It had never been a Royal Navy in the modern sense of the word. The King's ships were the personal property of the monarch, and on the accession of Henry VI the Council of Regency put them up to auction for the benefit of the late King's creditors. Once again English shipping was left without any protection other than that afforded by armed merchantmen, serving under contract. In other ways England was passing through troublous times. A long minority was followed by the reign of a weak and incompetent monarch; the civil Wars of the Roses succeeded to the disastrous campaigns by which England lost all her French possessions except Calais. Yet the impetus given to trade and navigation during the reign of Henry V seems to have persisted. The loss of the French provinces was a blessing in disguise —for they had become a drain on the National resources rather than an asset. The Wars of the Roses—fought out between the nobles and their retainers—did little to check the progress of the cloth industry, and the Merchant Adventurers (founded or refounded in 1407 with a factory at Antwerp) were rich enough and enterprising enough to keep a part, at least, of the cloth export in English hands.

Some evidence of the growth of shipping is afforded by the lists of vessels requisitioned for transport purposes. Down to the end of the fourteenth century, English ships had rarely exceeded 100 tons, and there were not many ships even of this size. But a list of ships taken up in 1439 for the transport of troops to Aquitaine includes eleven vessels ranging between 200 and 360 tons, and a similar list of 1451 contains twenty-three of from 200 to 400 tons. Some great shipowners, such as William Canynge of Bristol, are known to have possessed still larger ships.

Most of these larger ships probably found their chief employment in the Bordeaux wine trade and the pilgrim traffic to Saint James of Compostella. A contemporary ballad, describing one of these pilgrim voyages, gives a very vivid picture of the traffic, and an almost unique glimpse of the fifteenth century seaman going about his work. It is written from the standpoint of someone who has made the voyage; who has a very strong recollection of the discomforts of the stormy passage in a crowded ship no larger than a modern coaster, but, having found his sea legs, is ready to take on himself the airs of a sailor and poke fun at the terrors and sufferings of landlubbers.

Men may leve alle gamys
That saylen to Seynt Jamys

he tells us. The pilgrims come aboard at Bristol, or Sandwich, or Winchelsea (these last two not yet choked up by the shifting of the coast), and hardly has the ship cast off before "Theyr hertes begyn to fayle."

However, there is all the bustle of getting under way to distract their attention. The "Mastyr" calls his sailors together about the mast and orders them to make sail.

With "howe! hissa!" then they cry

for chanteys had not yet come in. One or two climb out on the yard to shake loose the great single square sail:

> "Y howe! taylia!"[1] the remenaunt cryen,
> And pulle with alle theyr myght.

While some of the crew are getting the ship under sail, others are looking after the comfort of the passengers:

> "Bestowe the boote, Bote-swayne, anone,
> That our pylgryms may pley thereon:
> For som ar lyke to cowgh and grone,
> Or hit be full mydnyght."
>
> "Hale the bowelyne! now, vere the shete!
> Cooke, make redy anoon our mete,
> Our pylgryms have no lust to ete,
> I pray god yeve hem rest."
> "Go to the helm! what, howe! no nere?[2]
> Steward, felow! a pot of bere!"
> "Ye shall have, sir, with good chere
> Anone all of the best!"
>
> "Y howe! trussa![3] hale in the brayles!
> Thou halyst nat, be god, thow fayles!
> O se howe welle owre good shyp sayles!"
> And thus they say among.
> "Hale in the wartake!"[4] "Hit shall be done."
> "Steward! cover the boorde anone,
> And set bred and salt thereone,
> And tary nat to long."

In spite of all these cheerful preparations, the pilgrims have still "no lust to eat." The inevitable Job's comforter is going round assuring them that a storm is at hand, and most of them are already seasick.

[1] Tally on, take hold and haul.
[2] No nearer the wind.
[3] Haul, as in "O truss her up."
[4] A Warp.

And some wolde have a saltyd tost
Ffor they myghte ete neyther sode ne rost;
A man myght sone pay for theyr cost,
  As for oo day or twayne.
Some layde their bookys on theyr kne,
And rad so long they myght nat se:—
"Allas! myne hede wolle cleve on thre!"
  Thus seyth another certayne.

The shipowner, however—some great merchant prince like William Canynge—is making the voyage with the ship and is ready to relieve the master of some part of his cares. It is his business to look after the comfort of the passengers and to see to the erection of the temporary cabins or cubicles provided for them. Like a good fellow and a business man with an eye to future custom, he tries to cheer up the pilgrims:

Then commeth owre owner lyke a lorde,
And speketh many a Royall worde,
And dresseth hym to the hygh borde,
  To see alle thyng be welle.
Anone he calleth a carpentere,
And byddyth hym bryng with hym hys gere,
To make the cabans here and there,
  With many a febylle celle.

Those who have brought a sack of straw or other bedding with them are lucky—for there are no bunks or hammocks and the rest must lie down in their hoods on the bare deck. But this is not the worst, and the ballad ends with what was evidently its maker's most bitter memory of the voyage:

For when that we shall go to bedde,
The pumpe was nygh oure beddes hede,
A man were as good to be dede,
  As smell thereof the stynk!

Despite all his discomforts the ballad-maker seems to have enjoyed this glimpse of a new life and to have kept his eyes well open. He sketches the sailors as a hearty, cheery crowd, with their cries of "Howe! hissa!" as they haul on the ropes, their mutual recriminations, their pride in their ship, and their delight in mocking the seasick landsmen. We have to thank him, too, for his care in recording the internal economy of the ship, the owner-manager, the master, boatswain (still essentially the petty officer in charge of the ship's boat), carpenter, cook, and steward.

He does not tell us what the seamen were paid; but from such scanty evidence as is left to us, we can gather that it was no bad trade in those days to be bred to the sea. The "Inquisition of Queenborrow" has preserved for us the customary rates for some of the more usual voyages in 1375. The rates quoted are all lump sum payments for a round voyage, and it must be remembered that they must be multiplied by fifteen, at least, to get an equivalent in modern money.

For the Bordeaux trip in "vintage time," the mariner had 8s. and the freight of a tun of wine; at other seasons he had to be content with 7s. and the freight of a pipe. A voyage to Brittany for salt brought him 5s. and the privilege of three quarters of salt at first cost. For the round voyage to any port on the south coast of Ireland he received 10s. and the freight on thirty hides; but if the voyage were extended west of the Old Head of Kinsale or north of the Tuskar, 2s. was added to the pay. The payment for a round trip in the Newcastle coal trade was 4s. and free space for two quarters of coal; for a voyage to Scone, in Scotland, 8s. in cash, and the freight of a last (4,000 lb.) of herrings between three men. Five shillings was paid for the London–Calais trip, and 6s. for a voyage to Flanders; but in these trades there were no freight privileges.

The value of these payments and allowances depended, of course, on the length of the voyage, and the profits of the seaman's private trading, or the amount of freight he received in lieu of free space. The latter was well worth having; for the "Inquisition of Queenborrow" records that the sailor was entitled to expect 10s. as the freight of a ton on the voyage to Bayonne; and 20s. on a voyage to Lisbon.

Perhaps the best way of measuring the seaman's real economic position is to take the wages he received when serving the Crown, as these are not complicated by privileges, other than a chance of prize money. During the thirteenth and fourteenth centuries, the rate of pay was 3d. a day, with usually an additional "reward" or bonus of 6d. a week, making a total of 9s. for a month of 28 days. This does not look much to us, but it compares well with wages ashore. In 1351, a mason, the best-paid type of artisan, could look for no more than 3d. a day *without food* (or 4d. if he were a master-mason). A master carpenter received 3d., an ordinary carpenter 2d., and a labourer only 1½d. a day. By the last quarter of the fourteenth century wages had risen, and a mason might look for 3d. a day with food, or 5d. a day without; but on the whole, the seaman still had a slight advantage.

In 1440 the sailor's wage was reduced to 1s. 6d. a week (the same amount being allowed for victualling); but in 1445 it was again raised to the old level of 1s. 9d. per week plus 6d. "reward"; boys received 1s. 1½d. a week; masters 6d. a day (or 14s. a month). By this time there had been a still further rise in shore wages, but the seaman's pay, when allowance is made for his food, put him at least on a level with the average skilled artisan, and much above the common labourer.

Under Edward IV, another strong ruler, the progress of trade and shipping became more rapid. Edward owed his accession largely to the support of the commercial classes, and he repaid that support by the adoption of a strongly protectionist policy and by withdrawing many of the privileges granted to foreign merchants. He gratified the shipowners, too, by a new Navigation Act, forbidding the chartering of foreign vessels by English subjects, either for export or for import, so long as "sufficient freight" was available in English ships. This Act, however, was allowed to lapse after three years, and did less for the shipping industry than the series of commercial treaties which Edward concluded with Burgundy, Brittany, Castile, Zeeland, and Denmark, providing for freedom of intercourse on a basis of reciprocity.

One great grievance to English traders and shipowners still remained. When a Lancastrian rising drove Edward from the country in 1470, it was by the aid of the Hanseatic capitalists that Edward had procured men and money for his return and for the victorious campaign of Tewkesbury. They reaped their reward in the Treaty of Utrecht which confirmed and extended their privileges in England and enabled them to compete on more than equal terms with English merchants in the export of cloth to the Continent. English traders and shipowners might grumble and curse as they passed the Steelyard—the London headquarters of the Hansa—but, strong in the Royal favour, the German merchants could afford to regard their jealousy with contempt.

In truth, England was not yet strong enough to quarrel with the League. It controlled, in large measure, the supply of indispensable commodities such as shipbuilding materials, wax, honey, high quality Swedish iron, and yew staves from the Carpathian forests, shipped through Dantzig for the making of English long-bows. Its political influence, and its naval power (which England had as yet no fleet capable of challenging) might be used, in the event of a break, to exclude English ships and traders from every port of North-eastern Europe. Englishmen might grumble at its privileges, but England could not afford its enmity.

It is strange to us to-day to read of Englishmen playing

second fiddle to foreigners in the export of their own goods, and of English ships trading at peril and on sufferance in European waters; and we are apt to think of the Hanseatics as the Merchant Adventurers thought of them in the reign of Elizabeth—as a selfish and rapacious group of foreign monopolists whom it was the duty of every patriotic Englishman to oppose with every weapon fortune put into his hands. There is an element of truth in this. The Hanseatics—like all mediaeval traders—were monopolists, and it was their folly and misfortune to cling to the idea of monopoly long after the progress of the nations with whom they traded had rendered monopoly impossible. But this is only one side of the truth. The Hanseatic League came into being because it was only by a strong and wealthy association of merchants, backed by diplomatic adroitness, and if necessary by force, that commerce on a large scale could be carried on at all in the chaotic conditions of feudal Europe. Selfish and unscrupulous as the Hanseatics often showed themselves, they conferred inestimable benefits on Europe and on England by promoting an exchange of products which raised the general standard of life, and by the lessons which they taught in commercial organization. They live in the history of the world by the part they played in the development of material civilization. In the history of the world's shipping industry they occupy a still higher place, as the first people of Northern Europe to show that national prosperity and political greatness could be firmly based on enterprise and ability in the carrying trade.

SOME BOOKS ON THE PERIOD

The best authority for the early history of the Fisheries is *The Sovereignty of the Seas* by T. W. Fulton, London, 1911. *The Hansa Towns* by Helen Zimmern ("Story of the Nations" series), London, 1904, and *The Hansa,* by E. G. Nash, London, 1929, are useful for the general history of Hanseatic trade, but not very strong on the shipping side. For the maritime laws of the Hansa it is necessary to go to the collection by Pardessus already cited. There is another version of the laws of Oléron, with English translation, in the Rolls edition of *The Black Book of the Admiralty*, which also gives the "Inquisition of Queenborrow." For the relations between Shipping and the State, seamen's wages in Crown service, and much incidental material relating to the growth of shipping, see Professor Oppenheim's *A History of the Administration of the Royal Navy and of Merchant Shipping in relation to the Navy*, London, 1896, and the Chapters which he contributed to the *Victoria County Histories*. For comparative shore wages, see Thorold Rogers's *A History of Agriculture and Prices*. The edition of Barnard's *Companion to English History* edited by H. W. C. Davies, London, 1924, has valuable chapters on mediaeval shipping (by Professor Oppenheim), trade, and industry. I have taken the Pilgrim ballad from *The Stacions of Rome*, ed. F. J. Furnivall, E.E.T.S., 1867. It is most accessible in *A Sailor's Garland*, ed. John Masefield, London, 1908.

CHAPTER IV

THE WEALTH OF THE INDIES

THE OPENING OF THE OCEAN ROUTES

It was a thing more divine than human to have found that way never before known to go to the east where the spices grow.
Letter quoted in Hakluyt

Consider the fruites, the drugges, the pearle, the treasure, the millions of gold and silver, the Spanyardes have brought out of the West Indies since the first viage of Columbus.
RICHARD WILLES, Dedication of *The History of Travayle*, 1577

THE closing years of the fifteenth century and the opening years of the sixteenth were marked by the greatest of all revolutions in the world's carrying trade, the opening of the ocean routes. It is one of the curiosities of history that neither the Italians and Hanseatics who were the leading shipowners of the time, nor the Dutch and English who were ultimately to reap the chief profit from the new discoveries, were responsible for bringing them about. The expeditions which turned the main current of the world's sea-borne commerce into new channels were equipped by the rulers of nations which have never before or since stood in the front rank as traders or seafarers. The first impulse came from a studious young prince whom the hard-headed, practical merchants of Venice or Lubeck would have despised as a theorist and a dreamer.

It was in 1418 that Henry, the fifth child of King John of Portugal and Philippa the daughter of John of Gaunt, turned aside from a brilliant career as a soldier to meditate, in his quiet retreat at Sagres, near Cape St. Vincent, on the problems of ocean navigation. From that date his whole life was consecrated to the achievement of a threefold ambition. He wished to turn the flank of the "Moors," the common enemies of Christendom. He longed to spread the true faith among the Moslems and pagans of unknown lands along the African coast. Deep in his heart, he cherished a more ambitious purpose. The circumnavigation of Africa by Necho's ships had long ago passed into a myth, and two Genoese galleys which had sailed, in 1291, on a mad expedition to the south, "that they might go by sea to the ports of India," had never returned. It was commonly held that, even if the Atlantic and Indian Oceans were connected, the burning heat of the sun would make navigation in the tropics impossible. Yet Henry believed that a direct sea route to India was to be found, and that its finders might wrest from the Venetians and Genoese the commercial supremacy which they enjoyed as carriers and middlemen for the Eastern luxuries which fetched so high a price in the markets of Europe.

Inspired by the faith of a visionary, he set about translating his dreams into practice like a scientist and a statesman. For oceanic voyages two things were necessary; better ships and more scientific navigation. He set himself to supply both. He founded at Sagres a shipbuilding yard, an observatory, and a school of navigation and chart-making. He enticed experienced Italian pilots into his service as navigators and teachers.

The single-masted, basin-shaped round ship of the early Middle Ages was already giving way to a handier vessel with more complicated rig. Two types attained special prominence in the fifteenth century. One was the carrack, a term used rather loosely to describe any large merchantman, but generally denoting a broad, very deep vessel with great carrying capacity. The other was the caraval, a type developed by the Spaniards and Portuguese for coastal trade in the Atlantic. She was a smaller, handier, and faster vessel than the carrack, single-decked, with a high square forecastle, which served to break the force of a head sea, high freeboard, and a high tapering poop. The earlier Portuguese caravals were lateen rigged; as later developed, the typical caraval had three or four masts, of which the foremast was square-rigged, while the others carried lateen sails. She was not a big cargo carrier, but her rig made her more manageable than the carrack, and she was better suited to the stormy waters of the Atlantic. Prince Henry set himself to develop and improve her.

Some progress had also been made in navigation. The compass was already in use in Italy in the twelfth century, though Brunetto Latini, the tutor of Dante, declared, a hundred years later, that "no master-mariner dares to use it, lest he should fall under a supposition of his being a magician." Custom had robbed it of any connection with the Black Art, and successive improvements had rendered it a more reliable instrument for use at sea. By Henry's time, too, the astrolabe of the astronomers was already being adapted to the purpose of ascertaining latitude, with a fair degree of rough accuracy—longitude remained a matter of dead-reckoning, or of guess-work. Maps, too, were coming into wider use, and the improvement both of nautical instrument making and of cartography was among the chief objects of the school at Sagres.

Having thus laid firm foundations for a system of oceanic exploration, Henry pushed out expedition after expedition down the African coast, and the discoveries of each expedition were carefully recorded and plotted. By his death in 1460, the Portuguese had already penetrated as far as Sierra Leone, discovered the Cape Verde Islands, and opened up a regular trade with the inhabitants of Senegambia, who supplied them with gold and slaves.

By this time the search for a direct sea-route to India had become a vital matter. Constantinople had fallen in 1453 before the onset of the Ottoman Turks, who cared nothing for trade, and were implacable in their hatred of the Christians. By the end of the century the transhipment route to the East through Syrian ports and the long land routes from Novgorod and the Black Sea ports had all been blocked, and that through Egypt was already threatened. Patriotism, crusading zeal, and self-interest all spurred on the Portuguese Kings to follow up the work of Henry the Navigator, and in 1498 the long-sought goal was reached at last, and Vasco da Gama arrived at Calicut with the first European ship to load a cargo at an Indian port.

Meanwhile, others were seeking the same goal by another route. All through the fifteenth century vessels had been growing in size and improving in rig. Geographical and navigational science had kept pace with the advance in ship-building; in particular, an adaptation of the astrolabe to nautical use by Martin Behaim in 1480, had brought it into general use at sea. The time had come when daring seamen could venture out into the open ocean with some degree of confidence, and as it was now generally accepted that the earth was round, they began to argue that if you sailed due west from Europe, you must come in time to the fabulous riches of Cathay and Zipangu (China and Japan). So, at least, argued Christopher Columbus, a Genoese pilot who had succeeded in obtaining the ear of King Ferdinand of Spain.

No one had the least idea that between Europe and Asia there lay an undiscovered continent. Greenland was known; for it had been discovered by the Icelander, Eirik the Red, in A.D. 981, and down to the middle of the fourteenth century fairly regular communication had been kept up between Norway and Iceland and the colony founded by Eirik a year or two after his discovery. This trade, in which the colonists exchanged hides and skins, walrus tusks, and ropes of walrus hide for iron, building materials, grain, and other necessaries, gives astonishing evidence of the boldness of the Norsemen as navigators; and some of them had gone even farther, for in or about the years A.D. 1000–1010, Leif Eiriksson, Thorfinn Karlsefni, and others had explored the coast of the American mainland from Labrador to, probably, as far south as Maine.[1] This, however, led to nothing, for the attempt to colonize "Wine-land the Good" from Greenland proved a failure, and in the course of the fifteenth century the Greenland settlements themselves died out. Even if Columbus had heard, from some English sailor trading to Iceland, the story of the Wine-land voyages, he would only have regarded it as a confirmation of his belief that Asia lay on the other side of the Atlantic. He was still firmly of this opinion when he actually discovered the West Indies in 1592, six years before Vasco da Gama arrived at Calicut, and the very name of the Islands preserves the memory of his error.

Those who followed in the wake of Columbus soon discovered that he was wrong, but it was not long before they made another discovery that fully made up for the disappointment. They found that the "New World," now added to the map, was rich in the precious metals. To realize the significance of this, we must remember that, although the Italians had made some progress in the science of banking, the credit system was practically non-existent. All commercial transactions and all Government obligations had ultimately to be settled in hard cash, and the supply of gold and silver in circulation was becoming inadequate to the growth of commerce and the rising military and administrative expenditure of the European States. The annual output of the European mines was small, and the stock accumulated in classical times had been depleted by centuries of trade with Asia and by lavish use in the arts. Thus the discovery of a new source of bullion held out

[1] See W. Hovgaard, *The Voyages of the Norsemen to America.*

promises of almost unlimited wealth and power to its lucky possessors.

For the Portuguese the prospect was no less brilliant. Vasco da Gama had returned with a cargo which is said to have repaid sixty-fold the expenses of his voyage, and it was obvious that even if the Turks should learn in time to tolerate Christian merchants, the old routes to Asia could never compete successfully with the new. In the first place, the elimination of land transport enabled a larger body of trade to be carried. In the second place, it enabled it to be carried at a lesser cost. Finally, it concentrated the whole profits of the trade in a single set of hands. Asiatic, Syrian or Egyptian merchants, Arab shipowners trading between India and the Red Sea or Persian Gulf, local rulers and governors imposing port and transit dues, had all taken toll of the goods before they came into the hands of the Genoese and Venetians; the Portuguese could purchase the goods in Asia at first cost, and all freight charges and customs would go to swell their own revenues.

Fired by such hopes, as well as by a crusading zeal for the conversion of the heathen, which was not the less sincere because it led to the commission of horrible atrocities, the Spaniards and Portuguese followed up the discoveries of Columbus and Vasco da Gama with an energy which is really astonishing when we remember that European navigation had hitherto been confined mainly to port-to-port coasting. Despite all improvements, the ships were still clumsy and unweatherly. Navigation was still so rudimentary that an error of 600 miles in the longitude was nothing uncommon, and when Columbus was approaching the Azores on his return passage, his second-in-command was firmly convinced that they were still off Madeira. Of all the ships which sailed from Portugal for the Indies between 1497 and 1612, no fewer than 12 per cent. were lost.[1]

[1] Sailed 806; remained in Asia for local traffic 285; returned 425; lost 96.

Hygiene was practically unknown and on long voyages leading through tropical waters, the tightly packed crews died like flies from fever and scurvy, so that many a ship limped home with hardly enough men alive to take her into port. Yet by 1535 the Spaniards had conquered not only the West Indies but Mexico and Peru, and the Portuguese had extended their chain of fortified naval bases and trading stations from the Persian Gulf to the Moluccas, and brought all the trade routes of the Indian Ocean under their control.

Naturally enough, from the standpoint of their time, both Spaniards and Portuguese sought to maintain a monopoly of the routes they had discovered, and they regularized their position by obtaining from the Pope, the supreme international authority, a series of Bulls which practically divided between them the whole of the unknown world. This for a long time sufficed to warn off all rivals. England, it is true, made one brief appearance on the scene, when John and Sebastian Cabot, Italians in the service of Henry VII, sailed from Bristol on voyages of exploration in 1497 and 1498, and discovered Newfoundland and part of the mainland of North America. But the discoveries of the Cabots were not followed up. One reason, undoubtedly was that Henry was afraid of provoking the jealousy of Spain. Another, probably, was that the new found lands lost their attraction when it became clear that they were neither rich in the precious metals nor a stepping-stone to Cathay and the Spice Islands.

Yet the ferment set up by the great oceanic discoveries could not permanently be confined within the narrow limits of a national monopoly. At a stroke, the whole political and commercial balance of Europe had been upset, and the centre both of trade and of naval power shifted from the Mediterranean to the Atlantic. The richest trades in the world could now be carried on only by ships and seamen equipped for long ocean voyages and prepared, at need, to accept the risks of winter navigation. On these voyages, galley fleets of the Mediterranean type could do nothing to protect them.

It took the best part of a century for the full implications of this change to be realized; but from the first the new discoveries gave an unprecedented impetus to the study of geography, scientific map-making, shipbuilding, and navigation. Hard as the Spaniards and Portuguese might strive to keep the secrets of the new routes to themselves, they could not prevent them from leaking out; for there were many foreign merchants resident in the Peninsula, and many foreigners were employed as seamen or pilots in the Indian and American trade. Even native pilots were not always incorruptible, and the closest censorship failed to prevent manuscript works on the navigation of the Atlantic from being seen and copied. In England, in France, in Germany, and in Flanders, men of science set themselves to piece together the new knowledge about the world they lived in, and the newly discovered art of printing enabled the results of their researches, especially the maps produced by Flemish cartographers at Bruges and Antwerp, to be widely circulated. Others set themselves to solve the problems of ocean navigation; to study the variation of the compass, and to improve the design of nautical instruments.

In shipbuilding, the chief new development was the introduction of the galleon—a ship of greater cargo capacity than the caraval; longer, less top-heavy, and much faster and handier than the carrack or the ordinary roundship. Italian in origin, the type seems to have been first perfected by French corsairs, but in the second half of the sixteenth century it was widely adopted as an ocean-going warship. It seems, however, to have been only in England that it seriously affected the design of the larger merchantmen.

In all these developments the old rulers of the seas took

little part. Venice, exhausted by long warfare with the Turks, and heart-broken at the loss of her supremacy, sank into lethargy and decay. The clumsy Hanseatic hulks, built with a single eye to cargo capacity, were ill-suited to ocean navigation, and the merchants of the Hansa were too much absorbed by the struggle to maintain their old monopolies, to see that the future of the carrying trade lay with the ocean routes. A further blow was dealt to the position of both Venice and the League cities when the Portuguese selected Antwerp as their emporium for the distribution of Eastern products. Their choice was, on the other hand, beneficial to the English merchants, who had old connections with Antwerp, and whose trade with that city rapidly increased.

It was in England that the challenge to oceanic expansion met with the most response; but Englishmen were shown the way in the Atlantic by the French corsairs of La Rochelle and other Huguenot ports, who got on to the track of the Spanish colonial trade about the middle of the century, and harried it with an energy equally inspired by greed and fanaticism. For a time the English held their hand. They fished, like the French and Spaniards, on the banks of Newfoundland; they discussed projects of colonization in North America, and they sought out a passage to Asia round the north of America or the north of Europe, that would not bring them into direct conflict with the Spaniards and Portuguese. But it was inevitable, well placed as they were for Atlantic navigation, that they should ultimately follow in the steps of the French, and even, more ominously, assert their right to trade themselves with the newly discovered lands. This, however, is a story for another chapter. Before discussing the beginnings of England's ocean trade, we must form some picture of the commerce and shipping of the new routes as they existed when the storm broke from the north.

The fundamental fact about the Portuguese trade with the Indies is that it was an artificial growth, due to the persistence and energy of the ruling house rather than to any strong commercial instinct in the people. The fundamental fact about the Spanish colonial traffic was that neither Government nor people cared a jot for ordinary commerce in comparison with the quickly acquired wealth to be drained from the gold and silver mines of Mexico and Peru.

Spain and Portugal were, in the main, pastoral countries, with comparatively little to export, and with no strong mercantile class. Both countries produced some good seamen, the best recruiting grounds being the fisheries of the Biscay provinces and southern Portugal; but the complements both of the Portuguese carracks and the Spanish treasure fleets had to be made up by the employment of foreign seamen. Neither people stood in the front rank as shipowners. Even in 1586, when the new routes had been exploited for more than three-quarters of a century, there were only 104 ships in Spain of 100 tons and upwards, and only 92 in Portugal, while an incomplete return of 1582 shows 177 belonging to English ports. Despite laws prohibiting the employment of foreign ships, Flemish, German, French, and Italian vessels had often to be used in order to make up the fleets.

From the first, the Portuguese trade with Asia was carried on at the King's risk and for the King's profit. An attempt to form a big trading company for the purpose failed completely, owing to the lack of mercantile support, and the Royal family, who had promoted the discoveries, were forced to keep the traffic in their own hands. The import of spices was an absolute monopoly of the Crown, but for general traffic, and especially for the lucrative local trade between Asiatic ports, trading licenses were often granted to syndicates or individuals. Freights seem to have been the perquisite of the captains, who were also allowed to carry a certain quantity of goods for their own profit. This private trade, which could never be effectively supervised, led to gross abuses which robbed the King of a large share of his profits and ended by completely demoralizing the captains and officials. A typical instance of its results is the Bengal voyage from Malabar in 1530, which yielded £2,450 to the captain, and only £78 to the King.

The actual sailings from Portugal to India during the sixteenth century averaged no more than seven ships a year. Some of the earlier fleets are said to have included as many as twenty vessels, but as time went on, the desire to economize in officers and to minimize the risks of shipwreck or capture led to the replacement of the earlier caravals by much larger ships, with a consequent reduction in the number of sailings.

Down to the close of the sixteenth century a ship of 100 or 150 tons was considered large enough for any voyage. The biggest English merchantman in 1588 was no more than 400 tons, and the Levantine squadron, which contained the largest ships in the Spanish Armada—brought together from every part of Europe—averaged probably no more than 600 tons by English measurement. Yet some of the Portuguese carracks in the East Indies trade are estimated at anything between 1,500 and 2,000 tons. They were singularly unweatherly craft, very broad, very deep, with a great overhang fore and aft, and immense upper-works. The *Madre de Dios*, captured by the English in 1592, will serve as an example. With a keel only 100 feet in length, she was 165 feet long over-all, her extreme breadth was 46 feet 10 inches, and her maximum draught 31 feet. She had four complete decks and a high forecastle, poop, and top-gallant poop. Her mainmast, 121 feet in height, carried a mainyard 106 feet long. It is hardly surprising that these clumsy, top-heavy vessels found great difficulty in keeping company, or that 22 of them were wrecked in the thirteen years 1579–1591.

Nevertheless, such ships, when laden with costly luxuries for the return voyage, could carry an enormously valuable cargo. That of the *San Felipe*, captured by Drake in 1587, realized £108,000, exclusive of bullion and gems to the value of another £3,900. The *Madre de Dios* carried 8,500 quintals (nearly 400 tons) of pepper, 900 quintals of cloves, 700 of cinammon, 500 of cochineal, and 450 of general cargo, such as porcelain, silks, and velvets, together with amber, musk, and precious stones which brought up the total value (apart from private plunder) to £140,000, or over a million of modern money.

Even for the Indian trade few such ships were necessary; for though they carried, on the outward voyage, cargoes of manufactured goods, mainly purchased from Flanders or Italy, a great part of the imports were paid for in silver, so that the bulk of the traffic either way was small. On the average about five of them sailed annually from Lisbon, returning, with luck, in the following year. On the outward voyage they sailed in company. On the return, they seem usually to have sailed independently as far as St. Helena, where they rendezvoused. Both on the outward and the homeward passage they called at Mozambique to water, provision, and refresh the crews, and homeward-bound ships which found the season too advanced would sometimes winter there.

The Spanish trade with the New World was not, like the Portuguese trade with the Indies, a Royal monopoly; the King was content to take a fixed proportion, usually one-fifth, of the produce of the American mines, and to levy duties on the remainder of the trade. These duties were very heavy; they amounted in 1566 to 17½ per cent. on the homeward and 7½ per cent. on the outward trade, in addition to transit duties in the colonies. It may be added that, whenever the Crown was pinched for money—as it nearly always was—the Kings had a pleasing habit of sequestrating private imports of treasure as a forced loan; granting to the involuntary lender an annuity which might or might not be paid.

The King's interest in the trade was thus very great, and as a result, the whole traffic was enmeshed in a network of regulations which did much to stifle it. In order to ensure delivery of the Royal quota and to facilitate the collection of the duties, the entire traffic was confined to the single port of Seville, the definition of which was reluctantly extended to include Cadiz and San Lucar. Seville itself was the seat of the *Casa de la Contratación*, or House of Commerce, a remarkable body, half Chartered Company and half State Department, to whom the whole regulation of the trade was entrusted. Every merchant and every ship engaged in the trade had to receive a licence from the *Casa*; a register, or manifest of all inwards and outwards cargo had to be handed to it, and no cargo could be loaded or discharged except under its inspection. It maintained a Hydrographical Bureau and School of Navigation, issued charts and instruments, examined and certified pilots, prescribed sailing dates and courses, and organized the protection of the trade.

The sailings, in the second half of the sixteenth century, were organized in two annual fleets. The *flota* of New Spain sailed in the spring or early summer for San Juan d'Ullua (later Vera Cruz), the port of Mexico, detaching on its way the ships bound for the Greater Antilles. The *flota* of Tierra Firme or the Spanish Main sailed in August or later for Cartagena (in Colombia) and the isthmus of Panama. Its importance was derived from the carriage of the Peruvian treasure; for the Spaniards dreaded the stormy passage round Cape Horn or through the Straits of Magellan and preferred the transhipment route. From Valdivia, where the gold of Chile was shipped; from Callao, the outlet for the seemingly inexhaustible silver mines of Potosi; from Guayaquil in Ecuador, and from other South American ports, the treasure was shipped to Panama, whence long trains of pack mules carried it to Nombre de Dios on the Atlantic coast.

Normally, both fleets wintered in America, and on the homeward voyage, rendezvoused at Havana, whence they came home in company, sailing from Havana about the middle of March. The sailing arrangements, however, were frequently altered. There were times when the outwards *flotas* sailed together, for better protection. Occasionally the *flota* of Tierra Firme sailed in January and returned in July, August, or September of the same year. After about 1585, when the English privateering developed into open war, the sailings both out and home became very irregular, and were sometimes held up altogether for a year.

All vessels in the trade mounted a few guns for protection against pirates; but this proved a very inadequate defence even against the French corsairs, and the flagship and vice-flagship of each fleet were accordingly exempted from the carriage of cargo, other than treasure, and supplied with a heavier armament and a strong complement of soldiers. Further, a force of regular warships, the Galleons of the Indian Guard, was provided to meet the home-coming convoys at the Azores and bring them into Seville. Later, when the English also joined in the attack, arrangements were made for the Galleons of the Indian Guard to accompany or follow the *flota* of Tierra Firme, and bring home the combined fleets from Havana, and for other squadrons to cruise off the Azores and Cape St. Vincent, to drive off raiders and shepherd the convoys home. A service of fast transatlantic packet boats, using both sails and oars, and able to make the passage from Havana to Spain in 28 days, was also organized, and linked up with a local packet service in the Caribbean, so that intelligence of enemy squadrons and routeing orders for the *flotas* could be quickly disseminated.

These protective measures were mainly, if not wholly, paid for by a special tax, the *averia*, levied by the *Casa de Contratación* on the value of all ships and cargoes in the trade. In 1596, at the height of the war with England, this tax amounted to as much as 7 per cent.

Finally, it became the custom for a large part of the treasure, including the whole of the King's share, to be unloaded at Havana, and transferred to specially constructed, well-armed, fast-sailing ships of about 200 tons, known as *fregatas*. As these ships could run from anything they could not fight, they often sailed independently of the convoys.

The ordinary merchantmen employed in the trade seem mostly to have varied from about 200 to 500 tons, though both smaller and larger vessels were employed. They were fairly numerous, for the volume of traffic was considerable. In addition to bullion and the produce of the Caribbean pearl-fisheries, the homeward-bound *flotas* carried hides, dye-woods, sugar, cotton, and other colonial produce. The Mexican ships might also carry some quantity of Chinese silks and porcelain; for a regular traffic had sprung up between Manilla (the Spanish entrepôt for the Chinese trade) and Acapulco on the Pacific coast of Mexico. This traffic, however, was latterly confined, in order to avoid a drain of silver to Asia, to one big ship a year, and most of its cargo was probably bought up by the colonists.

The outward cargoes from Spain were heavier. The colonists were rich and luxurious, and cargoes of every kind of European and Eastern goods had to be collected at Seville to supply their wants. They required slaves also, in ever-increasing numbers, who were usually supplied under licence by Portuguese and other foreign contractors. A typical outwards *flota* in the second half of the sixteenth century would consist of anything from 30 to 45 ships. If the sailings for a particular year were stayed, the next year's *flota* might comprise double that number. The homeward *flotas*, at first, at any rate, were a little smaller, as owing to the discrepancy in bulk between the outward and homeward cargoes, many owners put old ships into the trade, and sold or scrapped them on the other side.

This was a paying game, for by a curious exception to the Spanish mania for regulation, freights were not controlled, and they were so high that a vessel could sometimes earn her whole value on a single voyage. The custom, however, did not make for safety; nor did another consequence of the high freights—the tendency to increase the carrying-capacity of vessels by building up the superstructure, thus rendering them intolerably top-heavy. Regulations intended to check these practices were issued in 1557, but the general quality of the fleets was always bad. Spanish shipbuilding was poor, both as regards design and material, and the shortage of native shipping frequently led to the purchase or hire of German and Flemish hulks ill-suited to ocean voyages. High freights and the smuggling of unauthorized cargo, to escape the duties, led to persistent overloading. The crews were often polyglot; the seamen were looked down upon by the officials and soldiers and the standard of seamanship was low. It is not surprising, therefore, that wrecks were very frequent. Few years went by without a casualty, and there were many such disasters as those of 1590 when fifteen ships were wrecked by a "norther" in the harbour of Vera Cruz, and 1591, when seventeen ships of the *flota* of New Spain were sunk or stranded in a storm at the Azores.

The shipowners were sometimes merchants; but the demand for tonnage in the American trade gave a stimulus to the shipping industry proper, and there were many people who made their living solely by owning and running ships. The master, who was often a part-owner, corresponded to the mediaeval *patronus* or managing owner rather than to the English sailing-master; all details of navigation being left to the pilot, who gave his orders to the crew through the *contramaestre* or mate. The functions of master and pilot were, however, sometimes united in the same person. The title of "captain" was reserved for the military commander of an escort ship, or for an owner who accompanied his vessel without drawing pay.

Crews, in the earlier days of the trade, were sometimes hired on shares; officers and seamen dividing between them one-third of the net freights, after certain deductions had been made. Latterly, they were paid a fixed wage which, for the able seaman, amounted about 1550 to 2½ ducats a month.[1] Petty officers, such as the mate, gunner, or carpenter, received 4 or 5 ducats a month, while a pilot might get from 110 to 180 ducats per voyage, according to the size of the ship. By way of contrast, the services of the "General" commanding the escort were valued at 1,875 ducats a year.

Behind the shipowners and merchants stood the financiers. As only a small proportion of the freights was paid in advance, shipowners borrowed money on bottomry for the expenses of the voyage. As the perils of the sea and the risks of capture were enough to daunt the boldest adventurer, the risks had to be spread by insurance. When Drake's West Indian raid of 1585 made insurance unprocurable, the effect, for the time being, was absolutely to paralyse the traffic. But Spain, as we have seen, had no large mercantile and banking class. The Andalusian merchants who provided the outward cargoes of the *flotas* were often, in effect, mere agents for the foreigners who provided the goods. In like manner the trade was largely financed and insured by

[1] The Spanish ducat was reckoned in Elizabethan times as about 5s. 6d. English.

Germans and Italians. Further, the military expenditure arising from the insatiable ambition of Charles V and the religious bigotry of Philip I outstripped even the output of the American mines. The treasure brought by the *flotas* and (after the union of the Crowns of Spain and Portugal in 1580) the costly cargoes of the Portuguese carracks, were often mortgaged in advance as security for loans from the great European financial houses, such as the Fuggers of Germany and the Grimaldi of Genoa.

This dependence on foreign merchants and financiers defeated all the laws made against export of the American treasure. Payment for foreign goods, premiums on insurance policies, interest on and repayment of loans, and the expenditure of the Spanish armies in the Low Countries, steadily drained away a substantial proportion of the receipts from Mexico and Peru to countries better able to make commercial use of it than Spain herself. To the amount thus brought into circulation outside the Peninsula, must be added the plunder secured by the French, English, and Dutch privateers who harried so relentlessly the Atlantic trade routes and the Spanish colonies.

The universal effect of this influx of treasure was a rapid rise in money values which caused a great deal of economic distress, since prices rose faster than wages, but gave an immense impetus to the accumulation of capital and afforded an unprecedented stimulus to business enterprise. The second half of the sixteenth century was a period of much suffering in Europe; but it was also a period when large fortunes could be made quickly by long-headed men, and the employment of these fortunes to finance commercial expansion brought profit ultimately even to those classes who were temporarily depressed.

In all this the Spaniards and Portuguese had little part. They will always hold a very honourable place in the history of the shipping industry, as the men who first extended the carrying trade from the coastal to the ocean routes; but great as they were as pioneers, it was not until others had entered into the fruit of their labours that the full worth of those labours could be seen.

One revealing sentence by a seventeenth-century Portuguese historian sums up the weakness that held them back from following up effectively their great work of exploration and discovery. In his account of the Indian voyages, he apologizes for mentioning the expeditions of certain years because, "what they did was in relation to trade, a subject unbecoming a grave history." No healthy sea-borne commerce can be developed in a country where an apology is necessary for mentioning it.

The Portuguese went to India in the spirit of crusaders; they remained there as tyrants and plunderers, and while the expenses of their armaments ate away the profits of their trade, the trade itself gradually stagnated. The Spaniards looked upon their colonies in the New World as fields for exploitation rather than as markets and sources of raw material, and it was not so much the attacks of their enemies that prevented them from becoming a really great ship-owning Power as the subordination of every ordinary commercial interest to the extraction and transport of the Mexican and Peruvian treasure.

It must be said, in fairness, that the nations who supplanted them had, at first, little wider views. It was the lure of the treasure fleets that first brought the French, the English and the Dutch rebels against Spain onto the Atlantic routes. What made the difference was that in England and Holland, though hardly as yet in France, there was a mercantile class sufficiently enterprising, wealthy, and experienced to take full advantage of the opportunities opened up by the Spanish and Portuguese discoveries, and strong enough to obtain the backing of their Governments for purely commercial ventures.

"Pride and Prejudice"

SOME BOOKS OF THE PERIOD

The story of Prince Henry the Navigator and of the Portuguese in Asia is well told by Sir William Hunter in the first volume of his *History of British India*, London, 1899. A very full account of the Spanish Colonial trade is given in *Trade and Navigation between Spain and the Indies* by C. H. Haring (Harvard Economic Studies), Cambridge, 1918. *The Sea Trader* by David Hannay, London, 1912, gives some lively pictures of Spanish and Portuguese ships and navigation. Some details have been taken from books by Sir Julian Corbett and Dr. James A. Williamson, which are cited in the note to the following chapter.

CHAPTER V

MERCHANT ADVENTURERS

THE RISE OF ENGLAND

> I make no doubt but, in the meantime, to do such feats of merchandize as shall be to the King's great advantage in His Grace's custom(s). WILLIAM HAWKINS TO THOMAS CROMWELL

WHILE the Spaniards and Portuguese were discovering a New World and opening up a sea-route to the Indies, English merchants and shipowners were still absorbed in their struggle for a fair share in the distribution of English cloth to the continental markets. For more than half a century after the voyages of Columbus and Vasco da Gama they made but little attempt to follow in the footsteps of the great explorers, and the bulk of their trade continued to follow the old mediaeval lines. None the less, the accession of Henry VII in 1485 may be taken as the first great turning-point in the history of English shipping. It was the supreme merit of the hard-headed, hard-hearted, Tudor monarchs that, with all their imperious arrogance, they could understand, share, and direct into the most profitable channels the new consciousness of national unity and national destiny which followed the decay of feudalism in England. It is not their least title to greatness that they directed it steadily towards the sea.

Their attitude towards shipping and commerce differed widely from that of the Plantagenet Kings. In the past, foreign merchants, such as the Hanseatics and Lombards, had done services to England which went far to justify the privileges conferred upon them; but Englishmen were now beginning to feel able to stand upon their own feet, and were no longer satisfied merely to provide raw materials for foreign looms and cargoes for foreign ships. The Tudors themselves owed the security of their throne largely to the support of the new generation of monied men—the trading, manufacturing, speculating middle class, who were steadily supplanting the old territorial nobility as the chief power in the State. Moreover, England, after a long period of weak Governments and civil wars, was again prepared to assert herself in the affairs of Europe, and her rulers were thinking less of cheap and plentiful supplies than of how to increase the power and wealth of England as compared with those of her neighbours. All these considerations combined to make the policy of the Tudors strongly protectionist, and shipping, as a source both of wealth and of power, was an object of their special care.

At first they had to walk warily. Although Henry VII set himself to play the game of differential duties, retaliatory tariffs, and diplomatic bargaining, with a vigour and astuteness worthy of the Venetians themselves, he was far too prudent to risk quarrels for which England was not yet prepared. The fear of Spain checked his encouragement of oceanic exploration. Fear of the Hansa drove him to exempt the German merchants from most of the restrictions placed on foreign traders. Even Henry VIII, masterful as he was, had continually to trim his sails. In 1539, when he was seeking support against the alliance of France with the Empire, he actually threw open the whole trade of the country to foreigners, practically on terms of equality, for a period of seven years, and to the end of his life he maintained the Hansa in hardly diminished enjoyment of their privileged position.

Within the limits thus imposed upon them by their foreign policy, the first two Tudors did everything they knew for the encouragement of English shipping. To judge by the preamble to the various Navigation Acts of the time, such encouragement was very badly needed. An Act of 1531, for instance, recites dolefully that:

> the multitude of Shippes which tofore this tyme hath ben not onely a greate defence and suretie to this Realm of Englande in tyme of warre, but also a high commoditie to all the Subjectes of the same for transporting and conveyance of merchandises in and from this Realme, is nowe marvelously decaied . . . (so that) within fewe years there shalbe fewe Englisshe men that shalbe experte in the Seas.

Again, in 1540, it was alleged that the Free Trade Proclamation of the previous year had so gravely diminished the demand for English tonnage, owing to the preference given by foreign merchants to ships of their own nationality that

> townes villages and inhabitations nere adioyning to the sea costis ben utterly fallen in ruyne and decay.

We need not take these laments too seriously. Everybody, in Tudor times, who wanted assistance from the Government, declared that they were on the verge of bankruptcy. Still there is some evidence that the progress of English shipping had been arrested during the confusion of the civil wars, and that foreign competition was beginning to make itself felt even in the Bordeaux trade, which had hitherto been more or less an English preserve. This was a serious matter, for the importance of the Bordeaux trade as the chief school of ocean navigation and the chief stimulus to the building of large ships was greater than ever, as woad for dyeing, which had formerly been imported in the Genoese carracks, was now being drawn chiefly from Toulouse. This danger, at any rate, could be drastically dealt with, for the Hansa were not concerned in the traffic, and French commerce and shipping were not sufficiently developed to make effective retaliation possible. An Act was accordingly passed in the first year of Henry VII, confining the import of wines of Gascony and Guienne to:

> such as shall be aventured and brought in an Englisshe Irisshe or Walshmannys Shippe or Shippes, and the Maryners of the same Englisshe, Irisshe, or Walshemen for the more part.

This Act was only to be operative for three years, but in 1489 the restrictions were made permanent and extended to the import of Toulouse woad. At the same time, the old laws were revived which prohibited anyone, except merchant strangers, from importing or exporting any goods whatsoever in foreign ships so long as English tonnage was available.

The effect of these Acts was nullified to some extent by the sale of licences to disregard them, but so far as the Bordeaux trade was concerned, the laws seem to have been enforced fairly consistently, and with good results. They were almost certainly responsible for a notable revival in the trade of Bristol, where the merchants were largely concerned in this traffic.

The more general provisions of the Act of 1489, which was revived and confirmed in 1531, were rendered largely nugatory by the exception in favour of merchant strangers; but in 1540, in response to the shipowners' complaints, it was enacted that the Customs concessions made to foreigners in the previous year should only be granted on condition of their shipping the cargoes in English vessels. The Hanseatic merchants alone were allowed to ship goods in their own vessels without payment of penal dues, when no English ships were available.[1]

In this Act of 1540 there were two novel provisions. Most of the trade carried on by the foreign merchants passed through London, and in order to prevent any complaints as to lack of information concerning the available shipping, all owners of ships sailing from London were ordered to post

[1] It must be remembered that duties were payable on exports as well as imports.

up in Lombard Street particulars of the voyages to be undertaken by their vessels—a very early anticipation of *Lloyd's Loading List.* Further, in order to prevent profiteering by the shipowners, maximum freights were fixed for all the leading articles carried on the ordinary voyages from and to London.

The schedule of maximum freights is distinctly interesting, as showing the narrow limits within which English trade was still confined in 1540. The only voyages covered by the schedule are those from and to Flanders, Denmark, Bordeaux, Spain, and Portugal. The only exports it was thought necessary to specify were woollen cloth and rabbit skins; for tin and lead were shipped mainly from the Western ports. The import list, of course, is more varied: velvets, silks, and other manufactured goods, sugar, dates, prunes, almonds, currants, and pepper from Flanders; grain, pitch and tar, flax and canvas, iron, wax, eels and sturgeon from Denmark; wine and woad from Bordeaux.

Most of the freights were based on customary measures, such as the "fardel" or bundle of broadcloth, the "maunde" or basket, and the "dryefatte," or barrel of dry goods, and it is often difficult to work out their equivalent in modern weights and measures. Still, a selection of typical freights will give some idea of the cost of sea-transport in the sixteenth century—always remembering that every charge must be multiplied by eight or nine, at least, to give its present value.

	s.	*d.*
Flanders–London:		
Silks, per Bale of six feet in height	5	0
Sugar, per Chest	2	0
Dates and Prunes, per Hogshead	1	8
Trussing Chests (Chests for Clothes, etc.) ea. ..	2	0
London–Denmark:		
Cloth, per Broad Woollen Cloth	0	8

		s.	d.
Denmark–London:			
Wheat and Rye, per Last (12 quarters)	..	26	8
Flax and Canvas, per "Packe"	.. ..	30	0
Pitch and Tar, per Last (14 barrels)[1] ..	..	12	0
Osmunds (small bars of high quality iron) per Last (14 barrels)	.. ..	8	0
"Faggots" of Iron (Pig-iron) per Last ..	..	4	0
Feathers, per Cwt.	.. ..	1	6
Wax, per "Straw" of 16 cwt. ..	.. ..	14	0
Bowstaves, per 24 Bundles	.. .. ..	26	8
Bordeaux–London:			
Wine, per Tun,[2] first vintage ..	.. ..	18	0
later vintages ..	.. ..	16	0
Woad, per Ton ..	.. ..	20	0
London–Portugal and South of Spain, outside Straits:			
Broad Cloth, per Bundle of 15 cloths ..	..	10	0
(The merchant to be entitled to load one bundle freight free for every 5 tons loaded.)			
Biscay–London. All goods, per ton ..	..	13	4
Ayemonte–London. ,, ,,	.. ..	20	0
Seville–London. ,, ,,	.. ..	23	0
Malaga–London. ,, ,,	.. ..	25	0

In addition to the freights, a rate was fixed to cover "Lodemenage" (Pilotage Charges) and "Primage" (allowance to the ship for stowing and care of cargo). From Denmark, Primage was 4d. and Lodemenage 6d. per Last; from all named Spanish ports, both charges were covered by a single payment of 6d. per ton. Other petty charges were covered by the clause, "with averages according to custom." The freights from Seville and Malaga were subject to the proviso "pesterable wares (goods taking up an abnormal amount of space) only excepted."

As the Free Trade Proclamation of 1539 was not renewed when it expired in 1546, this Act of 1540 had no long life; but the earlier laws remained, at least nominally, in opera-

[1] As a measure of weight the "Last" was usually 4,000 lb.

[2] The Tun of 252 gallons occupied about 60 cubic feet.

tion until the reign of Elizabeth. The only modification was made by an Act of Edward VI in 1551, providing that foreigners might participate in the carriage of Bordeaux wines, except for the first cargoes of the season. This concession was justified in the preamble to the Act by a statement that the restrictions on the trade had caused wine and woad to be sold "at such excessive price as hath not before been seen within this realm." Dr. Williamson thinks that the real explanation was that the Council had been bribed. Both explanations are quite probable.

Apart from the original laws relating to the Bordeaux trade it is doubtful whether any of these Acts did much for English shipping; for their operation was continually modified, in practice, in deference to the complaints of foreign Powers. The preamble to an Act passed in the first year of Elizabeth, by which the whole of this restrictive legislation was swept away, sets out the real weakness of the Navigation Act policy with a quite delightful simplicity. Its effect, so runs the preamble, was that:

> Other forreyne Prynces fynding themselves agreaved withe the sayd severall Actes, as thincking that the same were made to the Hurte and Prejudice of their Countrye and Navye, have made lyke penall Lawes agaynst suche as shoulde shippe out of their Countreys in any other Vesselles than of their severall Countreys and Domynions; By reason wherof ther hathe not onely growen great displeasure betwene the forreyn Prynces and the Kinges of this Realme, but also the Marchauntes have been sore greved and endomaged.

This ineradicable tendency of foreign princes to render tit for tat has spoiled many a pretty scheme for the encouragement of national shipping.

The Tudors, however, had other and more effective ways of fostering the growth of shipping. When, for instance, Henry VII heard that,

> Our welbeloved Nicholas Browne of Bristoll merchant hath to his grete costes and charges made a newe ship called the Michall Browne of bristoll of the portage of cxl tonne to our grete pleasure and also to doo us service when the case in that behalve shal require,

he was so pleased with this example of enterprise that, "willing the comfort of al merchauntes in accouraging of them willing to make any ship or shippes, and also towardes the supportacion of the costes and charges of the said Nicholas," he granted him the sum of £26 13s. 4d. to be allowed out of the dues on the first cargo of the *Michall Browne*.[1]

This system of shipbuilding bounties initiated by Henry VII was carried on still more vigorously by his son; but the greatest service rendered by Henry VIII to English shipping was to give it, for the first time, the protection of a permanent fleet of genuine warships.

The invention of port-holes, which made it possible to carry heavy guns at sea, had paved the way for a sharper differentiation between the trading and fighting fleets, and Henry, with his strong military instincts, was the first ruler in Europe to appreciate the possibilities of this new development. He inherited from his father about half-a-dozen ships. He left to his successors incomparably the most powerful navy of sailing-vessels in Europe; composed mainly of ships designed and built specially for war, and provided with a permanent naval and dockyard administration.

This was a real landmark in the history of English shipping as well as in the history of England as a world-Power. For one thing, the burden of requisitioning was reduced; for although all merchantmen still went armed, and the Royal Navy was still supplemented by merchantmen whenever a big fleet was required, the Royal ships sufficed, to an

[1] Abstract of the warrant printed in Appendix A to *Bristol Privateers and Ships of War*, by Commander J. W. Damer Powell, Bristol, 1930.

ever increasing degree, for the normal police of the seas and for the ordinary operations of war. What was even more important, the permanence of the naval administration and the strong nucleus of Royal ships available, enabled much more regular and efficient protection to be given against pirates and enemies. Most important of all, English traders became assured of a vastly more effective diplomatic backing. Elizabeth could take a stronger line with Spain and the Hansa than was possible for Henry VII because she had at her disposal a fleet of real war-ships, fast, handy, and heavily armed, to serve as the spear-head of her naval power.

Nevertheless, the merchant service was still of immense importance as a second line of naval defence. It provided armed auxiliaries, transports, and victuallers. It provided, too, the crews of the Royal ships, for there was no permanent establishment for the personnel of the fleet. Thus for military as well as commercial reasons, the encouragement of merchant shipping remained one of the chief objects of English policy.

In order to maintain the supply of seamen, various measures were passed to assist the fisheries, especially by the enforcement of fast days which, since the change in religion, were no longer being generally observed. The general provisions of the Navigation Laws were not revived after their repeal in 1559, and foreign ships were free to carry English goods, subject to the payment of Aliens' duty; but in 1563 the monopoly of imports of wine and woad from Bordeaux was again conferred upon English shipping. This Act of 1563 never seems to have been formally repealed. It was probably allowed to lapse, as other wines began to supersede those of Gascony and Guienne in popularity, other methods of dyeing to replace the use of woad, and other trades to afford still greater opportunities for English shipping. Even at the time it must have counted for much less than the shipbuilding bounties, which had now crystallized into a fixed allowance of 5s. a ton on all new vessels of 100 tons and upwards, in return for which the owner was required to enter into a bond pledging him not to sell the ship to foreigners.

It is possible that the bounty system may have led at times to overbuilding, for in 1579 a speculative owner, one Olyffe Burre, a coppersmith of Southwark, who had received bounty on 790 tons of shipping in two years, found the freight markets so dull that he was driven to petition the Council to order the Spanish Company to charter his vessels. Generally speaking, however, the expansion of commerce provided ample employment for as much tonnage as could be built.

We have already seen what were the principal lines of commerce carried on by English shipping during the reign of Henry VIII: the trade with Flanders, the Baltic traffic, the Bordeaux wine trade, and the trade with Spain and Portugal. The trade with Flanders and the Baltic was carried on mainly from London. Other East Coast ports, such as Hull, Ipswich, Newcastle, and Boston, shared in the traffic; but as the exports of raw wool decreased, while those of manufactured cloth steadily rose, their relative importance declined. Bristol and the other West Coast ports, such as Exeter, Dartmouth, Plymouth, and Fowey, had a very considerable share in the Bordeaux trade, in the import of fish and salt from Rochelle and other Bay ports, and in the traffic with Spain and Portugal for oil, soap, iron, wine, sugar, pepper, and spices. They exported, in return, cloth, tin, and lead, and before the great development of sheep-farming in England made it necessary to take measures for conserving food supplies, they shipped considerable quantities of corn to Spain.

In addition there were the coastal and Iceland fisheries, the latter of which employed 149 ships in 1528, the trade with Scotland which employed 69 vessels in the same year, and the coasting traffic. The Iceland fishery and the trade with Scotland, in which comparatively small vessels were used, were carried on mainly from East Coast ports such as Cley (now an inland town), Yarmouth, Cromer, and Lynn.

These were all well-established trades, but Englishmen were now beginning to look further afield, and during the first half of the sixteenth century many new branches of commerce sprang up. It has already been noted that even during the fifteenth century isolated English ships had found their way to the Mediterranean; but so long as Venice and Genoa were at the height of their power and prosperity, there was little room for interlopers from the North. Both Venice and Genoa, however, were now on the decline. They were worn out by incessant wars, and the spread of Turkish domination in the Levant, coupled with the discovery of the sea route to India, struck at the very foundations of their greatness. On the other hand, the power of England was rising and English merchants were increasing in wealth and enterprise. Hakluyt, who had an opportunity of inspecting the books of the firms concerned, tells us that so early as 1511, during a period when the sailing of the Flanders Galleys was interrupted by war, "divers tall ships of London . . . with certain other ships of Southampton and Bristol, had an ordinary and usual trade to Sicily, Candia [Crete], Chios, and somewhiles to Cyprus, as also to Tripoli and Beyrout in Syria."

Once it had set in, the decline of the Italian City States was rapid. On May 22, 1532, the last of the annual fleets from Venice sailed on its return passage from Southampton, and though private Venetian merchantmen continued to carry Mediterranean products to London for another half-century, the Flanders galleys became a thing of the past.

To Southampton the loss of the Flanders galleys and the Genoese carracks was a fearful blow. The Customs of the port declined from an average of £10,341 for the five years

1504–1509 to £3,332 for the years 1533–1538, and though it remained for some time the second port in the Kingdom, it never recovered its old prosperity. The loss, however, was purely local. English merchants as a class rejoiced in their opportunity. Despite the diversion of a great part of the spice trade to the Cape route, the Levantine trade was still very profitable. The ships took out wool, either for their owners' account, or for the London agents of Italian merchants, cloth, hides, tin, and lead. They came back—after a round voyage occupying the greater part of a year—with cargoes of silks, cambrics, Turkey carpets, wines, currants, rhubarb, and spices, all of which fetched high prices in Northern markets.

Somewhat later, in 1551, came the beginning of the direct trade with Barbary—Morocco, Algeria, and Tunis. The exports in this trade included one rather surprising item—Hebrew Bibles for the Jews of Morocco. They also included large quantities of arms and munitions—a rather nasty early example of gun-running. The imports included gum, sugar, and molasses.

In all this there was no encroachment upon the Spanish and Portuguese monopolies; and the trade with the Canaries and Azores which sprang up early in the reign of Henry VIII was equally free from offence, for the Atlantic islands, alone among the Spanish and Portuguese colonies, were open to all comers. Canary wine soon came into favour, and the shipowners of the Western ports employed quite a number of small, fast vessels in the trade, making the round voyage in about three months.

Very soon, however, Englishmen began to go further afield. They had plenty of opportunity, in the trade with the Peninsula and the Islands, of picking up the secrets of the new Atlantic routes, and it was not very difficult to find Spanish and Portuguese pilots who were willing, if the terms offered were good enough, to betray their employers.

French freebooters from Rochelle and Rouen, who had early found out the way to Brazil, were another source of information.

The very first English trading voyage to the New World was made in 1530 by William Hawkins, a wealthy merchant-shipowner of Plymouth. He made three voyages in all, and when he himself retired from the sea, he continued to send his ships, under hired captains. His example was rapidly followed by others, chiefly from Southampton and the Western ports; but in one point Hawkins was shrewder, or better informed than his competitors. He took or sent his ships to Brazil by way of West Africa, and on the Guinea Coast he picked up valuable cargoes of ivory. It was a profitable trade. In February, 1540, his ship the *Paul* cleared from Plymouth with a miscellaneous cargo intended to delight the savages of Africa and South America. It comprised 940 hatchets, 940 combs, 375 pruning-hooks or knives, nineteen dozen nightcaps, 15 cwt. of copper and 15 cwt. of lead (one-third of each being made up into arm-rings), and three pieces of undyed cloth. The whole cargo, with the exception of the cloth, was valued for Customs purposes at £23 15s. In October 1540 the *Paul* was back at Plymouth with a hundred-weight of elephants' teeth and 92 tons of dye-wood from Brazil, with a total value of over £600. Even admitting that the outwards cargo was almost certainly undervalued through the good offices of a friendly official, Hawkins had good reason to refer with pride to his "feats of merchandize."

There was gold as well as ivory to be got on the Guinea Coast, and in 1553 there sailed the first of a long series of West African expeditions which cost heavily in men's lives (for the medical science of the time was ill-equipped to cope with the local fevers) and led to much acrimonious correspondence and a good deal of hard fighting with the Portuguese, but brought rich profits to the adventurers. Here for a time progress came to a stop. England was not yet in a position to challenge the power of Spain by attempting to trade direct with the West Indies or the Spanish Main, and the Cape Route to the East Indies was too little known and too strongly held by the Portuguese to tempt the most adventurous.

It remained to seek out a route to the Far East which should neither bring the traders into collision with the Portuguese at the Cape nor with the Spaniards at the Straits of Magellan or Panama. Such a route was sought by a North-West Passage through the ice floes of Arctic America, and by a North-East Passage along the northern coasts of Russia and Siberia. Hopeless as we now know these attempts to have been, they bore fruit not only in many feats of daring seamanship but in solid commercial results, for the search for a North-East Passage led to the opening up of direct trade with Russia by way of the White Sea.

Thus by the accession of Elizabeth, Englishmen had opened up trade with the Levant and Barbary, with the Canaries and Azores, and with Russia, in addition to the old mediaeval trade routes, and were making at least occasional voyages to West Africa and Brazil. With this the more conservative merchants would have been content. Their main interests lay in the trade with the Continent. They were doing very well in the North Sea, both as merchants and as shipowners; for the privileges of the Hansa had been drastically restricted under Edward VI and Mary, and the Merchant Adventurers were daily gaining ground. The trade with Spain itself was extensive and profitable, and many of the old-established merchants were very loth to risk it by a quarrel with the Spanish Government. There were many, however, especially among the merchants of the Western ports, whose minds were set on a more adventurous policy, and they had the spirit of the time with them. The growth of industry made new markets necessary. Economic distress at home, caused by the rise in prices and the enclosure of common land for sheep-farming, drove men to seek a living on the sea. The politician's dread of Spain was giving way to a determination to set some bounds to Spanish power and arrogance. Hatred of the leading Catholic power was fanned by the sufferings of Englishmen at the hands of the Inquisition. Behind all economic, political, and religious motives was the strong push of the new spirit of adventure and enterprise which called Englishmen to play their part in the opening up of the world.

This urge to adventure found two outlets. The fiercer and greedier spirits among the West Country seamen (who had always a bad reputation for piracy) set out to spoil the Amalekites by force of arms. Responsible merchants like John Hawkins (son of William) who could boast, "I have always enjoyed the name of an orderly person and have always hated folly" were nevertheless resolved to assert, if needs be by force, their right to trade with the New World. They knew that the monopoly bore hardly on the Spanish colonists. In particular the supply of slaves for working the sugar plantations in the West Indies was far below the demand. They had no scruples as to the morality of the traffic, and Hawkins found no difficulty in procuring powerful financial and political backing for a series of slaving voyages to Africa and the West Indies. From this moment war was inevitable, unless Philip of Spain could bring himself to make concessions which he would rather die than make.

We are not concerned here with the war, so much as with its effects on shipping. Yet the war itself does concern us, because it marked definitely the entry of England upon a policy of oceanic expansion, and because it marked the shifting of maritime power from Southern to Northern Europe. Drake's broadsides at Cadiz, in 1587, sounded the death-knell of the galley fleets, and soon even English merchantmen began to despise the type of warship that had once been supreme. The Armada campaign of the following year revealed England clearly to Europe as the leading oceanic Power. The exploits of the privateers taught Englishmen their way to America and the Indies, and paved the way to the first English attempts at colonization oversea.

All this implied a demand for more and bigger ships. As there was no Register of Shipping in those days, our information comes mainly from the Exchequer Warrants for bounty payments, and from a series of returns prepared for the Council, as an indication of the number of ships available for requisition. Neither authority is wholly satisfactory. We do not know definitely that the bounty was always paid, and we certainly cannot be sure that we have a record of all the payments. The lists of available shipping, too, are obviously incomplete, as in each list some ports seem to be omitted, and it is probable that ships absent on distant voyages were also left out. But, with all their imperfections, they do give good evidence of continuous growth. The three fullest of the returns may be summarized as follows:

	100–200 tons	200–300 tons	300 tons and upwards	Total over 100 tons
List of 1560:				
London	16	3	2	21
Other Ports ..	52	4	—	56
Total ..	68	7	2	77
List of 1577:				
London	35	7	2	44
Other Ports ..	86	3	2	91
Total ..	121	10	4	135
List of 1582:				
London	57	5	—	62
Other Ports ..	101	11	3	115
Total ..	158	16	3	177

The List of 1582 omits, among others, several London vessels, some of them over 300 tons, trading to the Mediterranean and elsewhere.

We have, unfortunately, no returns for the later years of the reign; but the bounty-warrants during those years show that the rate of progress was greatly accelerated by the rise of English naval power. During the four years 1592 to 1595 inclusive we know of 48 occasions on which the bounty was allowed, and between September 1596 and September 1597, it was earned by no fewer than 57 ships, including 8 of 300 or 400 tons, and 32 between 200 and 300 tons.

Whether all these ships would have earned the grant in a more scientific age may perhaps be doubted. At this time, the measurement of shipping was little better than guesswork. Two different tonnages were in use: "burden in merchants' goods" and "deadweight of ton and tonnage." "Burden in merchants' goods" was commonly calculated in casks of Bordeaux wine; the ship's capacity for the carriage of heavy cargo is more truly represented by her "deadweight of ton and tonnage" which was the burden plus one-third. One of the chief shipwrights, Mathew Baker, could give no better method of calculating the burden than to take a ship whose cargo capacity had been proved by experiment, measure her and compare the measurements of the ship to be rated. His examples would give as a formula: length on keel × beam × depth, over 97; but there was controversy and uncertainty as to whether length of keel should be measured with or without the false-post; beam with or without the plank; and depth by depth in hold or draught of water. So late as 1626, under Charles I, the leading experts recognized three different methods, according to which the ton and tonnage of a given ship, the *Adventure* of Ipswich, would be 244, 277 or 294 tons, respectively, besides a fourth "exploded" method, which would have made her 321 tons. In these circumstances it is not surprising that even the Queen's ships displayed a surprising elasticity when claims for prize-money were to be adjusted,[1] and we may be sure that shipowners claiming bounty or hire stuck out stoutly for the most liberal method of computation.

The rate of payment for hired or requisitioned ships under Henry VIII and Elizabeth had been 1s. per ton per month until about 1580, when it was doubled; no doubt to the great satisfaction of the owners whose ships were taken up in 1588 for the Armada campaign. A considerable proportion of the 164 ships which served during the memorable year 1588 were provided as the result of demands on London, the Cinque Ports, and other coast towns and districts for contingents to be equipped and provisioned at their own expense; but the actual owners of the ships received, as a part of the town's contribution, the customary 2s. per ton.[2] After the experience of 1588, when the Queen's ships bore the real brunt of the fighting, the carrying on of the war was left mainly to the Royal Navy; but every big overseas expedition entailed a big demand for transports and victuallers. For the Cadiz expedition of 1596, for instance, over 80 merchantmen were taken into pay, though only 12 of these served as fighting ships.

The payment of hire for ships in Crown service, whether requisitioned or chartered in the open market, seems to have been reasonably punctual, and the demand for such ships may have had something to do with the increase in

[1] The *Foresight*, for instance, was rated at 300 tons; but on the voyage in which she captured a great carrack in "consortship" with some privateers, the Queen received prize money on 450 tons.

[2] It is sometimes implied that the ships "set forth" by London and the Coast towns were requisitioned without compensation to their owners, but an account of the charges of the City of London, in connection with a reinforcement of ten ships, includes payment to the owners at 2s. per ton, and it may safely be assumed that this was the general practice. See Laughton, *Papers relating to the Defeat of the Spanish Armada* (Navy Records Society), I.251.

tonnage; but the attractions of Crown service paled before those of privateering pure and simple. The syndicate which financed Drake's voyage round the world is said to have received a net profit of £47 for every £1 invested, and a profit of 4,700 per cent. on a two years' voyage was enough to turn the thoughts of any bold speculator in the direction of such profitable patriotism. The line between public and private enterprises in those days is very hard to draw; Drake's brilliant campaign on the Spanish coast in 1587 was financed on the principles of a joint stock company with the Queen as chief shareholder, and Cumberland's expedition to Porto Rico in 1598 was a regular operation of war, with a real strategic purpose, though no Queen's ships were employed. Men like Drake, Hawkins, Cumberland, and the great London merchants were thinking of national interests as well as of what Drake called "a little comfortable dew of heaven"; but there is no doubt that the chance of intercepting a Spanish treasure ship or a Portuguese carrack deeply laden with the silks and spices of the East was a very big incentive. Some ships, like Cumberland's *Malice-Scourge,* a splendid galleon of 500 tons, equal to any middle-sized ship in the Royal Navy, were built purely for privateering, to the orders of men who would probably have disdained to engage in ordinary commerce, though they were ready enough to turn to attempts at colonization or to take a share in such a dignified adventure as an East Indies voyage. At the same time, the ordinary Elizabethan trading vessel, with an extra gun or two mounted, was quite capable of bringing in a rich prize, and there were probably few ship-owners who did not, at one time or another, take a hand in the game. A few of them made fortunes out of it; but many of those who devoted themselves to privateering on a big scale, from patriotic motives, lost more than they gained, and many smaller adventurers came back empty-handed. On the whole, while privateering no doubt increased the immediate demand for shipping it was harmful to the shipping industry. It led to much waste of men, money, and tonnage, and to a dangerous diversion of energy and ambition into channels that could not be permanently productive.

Apart from the privateers pure and simple, the Elizabethan shipowner was usually a merchant; but it did not follow that his ships were laden exclusively with his own goods. The cargoes carried by big ships on long voyages represented a larger sum than most merchants were prepared to risk on a single adventure. On the other hand, there were many merchants who had no vessels of their own and were eager to engage ships or space for the carriage of their goods. The usual arrangement was for a number of merchants to club together to charter a ship, appointing a captain, not necessarily a professional seaman, to control the business side of the voyage in their interests. The details of navigation were left to the pilot and sailing-master; but it was the captain, the charterers' nominee, who was responsible for deciding, subject to any instructions received from the merchants, on the ports of call and the sailing dates. It was his business also to supervise the sale of the goods and to arrange for a return cargo.

A big shipowner would thus have two distinct sources of revenue; his profits as a merchant from the sale of goods shipped in his own or other people's vessels, and his gains as a shipowner from freights, Crown hire, and prize money. Even apart from privateering, these gains seem to have been large enough to induce some men, such as our old friend Mr. Olyffe Burre, who stated that he had obtained a living for forty years "cheefely by the maynteyninge of shippinge and the navygacon," to make shipowning in the modern sense of the term their most important business.

Some merchant shipowners possessed considerable fleets. John Hawkins and his brother, William the Younger, were recorded in 1570 as owning, probably in partnership, nine vessels ranging from 100 to 500 tons, and four others of 60 or 70 tons, a total of thirteen. This list too is incomplete. It omits a number of smaller craft, from 20 to 50 tons, employed in coasting and short sea voyages and the Canaries trade, and it probably omits also some big ships then absent in distant waters.

Behind the merchant shipowner stood the financier; the big capitalist who might or might not be personally engaged in trade. Half-trading, half-exploring expeditions to new markets where the right to trade had often to be enforced at the cannon's mouth, required strong ships, strong crews, and carefully chosen equipment. All this meant heavy expenditure, and such voyages, like the more important privateering expeditions, were usually the work of powerful syndicates. As a rule, about half a dozen capitalists underwrote the capital required, each of them subsequently disposing of a portion of his interest in the adventure to personal or business friends. The original subscribers acted as a sort of Board of Directors, retaining the control of the venture in their own hands, but liable to account to their sub-shareholders for the profits earned. Among other things, they appointed the commander of the expedition, who was often himself a member of the syndicate. John Hawkins, for instance, was not only the promoter of the syndicates which financed his voyages to Guinea and the West Indies, but a large shareholder therein.

The Crown itself was sometimes a partner in the syndicate. It was essential that such voyages should include one or two ships of real force, and these were at times furnished by the Royal Navy. Both Henry VII and Henry VIII had continued the mediaeval practice of chartering the royal ships to merchants for the longer trading voyages, such as those to the Mediterranean, and during the early years of Elizabeth the older Royal ships were occasionally employed for pioneering expeditions into the Spanish and Portuguese preserves. In 1564, for instance, H.M.S. *Minion* was hired by a syndicate for a voyage to Guinea under a regular Charter-party, by which the Queen agreed to have the ship ready by a given date (except for sheathing) and to bear the whole cost of equipment and the whole risk on the ship. The charterers were to provide and pay the crew, to bear all running expenses, including victualling and repairs, and to load a cargo valued at not less than £5,000. At the end of the voyage they undertook to return the ship in good condition and to pay into the hands of the Treasurer of the Navy, for the use of his department, one-sixth of the net profits of the voyage.

When once a regular, long-distance trade had been opened up, these syndicates, formed for separate voyages, usually gave way to a Chartered Company. In the absence of quick and regular communications, of a properly organized diplomatic and consular service, and of naval protection for commerce in distant waters, the maintenance of a long-distance trade involved very heavy overhead charges. It had to be carried on in large, well-armed ships, sailing in company for mutual support. Factories had to be maintained abroad where the outward cargoes could be warehoused and disposed of, and where the homeward cargoes could be collected to await the arrival of the ships, and these factories had often to be fortified and garrisoned. Negotiations had to be carried on with Turkish, Asiatic, or African rulers, for freedom of intercourse, port privileges, and relief from onerous dues, and it was essential that those who carried on these negotiations should be able to make an impressive show of wealth and dignity, and to draw on ample funds for the gratification of any local magnate who had an itching palm.

All this work, so much of which the modern merchant or shipowner expects his Government to do for him, was very costly, and required a strong, permanent organization behind it. Individual merchants, however wealthy, lacked the necessary resources; syndicates formed for particular voyages lacked the necessary stability. The obvious thing to do was for those employed in the trade to form a company for the purpose, and in return for their outlay they naturally expected a monopoly of the traffic. The word "monopoly" has an ugly sound to-day, but the work done for the traders by the early Chartered Companies fully entitled them to expect all those who shared in its benefits to contribute to the upkeep of their organization.

Thus, the early Chartered Company was an association of merchants formed to exploit the trade of a particular route, to whom the Crown granted, permanently or for a term of years, a monopoly of the traffic and the right to make its own regulations therefor. As in the Corporation of Lloyd's to-day, each member traded on his own account and at his own individual risk, but under rules laid down by the governing body. Entrance fees and fees for licenses to trade were fixed either by the charter or by the Company's own Bye-laws (to use a modern phrase), and out of the revenue derived from these fees the Governors and Council paid the salaries of its officials at home and abroad, the upkeep of the factories, and other incidental expenses.

The actual constitution of the Companies varied widely. Membership of some of them, such as the Merchant Adventurers, was open to anyone who was willing to pay a moderate entrance fee or serve a period of apprenticeship. Others had a strictly limited membership and were very chary of admitting newcomers. It was the latter type which gave the chief occasion for discontent, by excluding from the traffic of a route, in favour of vested interests, men who were perfectly willing to abide by the Company's regulations and to pay a fair share of the overhead charges.

We have met already with two Companies established in

mediaeval times: the Merchants of the Staple, whose importance had greatly diminished as exports of cloth replaced those of raw wool; and the Merchant Adventurers, the great rivals of the Hansa, who flourished exceedingly in the times of Elizabeth under the able leadership of Sir Thomas Gresham, and to whose pressure was due the final expulsion of the Hansa from England in 1598. The Spanish Company, a loose association of merchants trading with Spain, was incorporated in 1530 and died out during the Spanish war.

These were all concerned with carrying on trades that were already long established when the first Tudor came to the throne. The Eastland Company, formed in 1579 for the Baltic trade, rose on the ruins of the Hansa. The first company formed in Tudor times for the exploitation of the new routes was the Russia or Muscovy Company, originally known as the "Merchants Adventurers of England for the discovery of Lands, territories, isles, dominions, and seignories unknown." It was formed in 1553, as a syndicate with a capital of £6,000, divided into £25 shares, to finance a voyage for the discovery of the North-East Passage, and re-formed in 1555, with a monopoly of the Russian trade which that expedition had opened up. It was followed by the Turkey Company in 1581, and the Venice Company in 1583, which were united as the Levant Company in 1592; by the first Guinea Company, which received a ten years' Charter in 1588, and by the East India Company in 1599.

The Chartered Companies did not, as a rule, own ships collectively and the shipowning members charged freight, in the ordinary way, on the goods carried for their colleagues, though the freight rates were sometimes fixed by the Governors and Council. What they did do, as Companies, was to stimulate the demand for larger vessels. In 1600 the members of the Levant Company owned fourteen ships, aggregating 2,790 tons, in the Mediterranean trade, and they employed, in addition, fifteen chartered vessels with a total tonnage of 2,500. These Levant merchantmen were stout ships which had proved themselves quite capable of beating off both the Spanish galleys and the galleons of the Ocean Guard. They must also have been profitable to their owners, for in 1624 freights on fine goods from the Levant were £7 per ton, and this seems to have been a rate of long standing.

Still larger ships were employed in the East India trade. The first English ship to reach India, the *Edward Bonaventure* of 250 tons, was normally a Mediterranean trader; but this was just before the East India Company was formed, and the first fleet sent out by the Company itself included the *Dragon* of 600 tons,[1] as well as four smaller vessels, from 130 to 300 tons.

The East India Company, in this opening stage of its great career, represented an improved form of the old "regulated" Company. A separate syndicate was formed for each voyage and the accounts were wound up and the profits distributed, as soon as the homeward cargo had been disposed of; but the Company itself was a permanent body with a Governor and Council who ensured continuity of management. The first syndicate instituted an important innovation, for it bought its ships outright, investing £45,000 in the ships and their equipment, and £27,000 in the outward cargoes. At this rate the cost of the fleet works out at over £31 per ton, but this included armament and stores.

The victualling of an Elizabethan ship was normally a simple matter: biscuit, salt beef, salt fish, and beer, with perhaps a few luxuries for the cabin. The victualling list for Hawkins's second slaving voyage in 1564 was a little more varied; but Hawkins was something of a pioneer, who looked carefully after the seaman's welfare and was always

[1] This was Cumberland's *Malice-Scourge*, which the Company had bought. It will be noted that her rating had increased by a hundred tons.

very particular as to the quality of the food. His crews, including the "gentlemen adventurers," numbered 170, and the voyage lasted eleven months. Hawkins would look, no doubt, to pick up some fresh provisions on the African coast and in the West Indies. The stores actually shipped at the beginning of the voyage comprised 25 thousandweight of biscuit, 120 barrels of meal, 20 quarters of beans and peas, 40 hogsheads of beef, 80 flitches of bacon, 6 lasts of stock-fish, 12 cwt. of ling, 40 tuns of beer, 35 tuns of cider, 40 butts of malmsey (no doubt for the use of the gentlemen adventurers), and various oddments, including a tun of oil, a pipe of vinegar, a hogshead of honey, and a quarter of aniseed.

The manning scale was still high. In spite of the improvements in rig, the ships required large crews to work them; the numbers had to be calculated for fighting as well as for navigation, and a margin for wastage had to be allowed on long voyages. The lists of the Levant Company's ships show that, in the Mediterranean trade, the scale was 20 to 24 men per 100 tons; but on more distant voyages, especially when fighting was expected, much larger crews were carried. The East India Company's *Dragon* of 600 tons had 300 people in her.

Over-crowding, a long-continued diet of salt food, and the absence of any proper sanitary arrangements, bred sickness rapidly, especially when voyages were made to tropical climates. On Wyndham's voyage to Guinea in 1553, 100 men died out of 140 who started on the voyage, and this was not so exceptional as one would like to believe. In general, however, the heaviest mortality from scurvy and fever occurred in the Royal fleets (manned on a scale of 50 men per 100 tons) and the big privateering expeditions whose numbers were swollen by the necessity of carrying a landing force. The experience of Hawkins, who set himself rigorously against overcrowding, and did what he could to keep down scurvy by procuring fresh meat and fruit whenever possible, shows that, even on the longer trading voyages, the health of the crews might compare well enough with some later periods. Of the 170 men whom he took out in 1564 he lost only 13 by disease.

From the money point of view, the seaman was decidedly worse off then he had been in the Middle Ages. Although prices and shore wages were steadily rising under the influence of the influx of precious metals, the pay of the sailor in Crown service, in or about 1546, was only 6s. 8d. for a month of 28 days; a drop of 2s. 4d. on the rate of a hundred years earlier. In 1585, it was raised, by the influence of Hawkins, to 10s. a month; but even so, seafaring could no longer be reckoned among the better-paid occupations.[1] Nevertheless, there seems to have been no difficulty in procuring men. For one thing, there was a chance of promotion. The officers were mostly men who had shipped before the mast, or had gone to sea as "pages" or ship's boys, and were in somewhat the same position as the modern apprentice. In addition to the captain and sailing-master, the *Edward Bonaventure*, in the Russia Company's first voyage, carried a master's mate, a master gunner and his mate, two gunners, a chaplain and a surgeon, a boatswain and his mate, four quartermasters, a steward and his mate, a cook, a cooper, and a carpenter, as well as 21 sailors. With the exception of the captain, chaplain, and surgeon all the officers and petty officers might well be men promoted from the forecastle.

There was a chance also of a little private trade, and if enemies were met or the ship was sent on a privateering cruise, of plunder and prize-money. And there was the interest and excitement, on the longer voyages, of sailing into unknown seas, treading land never before trodden by a

[1] By the end of Elizabeth's reign, even a labourer was getting 10d. a day (without food).

European foot, and coming into contact with strange peoples. It was probably this element of adventure, coupled with the economic distress at home, that accounted, more than anything else, for the large number of educated and highly intelligent men who were to be found serving in minor capacities afloat, and whose narratives, handed down to us in the collections of Hakluyt and Purchas, help to give life and colour to the story of the rise of England as a maritime Power.

SOME BOOKS ON THE PERIOD

Dr. J. A. Williamson's *Maritime Enterprise*, 1485–1558, Oxford, 1913, gives an excellent account of English trade, shipping and commercial policy, from the accession of Henry VII to the death of Queen Mary. His *Life of Sir John Hawkins*, Oxford, 1927, is not only a fascinating biography but rich in information as to trade and shipping. *The Early Chartered Companies*, by G. Causton and A. H. Keene, London, 1896, and *The Early History of the Levant Company*, by M. Epstein, London, 1908, are useful for this side of the story. Oppenheim's *Naval Administration*, already cited, is specially valuable for shipping statistics and for the bounty system. The background of war and privateering is brilliantly given by Sir Julian Corbett in *Drake and the Tudor Navy*, London, 1899, and *The Successors of Drake*, London, 1900. Hakluyt's *Voyages*, reprinted in the "Everyman Series," show how the various trading, and exploring, and privateering expeditions looked to those who took part in them.

CHAPTER VI

"THE PRODIGIOUS INCREASE OF THE NETHERLANDS"

THE DUTCH AS GENERAL CARRIERS

> The Prodigious increase of the Netherlands in their Domestick and Foreign Trade, Riches, and multitude of Shipping is the envy of the present, and may be the wonder of all future generations. SIR JOSIAH CHILD, *A New Discourse of Trade*

THE quotation from a great seventeenth-century merchant which stands at the head of this chapter sounds startling to us to-day. We are so used to thinking of Great Britain as the chief shipowning country that, from the moment when Englishmen began to find their way onto the ocean routes, we might expect the story of the world's carrying trade to turn into a history of British shipping. Yet for more than a hundred years after the first English ship arrived in India, Englishmen could claim to be no more than a bad second among the shipowning peoples.

We need not attribute this, as a contemporary writer attributed the failure of the first English attempts at colonization, to "the extreme beastly idleness of our nation." Yet there does seem to have been a certain reluctance among all classes to "get down to it." The nation's head had been a little turned by its sudden rise to power, and the Elizabethan orgy of privateering was as demoralizing as all other epidemics of get-rich-quick speculation. To make matters worse, the death of Elizabeth was followed by nearly half a century of very bad government under James I and Charles I, and the best energies of the nation had to be diverted from commercial expansion to the fight for civil liberties. Shipowners were among the chief sufferers from the misrule of the earlier Stuarts. The Navy became so inefficient that it could not even prevent Moorish pirates and Dunkirk corsairs from holding up the trade of the Channel and East Coast, and Government service was so unpopular, through failure to pay hire for requisitioned ships, that owners were found to be deliberately building ships unsuitable for troop-transport, in order to evade it.

Altogether, the conditions were not favourable to commerce, and behind all these incidental disadvantages lay two more deeply rooted handicaps; English industry had not yet made sufficient progress to provide a great variety of outward cargoes, and capital was still comparatively scarce and dear. English trade and shipping, despite all drawbacks, continued to increase, and the English East India Company, in particular, made some very successful voyages; but England was not yet ready to take the lead in oceanic expansion.

Of the other Powers, Portugal had shot her bolt, and the whole energies of Spain were concentrated upon the treasure fleets. France was yearly increasing her military and even her naval strength, but she had no bulky staple export and no large monied and commercial class to provide the foundations of a flourishing shipping industry. Only the Dutch were ready to take full advantage of the new era that was opening in the world's carrying trade.

With the help of England, Holland had thrown off the Spanish yoke, and the long struggle had proved the Dutch to be stout fighters and daring privateersmen; but among the burghers of Amsterdam and Rotterdam trade had always been not merely respectable but honourable, and once their freedom was won the whole nation settled down to make money with a wholehearted persistence that could not fail of its reward.

They found excellent cards in their hands. To begin with, the chief centre of the herring fisheries had tended, ever since the second quarter of the fifteenth century, to shift from the Baltic to the North Sea. Although very heavy catches were still made off Scania from time to time, the North Sea fisheries seem to have been the more reliable, and the discovery by a Dutchman of an improved method of curing the fish gave the Hollanders a further advantage. They were quick to take it. Either because, as contemporary English pamphleteers alleged, they were soberer and more industrious than the English fishermen, or because they had a greater inherited aptitude for business and more money behind them, they got the bulk of the North Sea fisheries into their hands, even off the English and Scottish coasts. During the sixteenth century they gradually ousted the Hanseatics as purveyors of salt fish to France, Flanders, and England, and from the beginning of the seventeenth century they began to conquer also the German and Baltic markets. They fished for cod and ling also on the Dogger Bank and off Iceland, and exported the catch not only to Northern Europe but even to Spain, Portugal, and the Mediterranean.

By 1620, the Dutch fishing fleet was said to number no fewer than 2,000 vessels, of which a large proportion were herring busses of 70 to 100 tons burthen. As the crews averaged about 15 men, this would mean that 30,000 were actually engaged in the fisheries, and in 1669 it was believed that the herring fishery and the trades connected with it, such as curing, cask-making, net-making, and buss-building, gave employment, directly or indirectly, to about 450,000 persons.

No great reliance can be placed on seventeenth-century statistics; but there is, at least, no doubt as to the importance of the fisheries to Holland, and especially to the development of Dutch shipping. The monopoly of the supply of salt fish gave to them, as it had given to the Hanseatics, a bulky export in very wide demand, which provided outward cargoes for a great number of ships, and which could be used to finance homeward cargoes of goods both for domestic consumption and for re-export, and to secure cargoes for Dutch vessels in the cross-trades. There was a great deal of truth in the contemporary Dutch epigram, "The herring keeps Dutch trade going, and Dutch trade sets the world afloat."

Even King Herring, however, would not have raised Holland to the position once occupied by the Hansa, had not Amsterdam and Rotterdam, like Hamburg, Bremen, and Lubeck of old, been natural entrepôts for the produce of Central Europe. The Hanse towns had now fallen into decay, and the ruin of their trade was completed by the desolation of a great part of Germany during the Thirty Years' War (1618–1648). The commercial life of Antwerp had been trodden out under the iron heel of Spain. Thus the Dutch ports became the chief outlets for the trade of a great part of the Continent; the more so because most of it could reach them by water, and the cost of water transport, according to the chief seventeenth-century writer on political economy, was only one-fifteenth or one-twentieth the cost of land carriage. Contemporary descriptions of seventeenth-century roads suggest that this is no very wild exaggeration.

Thus, while Holland itself was not specially rich in natural resources, Dutch ships need never lack for outward cargoes. Sir William Petty, whom we have just quoted, puts it picturesquely:

> There is much more to be gained by Manufacture than Husbandry, and by Merchandize than Manufacture; but Holland and Zealand being seated at the mouths of three long great Rivers, and passing through Rich Countries, do keep all the Inhabitants upon the sides of those Rivers but as Husbandmen.

That is to say, they skimmed the cream off the trade by taking the middlemen's and carriers' profits.

Even so they were not satisfied. Profitable as the European trades might be, there were richer profits to be earned on the ocean routes, and their European traffic supplied them with the shipping, seamen, and capital necessary for the vigorous exploitation of those routes. In the Atlantic they harried Spanish trade mercilessly, and at the same time carried on a lively contraband traffic with the Spanish colonists, whom they supplied with slaves and European goods in exchange for cocoa, tobacco, silver, gold dust, and pearls. They established their own colonies, too, in the West Indies and in North America, and from New Amsterdam (now New York), founded in 1624, they soon began to push their way into the commerce of the English colonies which were growing up on the other side of the Atlantic.

Yet it was the trade with Asia that still held the chief place in men's thoughts. Like the English, the Dutch formed syndicate after syndicate to promote voyages for the discovery of a North-East or North-West Passage, and like the English, they saved some solid profit from the wreckage of their hopes; for it was these voyages of exploration that introduced them to the whale, seal, and walrus fisheries of Greenland and Spitzbergen, in which they speedily outdistanced all rivals. Before the discovery of gas, electricity, or petroleum, whale oil was a very precious and necessary commodity; but the way to a still more lucrative traffic was opened in 1595, when John Huyghen van Linschoten of Haarlem, who had served with the Portuguese in the East, published a volume of sailing directions for the Indian Voyage.

It was the publication of an English translation of Linschoten's *Itinerario* in 1598 that was mainly responsible for the founding of the English East India Company in the following year; but meanwhile, the Dutch were already in the field. Between 1595 and 1601 no fewer than fifteen Dutch expeditions sailed for India and the Malay Archipelago, either by way of the Cape of Good Hope or through the Straits of Magellan, and a number of associations for trade with the Indies were formed in Holland. The Dutch, however, had an eye to business on the big scale, and they soon saw that the cut-throat competition between these associations was forcing down the price of Eastern products in Europe; while the companies were too small and weak to give their members the necessary backing in negotiations with native rulers, or to equip fleets capable of ousting the Portuguese from their commanding positions on the trade routes. The Dutch Government itself—a Government of merchant princes—took the lead in providing a remedy, and in 1602 all these local associations were merged in the United East India Company, with the colossal capital, for those days, of 6,500,000 gulden, or between £540,000 and £650,000 English. From the start this Company had the full backing of the State. It was empowered to make war or peace, to establish colonies, construct forts, and raise money. Its Directors were in close touch with the Government, and while they were left a free hand in the running of the Company's business, they knew that they could call on the whole strength of the Republic to support them against interlopers or foreign competitors.

One after another, the Portuguese trading settlements and bases were conquered, and native States brought into subjection. By the middle of the seventeenth century the Dutch possessions and spheres of influence in the East extended from Persia to the Malay Archipelago, trade had been opened with Japan, and the lines of communication were secured by settlements at the Cape of Good Hope, Mauritius, and Malacca. In Persia and Siam and on the mainland of India, their factories had to compete with those of the English Company, but the pearl fisheries and cinnamon trade of Ceylon had fallen wholly into their hands, and in the Malay Archipelago they were fast becoming not merely predominant but supreme.

This, and not the Indian trade proper, was their main object. All Eastern trade was profitable; but the products of the Spice Islands—the cloves of Amboina and Ternate, and the nutmegs and mace of Banda gave the best returns, and when Peter Both went out, in 1609, as the first Governor-General of the Dutch East Indies, he took with him explicit instructions, "That the commerce of the Moluccas, Amboina, and Banda should belong to the Company, and that no other nation in the world should have the least part." This applied to the Hollanders' old allies, the English, just as much as to anybody else. The English were cleared out of the Spice Islands by diplomacy, by fighting, and it must be said, by torture and massacre, and by the end of the century they had been expelled also from Java, the chief centre of the pepper trade.

Thus the Dutch had succeeded not only to the position of the Hansa as masters of the herring fishery and the carrying trade of northern Europe, but to that successively held by the Venetians and the Portuguese as the chief purveyors of Eastern products to the European markets. Both in volume and variety their trade exceeded any that the world had yet seen. Dutch ships carried to Western Europe the timber and shipbuilding materials, the iron, and wax, and grain of Scandinavia and the Baltic. Dutch ships distributed the produce and manufactures of Central Europe. The warehouses of Amsterdam and Rotterdam bulged with Spanish wool; with the wine, and olive oil, and honey of Spain and the Mediterranean; with spices and pepper from the Malay Archipelago; cinnamon, pearls, and areca nuts from Ceylon; cotton, calicoes, sugar, saltpetre, and opium from India; silks, porcelain, copper, tea, and lacquer from China and Japan; skins, dye-woods, and spelter from Siam.

As their contemporaries enviously acknowledged, the Dutch owed this predominance not merely to the natural advantages of their position but to wise commercial laws and skilful finance. Child attributed much of their success to their law for "Transference of Bills of Debt," which anticipated the operations of the modern bill-broker and enabled the Dutch merchant to turn over his capital quickly, while the English merchant had to wait six, nine, or twelve months for payment. They owed much, too, to the creation of the Bank of Amsterdam, founded in 1609, which had stood open for nearly seventy years when Petty still found it necessary to explain to English readers how a bank could be used, "to increase Money, or rather to make a small summ equivalent in Trade to a greater."

All this made for a plentiful supply of cheap capital. It was not because wages were low that Dutch merchants and shipowners could undercut their rivals. Child, who was stoutly of opinion that, "Where ever Wages are high universally throughout the whole world, it is an infallible evidence of the Riches of that Country," believed the general run of wages in Holland to be twopence in the shilling higher than in England, and states that many English seamen were drawn away into Dutch service by the lure of higher pay. The real determining factor was that when the rate of interest in England was 10 per cent., it was only 6 per cent. in Holland, and when the English rate fell to 8 and then to 6 per cent., the Dutch merchants and shipowners could borrow money at 3½ or 3 per cent. in time of peace, and 4 per cent. even in time of war. This gave them an immense advantage, for even in trades such as the whale fisheries, where the risks were big and the returns slow, they could be content with a lower rate of profit than their rivals. In shipping, their advantage was still greater than in commerce for, trusting mainly to convoy for protection against pirates and enemies, they built their ships with less regard to speed and strength than did the English builders, and the ships when built carried smaller crews. Lower costs of construction, lower running costs, and lower interest on borrowed capital made shipowning a far more profitable business in Holland than in England.

An older pamphleteer, whose *Small Treatise against Usury* Child bound up with his own tract, states that leading English merchants had assured him that "if they would Build a Ship, and let it to any other to employ," they could not look for a better return, after allowing for charges and depreciation, than 10 or 12 per cent., which made shipowning in the modern sense of the term "no gainful trade," seeing that they must pay 8 per cent. on borrowed money, or could obtain that rate by lending on good security. "But in the *Low-Countries*, where Money goeth at six, the Building of Ships and Hiring them to others, is a gainful *Trade*."

Nothing succeeds like success, and when the Dutch had once forced themselves into the first place as traders and carriers, the very extent of their operations gave them advantages which accelerated their relative progress. In those days when there were no trade journals or published volumes of commercial statistics, the information as to markets and sources of supply which can now be collected from such sources as the *Annual Statement of Trade* or the reports of the Overseas Trade Department, had to be obtained by observation at first hand, and as Petty observes:

> Those who predominate in Shipping and Fishing have more occasion than others to frequent all parts of the World, and to know what is wanting or redundant everywhere, and what each People can do, and what they desire, and consequently to be Factors and Carriers for the whole World of Trade.

He insists even more strongly on the advantage which their extensive carrying trade gave them, in being able to build ships specially suited to each branch of their commerce:

> Those who command the Trade of Shipping can build long slight Ships for carrying Masts, Fir-Timber, Boards, Balks, etc., And short ones for Lead, Iron, Stones, etc.

> One sort of Vessels to Trade at Ports where they need never lie a ground, others where they must jump upon the Sand twice every twelve hours; One sort of Vessels and way of manning in time of Peace, and for cheap gross Goods, another for War and precious Commodities . . . One sort of Vessels and Rigging, where haste is requisite for the Maidenhead of a Market, another where ⅛th or ¼th part of the time makes no matter. . . . And this I take to be the chief of several Reasons, why the *Hollanders* can go at less Freight than their Neighbours, viz. because they can afford a particular sort of Vessels for each particular Trade.

In particular, he believed the Dutch derived a great advantage from what he called "undermasting" vessels employed to carry "cheap and gross Goods, and whose Sale doth not depend much upon Season." His argument was that, in trades where a ship might be over three weeks in port for four or five days under sail (he was probably thinking of the Baltic routes), the gain of a day on the passage was a very trifling matter in comparison with the cost of the increased sail area, and the consequent increase in the manning scale, which was required to effect it.

It is impossible to measure the Dutch predominance arithmetically with any accuracy, for in days when ships were not registered, no statistics were much better than guess-work; but Petty's own guess gives at any rate an idea of how things appeared to a very shrewd observer. He put the whole shipping of Europe at about 2,000,000 tons; of which he thought about 900,000 tons belonged to the Dutch, 500,000 tons to the English, 100,000 tons to the French, 250,000 tons to the Germans and Scandinavians, and 250,000 tons to the nations of Southern Europe.

His proportions, at any rate, may not be far wrong; for there is no doubt that the Dutch fishing fleet was far bigger than that of any other country, and that Dutch merchant ships took the lion's share in the carriage of almost all the bulkiest European cargoes, such as fish, salt, grain, and timber. They predominated too in the whale fisheries and in the long-distance trade to the East. The Dutch East India Company's fleet was necessarily of great size, for in addition to the ships which sailed between Holland and Batavia or Ceylon, a large number of vessels, many of them big ships, were continuously employed in collecting the products of the Spice Islands, and in the very profitable local trade carried on from Batavia with ports in India, Persia, Siam, China, and Japan. The Dutch West India Company, formed in 1621 to organize the Atlantic trade, was also a large shipowner.

From the business point of view, then, the Dutch were the most successful shipowners the world had yet seen. No other nation had ever carried so large a proportion of the world's commerce or drawn such large profits from the carrying trade. When we turn, however, to the conditions in which the trade was carried on, we have no such progress to record. In the long-distance trades, at any rate, life on a Dutch merchant vessel was terribly apt to be "short, brutish, and nasty."

Although shipbuilding and navigation had made great strides since the days of Columbus and Vasco da Gama, the perils of the seas were still such as we can scarcely imagine to-day. By modern standards the ships were still clumsy and top-heavy, and the absence of fore-and-aft headsails restricted their power of sailing near a wind. The improvement of nautical instruments had made it possible to calculate latitude with greater accuracy, but the problem of longitude was still unsolved, and dead-reckoning gave very imperfect results. Moreover, the seas were still largely uncharted, and no sailing directions could give more than a very sketchy account of the winds, currents, reefs, and sandbanks in distant waters.

Thus every voyage was full of peril, and the keen business instinct of the Hollanders did not make Dutch ships safer than others; for greed often makes men short-sighted, and like many other shipowners before and after them, the Dutch were willing to run a big (insurable) risk, in order to snatch at immediate gain. Their ships were built to carry the last ton of cargo, with little regard to speed or handiness, and in the East Indies trade, at any rate, they were often overloaded. As with the Portuguese before them, the practice of allowing officials to carry private ventures in addition to the ordinary cargo, added to the perils of the homeward voyage.

Neither the material nor the personnel of the United East India Company's fleets was always of the best. There is clear evidence that worn-out and leaky ships were retained in employment, to save the cost of replacing them, and some of the officers seem to have been as worn-out as the ships. Christopher Frick, a German surgeon in the Company's service from 1680 to 1685, describes the Master of the ship in which he went out to Java as over 80 years old, and the Master of the ship in which he came home as "a good old Man of near 90 Years of Age." Such men can have been retained only because they were cheap, or because they had an interest with the owners. The native Dutch seamen were good, but there was also a foreign element among the crews which did not always make for discipline or efficiency.

Altogether, it is not surprising that casualties were frequent. Frick, a careful observer, and an adventurous young man who took kindly to the sea, remarks casually of a voyage from Java to Siam, "It is almost impossible for two or three ships to make so considerable a Voyage without some lett or misfortune." His own tale of vessels wrecked, stranded, burnt, or blown up, and of others narrowly escaping similar disasters fully explains his impression, and there is plenty of other evidence to support it.

Frick tells us, indeed, that:

> There are many hundreds, who when their time [in the Company's service] is expired, bind themselves afresh rather than venture the danger of going home again. . . . The frequent news of ships being cast away, and losing one half of the Fleets, and sometimes the whole ones, increases their fears daily.

There is no reason to disbelieve his statement; for even during the first half of the eighteenth century, the proportion of casualties among homeward bound Dutch East Indiamen was excessively high.

Shipwreck, moreover, was not the only terror of the passage. Neither medical science nor sanitation had made much progress since the sixteenth century, and no nation—at any rate no Northern nation—had as yet discovered how to victual ships suitably for long Eastern voyages.

This was the more serious because the poor sailing qualities of the ships made the passages immoderately long. It would be unfair to compare the performances of the Dutch East Indiamen with the records set up by the later China and Australian clippers, for the East Indiamen were not racing. On the homeward voyage, at least, they were always in convoy, and the best sailers had to wait on the laggards of the squadron. The reader may be reminded, however, that *Sir Lancelot*, when breaking the record from Fochow, ran home from Anjer on the Sunda Strait (between Java and Sumatra) in 68 days, and that anything much over 100 days from or to Anjer would have been considered, in the second half of the nineteenth century, a definitely bad passage. Frick arrived at Batavia in the *Europa*, 184 days out from the Texel, including a stay of some few days at the Cape. Schweitzer, another German, was luckier, arriving 162 days out from the Texel, and 55 days from the Cape, where she had spent a week; but his homeward passage from Colombo took no fewer than 231 days—108 days from Ceylon to the Cape, 7 days at the Cape, and 116 days from the Cape to the Texel, northabout. By way of contrast, the present writer, some thirty years ago, came home from Australia in the *Torrens*, then long past her prime, in 125 days, including a fortnight discharging cargo at Durban, and 10 days in quarantine at St. Helena.

Frick's and Schweitzer's passages do not appear to have been abnormal—others much longer are recorded—and on voyages of such length, bad and unsuitable food, dirt, and over-crowding were bound to take a heavy toll. These were not conditions confined to the Dutch service. Indeed, so far as victualling was concerned, English vessels, whether King's ships or merchantmen, were among the worst, though it must be admitted that the unsuitability of the food was not wholly the fault of the Admiralty or the shipowners. Naval experts were quite aware that a diet consisting chiefly of biscuit, salt meat, and salt fish was a sure breeder of scurvy; but however much they might desire to copy the Spanish and Italians, "who live most upon rice-meal, oat-meal, biscake, figs, olives, oil, and the like," they could not impose such rations on the seamen themselves.

> The common seamen with us are so besotted on their beef and pork as they had rather adventure on all the calentures and scarbots in the world than to be weaned from their customary diet.[1]

In the service of the Dutch East India Company the allowance of salt meat was only 2¼ lbs a week (three meat days) as against 6 lbs in the English Navy; the disparity being made good by larger rations of fish, butter, and pease, and by the use of boiled barley or oatmeal. On port-to-port voyages in the East, the salt fish was cut out, and pease and rice, with a small meat allowance, formed the staple diet.

Even the Dutch victualling was not very well suited to long voyages, and what was much worse, it was often

[1] *Boteler's Dialogues* (1634), ed. W. G. Perrin, Navy Records Society, 1930.

defective both in quantity and in quality. The seventeenth-century seaman was, in fact, abominably fed by all Governments and all shipowners. In the English Navy the beer stank, the biscuit crawled, and the beef was apt to turn out to be ox-hooves. Here there was at least the excuse that the Admiralty was usually desperately short of money to pay the victualling contractors; but in the merchant-ships things were little better. There were no merchants or part-owners among the crews as there were in the Middle Ages, and now that the ocean routes had lost their first glamour of adventure, few men of any education or standing shipped before the mast. The seamen were merely "hands," and although Petty reckoned their pay "as good as 12s. [per week] in Wages, Victuals (and as it were housing) with other accommodations," or three times the pay of an agricultural labourer, their position was declining as compared with the better-paid occupations on shore. They were treated by the shipowners as cheap labour was habitually treated in a hard age. "Only the East India Company," says Pepys, "victuals well." The same could hardly be said of their wealthier rivals at Amsterdam. Let us again summon Christopher Frick to the witness box:

The beef and pork, he tells us, were so salt, "having lain in the Salt it may be five or six years," that they lost about one-third of their weight when cooked. "The Beer is in common as long as it lasts"; but before his ship had reached the St. Paul's rocks, beer, brandy, tobacco, and cheese had almost given out, and the crew were left to subsist mainly on "Bacon as salt as Brine, Gray-Pease half boyl'd, Grout and stinking Water," and not too much of these. Add to the effects of such diet those of overcrowding (the *Ternate* had between 300 and 400 people on board), dirt and bad ventilation, and it is little wonder that "the Dropsie, the Bloody Flux and Scurvey" increased till "the Ship became a meer Hospital." Between St. Paul's Rocks and the Cape, small-pox also broke out on board, and with the Scurvy "carried off almost all of the oldest of our Men." Another German in the service of the Company, Christopher Schweitzer, had a still worse experience. On nine days in the doldrums his ship threw overboard sixty-two dead.

Schweitzer's experience, at least, was exceptional; but the general mortality from scurvy must have been very high. It would have been higher still but for the Dutch colonization of the Cape of Good Hope, where all ships called for water and provisions, and where they could obtain the priceless boon of "Sallads, Cabages, Turnips, Cowcumbers, and all sorts of Kitchen Herbs."

The "prodigious increase of the Netherlands" in shipping and commerce was thus purchased at a heavy cost in human suffering and in human lives; but, while the conditions on board the ships of the United East India Company may have been a little worse than the average, no shipowning State of the seventeenth century was entitled to cast the first stone. Such conditions were, and long remained the common lot of those whom preference or necessity drove to do their business in great waters.

SOME BOOKS ON THE PERIOD

Petty is quoted from *The Economic Writings of Sir William Petty*, ed. C. H. Hull, Cambridge, 1899. His *Political Arithmetick* was published posthumously in 1690, but was probably written about 1671–1676. Sir Josiah Child's *New Discourse of Trade* is quoted from the edition of 1698. Much of it seems to have been written about 1660–1669. For the Dutch Fisheries, see Fulton, *Sovereignty of the Seas*, and Jenkins, *The Herring and the Herring Fisheries*, London, 1927; and for the Dutch East India Company, Sir William Hunter, *History of British India*, and Clive Day, *The Dutch in Java*, London, 1904. The *Voyages to the East Indies* by Christopher Fryke and Christopher Schweitzer, ed. C. E. Fayle, London 1929, give very lively accounts of voyages in Dutch East Indiamen and of Dutch trade in the East.

CHAPTER VII

"SHIPS, COLONIES, AND COMMERCE"

THE ERA OF THE NAVIGATION ACTS

Profit and Power ought jointly to be considered.
SIR JOSIAH CHILD, *A New Discourse of Trade*

And some we got by purchase,
And some we had by trade,
And some we found by courtesy
Of pike and carronade.
KIPLING, *The Merchantmen*

WHEN the good people at Lloyd's put up illuminations to celebrate the Jubilee of George III, the central feature of their display was the fiery outline of a full-rigged ship. On one side of her blazed the loyal legend, "Long live the King"; on the other side, the words "Ships, Colonies, and Commerce." As a brief summary of the aims which inspired the statecraft of Western Europe from the middle of the seventeenth century to the end of the eighteenth, it would be hard to improve on the slogan adopted by the underwriters of 1809.

By opening up the ocean routes and showing the way to overseas expansion, the Spaniards and Portuguese had given a new direction to national and dynastic rivalries. The Dutch, as we have seen, were the first to exploit fully the possibilities of wealth and power in colonization and ocean trade; but as soon as England under Cromwell and France under Louis XIV had overcome their internal difficulties, it was inevitable that Dutch supremacy at sea should be challenged as fiercely as the Spanish and Portuguese monopolies. For a century and a half of almost incessant war, and of commercial competition hardly to be distinguished from war in its aims and methods, the chief

European Powers were engaged in one long struggle for the heritage of Henry the Navigator, and it is impossible to understand the history of the shipping industry during this period without some study of the attitude of the statesmen towards ships, colonies, and commerce.

To those engaged in these fierce national rivalries, commerce was not an end in itself but a means to an end. Wealth was sought chiefly for the military power and political influence which it gave, and progress was measured less by the actual increase in the national wealth than by the margin of superiority over the wealth of other States. To diminish the prosperity of a rival was almost as important an object of national policy as to increase your own.

Wealth itself was measured mainly in terms of gold and silver which, as Petty put it, "are not perishable, nor so mutable as other Commodities, but are Wealth at all times, and all places," and gave the necessary supplies of ready money for defraying the expenses of war. The object of commercial policy, therefore, was to secure an excess of exports over imports, thus creating a balance in your favour, which other countries would have to settle in hard cash.

This was one great reason for devoting special attention to the encouragement of the carrying trade; for, in Petty's words:

> The Labour of Seamen, and Freight of Ships, is always of the nature of an Exported Commodity, the overplus whereof, above what is Imported, brings home money.

There was an even stronger reason, however, for fostering the shipping industry. Not only did the ships earn freights which went to swell the "favourable balance of trade"; the ships themselves were a part of the national strength. Under the great soldier-admirals of the Commonwealth, the distinction between the fighting and trading fleets became much more rigid and the practice of putting merchantmen into the line of battle gradually faded out; but privateering still played an important part in war, merchantmen were still required as transports and storeships, and above all, it was only by maintaining a large mercantile marine that the fighting ships could be manned; for there was, as yet, no regular establishment for naval personnel.

Child put the whole argument very clearly:

> No trades deserve so much care to procure, and preserve, and encouragement to prosecute, as those that employ the most Shipping, altho' the Commodities transported be of small Value in themselves; For, *First*, they are certainly the most profitable; for besides the gain accrewing by the Goods, the Freights, which is in such Trades often more than the Value of the Goods, is all profit to the Nation; besides, they bring with them a great access of Power (Hands as well as Money) *many Ships and Sea-men being justly the reputed Strength and Safety of England.*

Both the balance of trade theory and the importance attached to naval power led the statesmen of the time to look with peculiar favour on the trade with distant colonies or factories. In the first place, the whole commerce of these overseas possessions could be regulated with a single eye to the interests of the mother country, whose merchants were thereby furnished with a sheltered market for their own goods, and with a monopolistic supply of rare products for re-export to other European countries. Secondly, the great length of the voyages created a big demand for tonnage, the whole benefit of which could be confined to ships flying the national flag.

Whatever their ostensible cause, all the great European wars of the late seventeenth, and eighteenth centuries, tended to develop into a struggle among the Western Powers for colonies and spheres of influence, and during the brief intervals of peace, their commercial policy was inspired by the same motives that actuated them in war. Indeed, the working of this spirit can best be studied in the English Colonial System, founded on the great Navigation Acts of Cromwell and Charles II.

The fear and jealousy with which Englishmen had watched the rise of Holland to maritime supremacy had been fanned into bitter enmity by the ruthless cruelty with which Dutch Governors had crushed out English competition in the Spice Islands, and as soon as England had a Government strong enough to protect her interests, the merchants began to clamour for effective support against their hated rivals. There was already a long lee-way to be made up. The trade of the Spice Islands was lost, and the position of the Dutch in the general carrying trade of the world appeared to be impregnable. The last hope for English shipping seemed to lie in the colonial traffic, on which the Hollanders were already beginning to intrude.

The first English attempts at colonization, in the days of Elizabeth, had been unsuccessful; but when the peace with Spain in 1603 put an end to privateering, other outlets had to be found for the spirit of enterprise and adventure, and syndicates, such as those which had financed the larger privateering expeditions, began to turn their attention to the founding of colonies. Successive waves of refugee emigration—Catholics, Puritans, and Royalists in turn seeking a safe asylum oversea—had given a great impetus to the work. By the middle of the seventeenth century, New England, Virginia, Maryland, the Carolinas, and several West Indian Islands had been at least partially colonized. Jamaica was conquered from Spain in 1655. In Asia and Africa, the East India and Guinea Companies had established posts and factories as depots and bases for the development of their trade. Thus the colonial traffic—the Plantation Trade as it was called—was already considerable, and it was bound to expand as the population and production of the colonies increased. The demand for slave labour in the sugar and tobacco plantations was alone sufficient to create a large and steadily increasing demand for tonnage.

In these circumstances, the defence of English shipping naturally took the form of a series of Acts designed to create for English merchants and shipowners a monopoly in the handling and carriage of colonial goods, and at the same time to do as much damage as possible to the entrepôt and carrying trade of the Dutch.

The basis of the whole system was Cromwell's Act of 1651, but this was so soon superseded by the Act of 1660, which modified and extended its provisions, that we need not pause to examine it in detail. The Act of 1660 which became, in the eyes of many generations, the Great Charter of English shipping contained seven main provisions.[1]

> (1) No goods or commodities whatsoever were to be imported into or exported from any of the English Possessions in Asia, Africa, or America, except in English ships.
> (2) No goods or commodities of the growth, production, or manufacture of any part of Asia, Africa, or America were to be imported into England and Wales or Ireland, except in English ships.
> (3) No foreign ship was to be allowed to participate in the English Coasting trade.

For the purpose of the Act, an English ship was defined as one which was owned, "truly and without fraud" in England and Wales, Ireland, or the Plantations, of which the Master and at least three-quarters of the crew were English subjects. The effect of these three provisions was to create for such ships an absolute monopoly in what would to-day be called the "Inter-Imperial" trade, in the entire foreign trade of the English oversea Possessions, and in the import trade from all countries outside Europe.

[1] In the Act the Clauses are not numbered, and they appear in a different order to that here given.

This was fairly sweeping; but in the eyes of those who framed the Act, it did not go far enough. The trade of the Dutch as middlemen and general carriers must also be attacked. This was done in two ways.

> (4) No goods whatsoever of foreign growth, production, or manufacture were to be imported, even in English ships, except from the place of origin, or the ports where such goods "can only be or are or usually have been first shipped for transportation."
>
> (5) No Russian goods, no Currants or other produce of the Turkish Empire, no Masts, Timber, Boards, Salt, Pitch, Tar, Rezin, Hemp, Flax, Raisins, Figs, Prunes, Olive Oil, Corn, Grain, Sugar, "Potashes," Wines, Vinegar, or Brandy were to be imported except in English ships or ships belonging to the country of origin or usual port of first shipment, as already defined.

The first of these clauses was aimed at the Dutch entrepôt trade. Central European goods might be shipped to England from Dutch ports, if these were the ports where they could only be or most usually were "first shipped for transportation"; but no shipbuilding material from the Baltic, or wine and oil from Spain could be re-exported to London from the warehouses of Amsterdam and Rotterdam. If a country had a seacoast, it must trade with England direct.

One big exception had to be made, though the Dutch reaped no benefit therefrom. The Spanish and Portuguese colonies were not allowed to trade direct with foreign countries, and it was accordingly provided that their products might be imported, but only in English ships, from any port in Spain, Portugal, the Azores, Madeira, or the Canaries. It was made clear also that goods could be shipped to England (in English ships) from the great collecting ports in the East Indies, the Levant, and Northern Africa, "though the said commodities be not of the very growth of the said places."

The second provision attacked the Dutch carrying trade.

If a Swedish merchant, for instance, had a cargo of timber to ship to England, and no Swedish vessel happened to be available, then the charter must go to an English merchantman, not a Hollander or a Lubecker. In the Cromwellian Act, the provision applied to all European goods whatsoever; but the Act of 1660 was really quite as effective, for the listed commodities included all bulky items of ordinary commerce which were likely to come on to the freight markets.

But the statesmen of the Restoration were as anxious to build up English as to damage Dutch trade, and they wanted to make London a great entrepôt port, rivalling Amsterdam and Rotterdam. So another clause provided:

> (6) No Sugar, Tobacco, Cotton, Ginger, Indigo, Fustick, or Dyewoods produced in the Plantations (that is to say, none of their most valuable products) might be shipped to any other destination than England and Wales, Ireland, or other British Possessions.

If, let us say, a German merchant wanted tobacco from Virginia, he must buy it from a correspondent in London or Bristol, and the transaction would carry with it middlemen's profits, warehousing and handling charges, and a double freight, from Virginia to London and from London to Hamburg—all remaining in English hands.

Finally, foreigners who wished to send their own goods to England in their own ships must pay for the privilege.

> (7) All goods mentioned in the Act, and permitted to be imported in foreign ships (belonging to the country of origin or usual first port) must pay Aliens' duty if so shipped. All Dried Fish, Fish Oil, or Whalebone imported in foreign ships were to pay double Aliens' duty.

Three years later a further turn was given to the screw by an Act providing that no goods of European origin should be shipped to the Plantations except from England and Wales, and in ships built, as well as owned, in this country. Still later it was provided that no Plantation goods might be shipped to Ireland direct—all must pass through the English entrepôts.

A more sweeping system of protection and flag discrimination could hardly be imagined. Yet, at the moment, the danger of retaliation was small. The trade of the Dutch, Spanish, Portuguese, and French colonies was governed by a system as rigidly exclusive as our own, and in respect of this trade we had nothing to lose. The direct Dutch trade with England, including the traffic in Central European goods, was too valuable to be risked by measures of commercial reprisal, and no other Power was much interested in the general carrying trade. It used to be said that the Dutch wars were the immediate consequence of the Acts, but recent investigation has tended to disprove this assertion, though the general spirit of commercial rivalry which led to the Acts was also a part cause of the wars. At any rate, the three hard-fought wars left the Acts in full operation, and it was not until the last quarter of the eighteenth century that any serious breach was made in the English monopolies.

It is not easy to say how far the Acts achieved their purpose. As a weapon of offence against Holland they must be written down a failure. It is true that the Dutch were ultimately excluded from the Plantation Trade, though it would probably have proved impossible to enforce the Act rigorously in the Colonies but for the capture of New York in 1664, during the Second Dutch War, which deprived the Hollanders of their commercial base in North America. This, however, represented a check to the growth of Dutch shipping rather than an actual diminution of its activities; for the effect of the Acts was to increase the severity of Dutch competition in all trades not specially reserved. So late as 1776, Adam Smith who, despite his Free Trade theories, approved of the Acts as a defence measure, admitted that the carrying trade of Holland was much greater than that of any other country. The subsequent decline of Dutch prosperity was due mainly to the cumulative strain of a long series of exhausting wars, in which their trade suffered severely, while they were obliged to make great military efforts for the defence of their weak land frontier.

It was not only Dutch competition that was intensified by the passing of the Acts. The exclusion of foreign shipping from the Plantation Trade led to a demand for tonnage which forced up the price of shipbuilding. English ships were always expensive, for owners were encouraged by bounties and regulations to build "ships of force"—strongly built vessels that could carry a strong armament. The new rise in construction costs, and the consequent rise in freights, proved a severe handicap in the unsheltered trades, and English shipping began to lose ground wherever it was not supported by a legal monopoly or by great natural advantages. For instance, the import of timber from Norway (then under Danish rule) fell almost entirely into the hands of the Danes. An Aliens' Duty which worked out at £5 or £6 a voyage was of little use, as Child bitterly complained, to check the competition of people who could build for £1,300 or £1,400 a 300-ton "flyboat" which would carry as much cargo as an English ship costing from £2,200 to £2,400.

This does not mean, however, that the Acts were, at the outset, a failure as a protective measure. The growing colonial traffic was probably able to absorb, during the second half of the seventeenth century, all shipping driven off other routes, together with as much new tonnage as English owners could build and run. It is beyond question that English shipping increased very rapidly during this period—it may even have been trebled—and the credit for a great part of this increase may fairly be given to the secure employment provided by the Plantation trade.[1]

It was admitted even by the warmest advocates of the Acts that their effect was to raise the cost of imports; but this did not trouble those who held with Child that "Profit and Power ought joyntly to be considered," and that the increase of English shipping was a more important matter than "the present Profit of the generality." The system bore hardly also on the colonists, who were often prevented from selling their products in the best market, or shipping them by the most convenient vessel; but this was not likely to trouble statesmen who looked on a colony as an estate to be farmed for the benefit of the mother country.

For good or ill, the spirit of the Navigation Acts continued to dominate British commercial policy throughout the whole of the eighteenth century. (We can now say British rather than English, for the Act of Union in 1707 threw open the whole of the reserved trades to the enterprising shipowners of Glasgow and Greenock.) It was not a spirit that was confined to Great Britain. Sweden imposed such drastic measures of discrimination against imports in foreign bottoms, that English ships, even when laden with English products, had to trans-ship their cargoes to Swedish vessels in a Baltic port, so that they might be entered under the national flag. Spain continued to prohibit all direct trade with colonies whose requirements she was unable adequately to supply, with the inevitable result that a vast organized smuggling traffic grew up, leading to perpetual friction, and occasional war. Holland continued to exclude all foreigners from traffic with the Dutch East Indies. France pursued the same policy in her Canadian and West

[1] The clearances of British shipping from ports in England amounted to 93,000 on an average of the years 1663–1669 and 274,000 on the average of the years 1700–1702. The percentage of British to total tonnage cleared increased from 65 per cent. to 86 per cent.

Indian colonies, and her ministers devoted a large share of their attention to building up a mercantile marine and a flourishing foreign commerce, by means of subsidies, protective duties, navigation laws, and the formation of privileged companies. The French and English East India Companies fought each other for trade concessions in India, even when their Governments were at peace. Commercial rivalry lay at the back of war after war, and in every treaty of peace colonies passed as the prize of victory.

It was a foolish game; but while everybody played it, those prospered most who could play it best. Every war left Holland, whether our enemy or our ally, a little more exhausted. Every war administered a check to the development of French commerce. Every peace treaty added to the markets open only to British traders and the ports open only to British ships. Canada and Newfoundland became British. The British East India Company found in the rapid growth of their possessions and spheres of influence in India a more than sufficient compensation for their exclusion from the Malay Archipelago. British shipping, which may have trebled during the last forty years of the seventeenth century, was again nearly trebled during the first three-quarters of the eighteenth.[1]

Successful war was related to the growth of shipping both as cause and effect. The naval and financial strength which gradually raised Great Britain to the leading place amongst the Powers was derived from her expanding commerce. Naval strength, combined with her insular position, preserved her commerce and the industries which fed it from suffering, in the same degree as those of her competitors, from the interruption caused by war. The prize of success in war was the opening of new fields of activity to her

[1] The clearances of British shipping from ports in England rose from 274,000 tons, or 86 per cent. of the total on the average of the years 1700–1702, to 798,000 tons, and 92 per cent. of the total, in 1774.

merchants and shipowners. Yet success in war would have availed them nothing but for the peaceful economic and social developments which placed them in a position to take full advantage of those opportunities. By the beginning of the eighteenth century, Great Britain had got over her political growing-pains and was settling down steadily to the task of developing her economic resources. Much waste land had been reclaimed for agriculture. Handicrafts were making rapid progress, largely as the result of the welcome extended in the sixteenth and seventeenth centuries to Flemish and Huguenot refugees. Although the scale of production was still small, the range of manufactures steadily increased. In the reign of Queen Anne woollen cloth still furnished two-fifths of the export trade, but it was no longer the sole staple of English commerce. In two respects English manufacturers were favoured above all their rivals. The Navy preserved them from the desolation wrought in almost all continental countries by repeated invasions, and the good sense of English politicians gave them the largest free-trade market in Europe. In 1706 a Venetian envoy reported that, thanks in large part to freedom from taxes on internal trade, "industry was further advanced in England than in any other part of the world."[1]

Financial progress went hand in hand with industrial. The founding of the Bank of England in 1694, the funding of the National Debt, the rapid growth of insurance, and an increasing use of commercial bills, all tended to cheapen the rate of interest and provide facilities for the accumulation and employment of capital. Englishmen had learned how to make money breed, and a large part of the accumulated savings of the trading and business community was invested in foreign trade and the shipping that carried it.

Thus, while war opened new markets to British goods and new ports to British ships, the consequent growth of British

[1] Quoted by G. M. Trevelyan, *Blenheim*, p. 13.

shipping was a natural growth, based firmly on the possession of an ever increasing volume of goods for export and on the activities of a rapidly increasing body of wealthy traders, restlessly seeking an outlet for their accumulated capital. It was not merely because the British fleets were usually victorious that Great Britain outstripped France in the race for ships, colonies, and commerce, but because British trade and shipping followed the lines of natural economic development, while French industry and commerce were still, to a great extent, artificial; stimulated into activity by Royal rescripts, subsidies, and grants of privilege, and at the same time shackled with a host of mediaeval regulations and imposts.

After, at latest, the middle of the eighteenth century, it is very doubtful whether the Navigation Acts were of much help to English shipping. Their provisions had continually to be relaxed during the course of the wars in order to permit the employment of neutral vessels, either for safety in the more dangerous trades or to take the place of British ships employed as transports and privateers, and to permit the employment of foreign seamen in place of British sailors who had been swept up by the press-gangs, or induced by bounties to volunteer for naval service.[1] Some more permanent modifications of the Acts had also to be made to meet the complaints of the West Indian planters, to whom their restrictions were becoming an intolerable nuisance. Apart from this the whole principle of the Acts was becoming out of date. British overseas trade was now too healthy and vigorous to need artificial support, and the high rate of profit in all the monopoly trades was definitely detrimental to the general expansion of British commerce, by attracting an undue proportion of the country's mer-

[1] In 1760, during the Seven Years' War, the percentage of foreign to total clearances at ports in Great Britain, rose to 20 per cent., as against 7 per cent. or 8 per cent. in times of peace.

cantile energies into a single channel. Most important of all, the North American Colonies were growing up, and were no longer content to be regarded as mere "Plantations," to be exploited for the benefit of the mother-country.

British statesmen were slow to read the writing on the wall, and they reaped the fruits of their folly in the revolt of the American Colonies and a new and perilous European war. British shipowners found some consolation for the final recognition of American independence in 1782, in the exclusion of the New Englanders—already dangerous competitors—from the reserved trades; but to many people it seemed that the sun of Britain's commercial prosperity had set for ever.

Never were pessimists more completely confounded. Even while the Colonial System was reeling from the shock of American independence, forces were at work that were to lift British shipping into a position of unchallenged supremacy. Four great developments marked the last half of the eighteenth century in Great Britain—the adoption of improved methods of agriculture, which enabled a largely increased population to be supported; the construction of canals which multiplied many times the volume of internal transport; the adoption of coal (hitherto used mainly for domestic purposes) as an industrial fuel; and the introduction of machinery in the textile trades. With these aids to production and distribution, iron-works, potteries, and cotton-mills sprang up apace, and by the end of the century Great Britain had available for export such a volume of surplus products as the world had never yet seen. The consequent growth in the demand for shipping was reflected in an increase of the tonnage cleared at ports in Great Britain from an average of about 900,000 tons just before the American war, to an average of over 1,700,000 tons, of which over 90 per cent. was British, in the last five years of peace before renewal of the struggle with France.

"Ships, Colonies, and Commerce"

The Industrial Revolution was already well under way in Great Britain, but had hardly begun to spread to other countries when the outbreak of the Revolutionary and Napoleonic Wars put a stop, for more than twenty years, to all progress on the Continent. In almost every commercial centre production and enterprise were stifled by wave after wave of invasion, by the drain of the conscription, and by the ruthless exactions of the invaders. The ships of France, of Holland, and of every country brought into the orbit of the Napoleonic system, were swept into British ports as prizes, or bottled up in their own harbours by blockading squadrons. Meanwhile British manufactures and colonial products were being distributed all over the world by British ships, or by neutral ships with a British license. Even countries under French domination drew their supplies of woollen and cotton goods, and hardware, and sugar from Great Britain, by means of a vast organized contraband traffic through neutral ports.

There were rich pickings in all this for neutral shipowners, such as the Americans and the Swedes, for many routes were very unsafe, and a great number of British ships were withdrawn from commerce to serve as transports and storeships. Nevertheless, it was British shipping that took the lion's share of the trade, especially the outwards traffic. During the years 1802–1811, when the attack on British commerce had reached its height, only 68·4 per cent. of the tonnage cleared at ports in Great Britain was under the British flag, but of the tonnage cleared *with cargoes*, the percentage was 77·8 per cent.[1] Two comparisons of figures sum up the effect of the war on British shipping. In 1792, the year before the great struggle began, there were 1,269,000 tons of shipping on the Register of Great Britain; in 1816,

[1] The British percentage of tonnage entered was 67·9 per cent. and of tonnage entered with cargoes 62·5 per cent.

the year after it closed, there were 2,417,000 tons.[1] The clearances of British shipping from ports in Great Britain during the five years 1816–1820, were nearly 42 per cent. greater than in the five years 1787–1792.[2] A century and a half of conflict, which began with the first Dutch war and the promulgation of the Navigation Acts, had ended by placing Great Britain in a position of supremacy as regards ships, colonies, and commerce, such as even seventeenth-century Holland had never enjoyed.

SOME BOOKS ON THE PERIOD

Those who wish to study the Navigation Laws and their working will find the texts in *Acts and Ordinances of the Interregnum*, ed. C. H. Firth and R. S. Rait, London, 1911, and the *Statutes of the Realm*. There is a very good summary of the Acts, and of subsequent modifications, in an anonymous pamphlet entitled *A Short Review of the History of the Navigation Laws of England*, London, 1849, contained in a volume at the London Library (Pamphlets 193) and attributed to the first Earl of Iddesleigh (Sir Stafford Northcote). In addition to the contemporary authorities cited in the text, reference may be made to Cunningham's *Growth of English Industry and Commerce*, 3rd edition, Cambridge, 1903, Vol. II (1)—"The Mercantile System." For the political and economic background and the great eighteenth-century wars no better brief survey can be found than that in G. M. Trevelyan's *History of England*, London, 1926.

[1] For the British Empire as a whole the figures were:

1792: 1,540,000 tons
1816: 2,784,000 tons

[2] The actual figures of tonnage cleared at ports in Great Britain are as follows:

	Average 1788–1792.	Average 1816–1820.
British	1,572,000	2,232,000
Foreign	150,000	436,000
Total	1,722,000	2,668,000
British Percentage	88·2	83·7

CHAPTER VIII

"THE SHIPPING INTEREST"

THE CARRYING TRADE IN THE EIGHTEENTH CENTURY

> The Office of Mr. Brigg (Notary Publick) for Buying, Selling, Hiring, Letting to Freight, all sorts of Trading Ships . . . is now kept in the Royal Exchange, London.
>
> *The City Mercury or Advertisements concerning Trade*
> 24th Feb./March 2, 1675/6.

WHEN we turn from the remarkable increase in British commerce and shipping between 1650 and 1815 to the way in which the business of overseas trade was carried on, we find the same influence at work—the growth of national power, the growth of colonization, and the growth of capitalism. By the latter half of the eighteenth century, British commerce had settled down into more or less regular channels; it was carried on, for the most part, with settled and orderly communities; it enjoyed the backing of an active and commercially-minded diplomacy, and the protection of a fleet capable of enforcing, even in distant waters, respect for the rights of British traders. The number of traders wealthy enough to invest large sums in a single ship or a single cargo was many times greater than it had been in the sixteenth and seventeenth centuries, and the risks of foreign trade, in themselves greatly diminished, could be covered by insurance at reasonable rates.

In these circumstances, the great Chartered Companies had ceased to be necessary either for the provision of capital or for negotiating trade agreements and organizing defence, and as soon as they ceased to be essential, their restrictions began to be felt as a clog on the expansion of commerce. Most of them lost their monopolies so early as 1689, by the Bill of Rights, and although some of them, such as the Turkey and Russia Companies, lingered on until the end of the eighteenth century, they preserved hardly a shadow of their former greatness.

The one great exception was the East India Company, which had been reorganized on a permanent joint-stock basis in 1657. The great distance of India from Europe and the necessity of providing for local defence and for negotiations on the spot with rulers who knew nothing of the Court of St. James's were conclusive arguments for the retention of the chartered company system in this particular trade, and after various vicissitudes and a long struggle with "interlopers," the Honourable the East India Company was finally reconstituted in 1708 in a form which endured until the early years of the nineteenth century.[1]

As an owner or employer of shipping, the Company had a curious history. It began, in 1599, by buying ships second-hand; later it acquired a shipyard for the construction of its own vessels; still later it took to chartering private ships, to the great advantage of those Directors who were also shipowners. An end was put to this scandal, after the settlement of 1708, by a by-law which prohibited any Director from being concerned in ships hired by the Company, and throughout the eighteenth century tonnage was procured under a system which may be defined as life-charter of ships built specially for the Company's service, under supervision of its surveyors. The contract for each ship was made with the prospective commander and two of the owners (who were also the builders) of the vessel. The owners provided the ship, complete with equipment, and the Company undertook to hire her, at a specified freight, for a fixed number of voyages, representing her effective life, in the India and China trades.[2]

[1] The Indian trade was thrown open in 1814. The monopoly of the Chinese trade was not rescinded till 1833, after which the Company sold off its ships and ceased to be a trading concern.

[2] By a by-law of 1773 ships were not to be engaged for more than four

The justification of this system lay in two facts; the Company's monopoly ensured continuous employment for the ships, and the character of the trade entailed the provision of ships too large and costly to be profitably employed on other routes. Its defect was that, although each contract was legally supposed to be fixed by open competition, the commander and owners of a worn-out ship came to be recognized, in practice, as having at least a moral right to replace her; with the result that the provision of tonnage fell into the hands of a small hereditary ring known as "The Marine Interest," who enjoyed all the advantages of monopolists in their dealings with the Company. In the absence of competition, freights were very high. In 1783, the Company had to pay as much as £33 per ton for the voyage out and home; in 1785 the rates were: £26 to China direct, Coast and China £27, Bombay £28, Coast and Bay £29. In time of war, these rates were subject to large additions to cover insurance and other charges for owners' account. When, in 1796, the system of "hereditary bottoms" was at last abolished, it cost the Company no less than £348,000 in compensation to commanders whose vested interests were thus extinguished.[1]

Apart from the East India trade and one or two others of special character—such as the Canadian fur trade, which was a monopoly of the Hudson's Bay Company—foreign commerce fell more and more into the hands of individual merchants and private partnerships. At the beginning of the eighteenth century, the adventure system—the formation of a syndicate for a particular voyage—was still in vogue; but as time went on it gave place more and more

voyages out and home. This number was increased to six in 1790, and to eight in 1803. In 1810 additional voyages were authorized.

[1] Peter Auber, *An Analysis of the Constitution of the East India Company*, London, 1826, pp. 648–663. Still higher freights are quoted by Lindsay in his *History of Merchant Shipping*, Vol. II, pp. 448–452.

to the establishment of solid, permanent firms, mostly specializing in some particular branch of trade, such as that with the West Indies, or the Baltic, or the Mediterranean.

These developments were accompanied by a growing tendency to separation between the mercantile and the shipowning interests. Even during the early years of the century, many ships were built as a speculation by syndicates comprising not only merchants but such people as shipmasters (active or retired) and those who acted as "ships' husbands" or agents at the ports. Such a syndicate would often buy a cargo for their vessel and look for their profit to trading in the goods; but they would be equally ready, when no advantageous bargain offered, to fill her up "on freight," and look for their profits to their remuneration as common carriers. As the volume of sea-borne commerce increased this method of employing tonnage became more and more profitable; mercantile speculations by shipowners as such became exceptional, and the carrying trade proper emerged as a separate, specialized branch of commercial activities. It might well happen that a member of a mercantile firm was part-owner, in his individual capacity, of a ship employed to carry his firm's goods; but even so the partnership owning the goods and the partnership owning the ship were separate entities, with separate interests, linked only by the contractual relations of a Charter-party or Bill of Lading.

Whether the merchants were interested in the ship or not, it was no longer customary for them to travel with the goods in order to seek out a market and conduct the sales; indeed, the volume and range of transactions now carried on by mercantile firms would often have rendered this impossible. None the less, it was still essential that a very wide liberty with regard to the sale of outward cargoes and the purchase of homeward cargoes should be left to someone "on the spot"; for although regular lines of postal packets ran to many of the chief ports abroad, communications were still almost incredibly slow from the point of view of a generation accustomed to the benefits of cables and wireless. By the time a ship reached her port of discharge, an outbreak of war, or a bad harvest, or a simple rise in prices, might have made nonsense of any instructions that she had brought out with her, or could receive in time, from the cargo-owners. To get over this difficulty, it was customary for the cargo-owners, whether owners or part owners of the ship, or merely charterers, to send out in the ship a "supercargo" who had the sole charge of all business relating to the sale and purchase of goods. As representative of the cargo-owners the supercargo had usually the right, under the Charter-party, to order the vessel to a second port of discharge, or to require the master to proceed in ballast to a port where a return cargo could be obtained.

All ships, however, did not carry supercargoes, for many ship-masters had acquired, in the course of trading to foreign ports, an excellent idea of market conditions and commercial practice abroad, and were quite competent, not merely to supervise the delivery of goods to a consignee or to the merchant's agents at the port, but to effect a sale of the goods in the open market and purchase a suitable return cargo within limits laid down by their instructions. It was quite common, therefore, to find the master acting also as supercargo, especially when he himself had an interest in ship and goods, or when he had long experience in a particular trade.

All these developments are well illustrated by the experience of two eighteenth-century ship-masters who have left us remarkably lively and vivid pictures of life at sea in the opening and closing years of the century. The first, Captain Nathaniel Uring, was born in Norfolk in or about 1682, and brought up by a London relative "who had part of several vessels and traded abroad." His career was varied and typical of his time. He found his sea-legs in the Newcastle coal trade—the favourite school of practical navigation; served twice in the Navy, once as a volunteer and once as a pressed man; commanded a Falmouth–West Indies packet and was captured, after a sharp fight, by a French privateer; and was latterly engaged in the logwood trade in the West Indies and the contraband traffic with the Spanish colonies. It is with his deep-water trading voyages, however, that we are now concerned; or rather with those of them that throw light on the trading conditions above described.

In 1698 we find him on board a ship which had loaded provisions in Ireland for Barbados. Here the proceeds were invested in rum, sugar, and molasses for the Newfoundland fishermen, from whom the supercargo intended to purchase a cargo of fish for Portugal. The Newfoundland market, however, proved to be overstocked with colonial products and the price of fish high, and the ship was accordingly directed to Virginia, where her lading was gradually disposed of, and a cargo of tobacco purchased.

Skipping ten adventurous years of trading, fighting, and slaving (the details of which readers will do well to seek in Captain Uring's own memoirs), we come to 1709, when a syndicate of his friends purchased a ship of 150 tons, of which he was made master. Uring, who was a shrewd, observant, businesslike man, never seems to have carried a supercargo, attending himself to the business, as well as the navigation of the ship. The most interesting part of his career (for us) begins in 1712, when he obtained the command of the *Hamilton* Frigate of 300 tons, with instructions to load logwood (dye-wood) at Campeachy for the Mediterranean, with discretion from the owners, "to dispose of the cargo where it was most for their benefit." He called first at Lisbon, where he sold 50 tons of logwood and filled up with sugar "upon freight" for Leghorn. At Leghorn he consulted the English Consul as to the respective advantages of Leghorn and Venice as markets for logwood, with the result that he sold the cargo at Leghorn, where he entered into a Charter-party to load 100 tuns of oil at Tunis for Genoa, "proposing to lade the rest of the ship either upon freight, or upon our owner's account." At Tunis, the Bey compelled him to make an intermediate coasting voyage, to fetch timber from Tabarca, for which he was duly paid. He then loaded the oil, and seeing no bargains about, filled up the ship with "what other goods I could procure upon freight" for Genoa.

At Genoa, Uring contracted "for the freight of a lading of wheat, which I was to carry first to Cadiz, and try the market there; and if that did not answer, to proceed to Lisbon." It is not clear whether any agent of the shipper accompanied him; but Uring himself evidently had wide discretionary powers as, the winds being unfavourable for entering Cadiz, he went straight on to Lisbon, where he discharged the cargo, presumably giving delivery to the shippers' agents. "Finding the ship perfectly worn out with age," he then sold her to Portuguese ship-breakers, "as I was empowered to do."

Uring had now saved money, and in 1715 he promoted a syndicate, of which he was a member, to buy a ship for the Portugal trade, "having great promises of being quickly despatched both at Lisbon and London." He does not say whether his syndicate owned the outward cargo; but after discharge at Lisbon, he "let the ship to freight for Madeira to lade wines, and thence to Boston in New England, and so to Fayal, where we loaded brandies for Lisbon," picking up ten passengers at the Azores. At Lisbon he loaded wine and wheat for London, where he arrived in January 1717, after a voyage of about eighteen months, during the greater part of which, at least, the ship was sailing under Charter-parties as a general carrier.

Finding the "chief owner," who was apparently a merchant, very dilatory in loading the ship, Uring sold his share to another master, and purchased another vessel, together with a cargo of calicoes, muslins, and linens for New England. This time Uring or his syndicate undoubtedly owned the goods as well as the vessel, and in the course of subsequent voyages of the *Bangor Galley*, we find him repeatedly disposing of cargo and investing the proceeds in a new lading; but ready also to "fill the ship up upon freight." One phrase he uses is curious: "Having delivered the freight wines and sold our cargo." "Cargo" to Uring always meant goods for owner's account, as distinguished from "freight," goods carried merely for hire.

We must not follow Captain Uring any longer, but may pass at once to Captain Samuel Kelly, who has left us an equally interesting account of a ship-master's life at the latter end of the eighteenth century. We need not follow Kelly's career in detail; for its present interest lies in the fact that it ran on much more regular lines than Uring's and reflects more settled trading conditions. Kelly himself was never personally interested either in ship or goods; he was simply the salaried servant of his owners. The owners themselves were shipowners in the strict sense of the word, looking to freights, and not to trading for their profits from the ship. Although Kelly, like Uring, seems always to have acted as his own supercargo, he was only once engaged in a definitely mercantile transaction. On that occasion, he had arrived at Barcelona, outward bound from Philadelphia with wheat and flour, and found there instructions, sent out by packet, "to load sea salt at the most eligible port of the Mediterranean and proceed as quickly as possible to Philadelphia." Accordingly, after he had "remitted what I could to my owners by a draft on London," Kelly proceeded to purchase salt at Yvica with the balance of the freight monies. He was not, however, required to supervise the sale of the salt; his responsibilities ended when it was delivered to the owners' agents in New England.

This was an exceptional transaction; but Kelly's normal duties included a good deal that now lies outside a ship-master's province. Forwarding agents had not yet come into existence, owners' instructions could seldom be received at a port abroad in time to be of service, and the ship-master had to be prepared to use his own discretion in fixing charter-parties and even to assist in collecting cargo for an outward voyage.

In 1789, for instance, Kelly found himself at Bristol as master of a coasting brig "laid on the berth to load for Liverpool"; but the freight markets were dull, and he was obliged "to cruise the city for goods." While thus engaged in tramping round from office to office, he received instructions to proceed to Liverpool by coach, to take command of the *John*, "a constant trader to Philadelphia"; breaking his journey at Birmingham, "to wait on several manufacturers who were in the habit of sending goods to America to solicit their favours for the *John*." It was easier, however, to arrange an outwards than a homewards cargo. The exports to New England always exceeded the imports therefrom, and even a regular trader did not necessarily return to her home port. Accordingly Kelly took out with him "liberty from my owners to embrace a freight for any port most eligible," and it was in the exercise of this discretion that he concluded the Charter-party which brought him to Barcelona on the voyage already cited.

By Kelly's time the distinction between the shipping and the mercantile interest was already well established. The great majority of the ships no longer corresponded to the van in which a shopkeeper delivers his wares, but rather to the lorry out of which a cartage contractor makes his living, by carrying other people's goods. By the opening years of the nineteenth century this distinction had become so clear that the General Shipowners' Society laid special emphasis, in an advertisement, on the fact that their members were all men whose business was confined to the running of ships, and who had no outside interests.

This gradual emergence of the shipping industry as a separate branch of commercial activities was accompanied by the rise of other classes of men, such as ship brokers, marine underwriters, and insurance brokers, whose business it was to facilitate the carrying on of the industry. All these, as well as the shipowners themselves, were greatly assisted by two very important developments in the social life of the country—the newspaper and the coffee-house—both of which date from the second half of the seventeenth century.

To people interested in shipping and foreign trade, prompt and accurate news is of first-class importance, and many newspapers of the late seventeenth and early eighteenth centuries gave a proportion of their very scanty space to such items as the safe arrival of ships or convoys. Moreover, the proprietors of these early newspapers were quick to discover that space could be sold as well as paid for, and among the earliest advertisements appear many which relate to shipping. Queerly named journals like *Smith's Protestant Intelligence* or *The Impartial Protestant Mercury* would contain announcements that freight or a passage on a ship bound for South Carolina could be booked at the Jamaica Coffee House, or that someone wanted to buy a ketch or pink and desired offers to be left at the same house. In the *Gazette* of July 22–26, 1680, Mr. Hive of "the Bee Hive on St. Marie Hill" announced to "All persons that have occasion to ship goods for Newcastle and Sunderland," that they should "repair" to him, "to be informed what ships are ready to take in both goods and passengers." In the *City Mercury* of February 24/March 2, 1675/6, Mr.

Briggs, Notary-Public informs all whom it may concern that his office, "for Buying, Selling, Hiring, Letting to Freight, All sorts of Trading Ships" is now kept in the Royal Exchange. The *City Mercury* was a pure advertisement sheet, run by a sort of "Exchange and Mart" office, and announced, in the issue for January 20, 1680:

> At this Office Merchants or Masters of Ships may be supply with Money upon Bottomare [Bottomry] be recommended to shipping or Freights for Ships, and have Polities, Charter-parties, or other writings made.

The most numerous class of shipping advertisements, however, related to the sales of ships by auction, always at a coffee-house. Although the prevalence of the coffee-house habit in the late seventeenth century and throughout the eighteenth is a commonplace of social history, it is not always recognized how completely it revolutionized business methods, especially in London. Before the advent of coffee-houses the Royal Exchange was practically the only central meeting-place for people interested in trade and shipping, and it must be remembered that, before the days of telephones and telegrams, personal intercourse was vastly more important in business than it is to-day. As business increased, the Exchange inevitably became overcrowded; it was only open for part of the day, and although separate "walks" were appropriated by special trades, it was too general a meeting-place to be really convenient for all purposes. The coffee-house supplied exactly what was needed. Most of the big City establishments laid themselves out to cater for a special class of customer, and the man who regularly frequented one of them knew that he would meet people with common business interests and could do business with them in quiet and orderly surroundings. They took in, too, all reputable newspapers, and they were convenient places for putting up advertisements or for holding auctions.

In this way the Jamaica Coffee House became the common resort for merchants and ship-masters in the West India trade, and Jonathan's the equivalent of the modern Stock Exchange, while the enterprise of Mr. Edward Lloyd in collecting and posting up accurate shipping intelligence made his establishment a sort of general headquarters of the shipping interest. Lloyd died in 1713, but the house continued to flourish under his successors. Throughout the eighteenth century it was at Lloyd's that practically all sales of ships were held, with the natural result, as shown by advertisements in the newspapers, that the house became the chief resort of ship brokers. Some of them, however, divided their time between Lloyd's and "Sam's next the Custom House," and it is worth noting that so late as 1786, advertisements show that Sam's was a place for doing business with ship-masters as to freights and passages.

During the first quarter of the eighteenth century Lloyd's Coffee House began to be known as, before all else, the headquarters of the marine insurance interest, and in 1734, Thomas Jemson, then proprietor, began to publish for the benefit of the underwriters a weekly sheet known as *Lloyd's List*, giving all arrivals and departures in the foreign trade at the chief British ports. The next big step forward was taken in 1760, when a number of the underwriters at Lloyd's formed a Society for the purpose of publishing a Register of ships insured by them or likely to be offered to them, with particulars of ownership, age, dimensions, and state of hull and equipment. Later still, in 1771, the leading underwriters formed themselves into an association with the object of procuring premises under their own control, and in 1774 they removed to the Royal Exchange, from which Lloyd's did not remove until 1928. Within a few years of their establishment in their new quarters the Subscribers to Lloyd's had become a power in the State, regulating all matters of marine insurance, and consulted by the Admiralty on every question relating to the protection of shipping.

It would be almost impossible to exaggerate the importance of these developments to the shipping industry. Without ample facilities for cheap, prompt, and safe marine insurance, and strict regulation of the underwriter's business, the vast commerce of Great Britain must have degenerated, especially in time of war, into a mere gamble, with the dice heavily loaded against both shipowners and shippers. Nor was this the end of the services rendered to shipping by the proprietors and customers of Lloyd's Coffee House and their successors, the subscribers to Lloyd's. The splendid service of shipping intelligence which was gradually evolved from very humble beginnings was of direct utility to shipowners and merchants, and was of incalculable value in assisting the Admiralty to furnish protection in time of war. Moreover, the Register Book with its classification of ships, crude as it was at first, and the prosecutions instituted by the Committee of Lloyd's in cases of fraud, were almost the only checks on unscrupulous shipowners and shippers, in days when British Governments (less enlightened than the Italian Republics of the Middle Ages) had not begun to concern themselves seriously with such matters as surveys and loadlines.

In matters of navigational science and hydrography, Governments had a better record. It was mainly the desire "to find out the much desired longitude of places for perfecting the art of navigation" that led to the establishment of Greenwich Observatory in 1675, and in 1714 an Act was passed offering the immense reward of £20,000 for a reliable and practicable method of ascertaining a ship's longitude, under all conditions, within half a degree. It was this offer which stimulated John Harrison to produce in 1759, the first successful chronometer, and in 1772 he finally satisfied the Board of Longitude that he had complied with every condition laid down by the Act. Meanwhile, Le Roy and Berthould had been at work on the same problem in France, and during the last twenty years of the eighteenth century men like John Arnold and Thomas Earnshaw were able to produce chronometers in some numbers, on a commercial basis. The cost of the instruments, however, was very high, and they were looked upon with suspicion, as new-fangled novelties, by tough old salts such as the American skippers who assured a French official, during the Napoleonic wars, that even a chart and sextant were wholly superfluous, on a trans-Atlantic passage, to any seaman "with common nautical knowledge." To explorers and people like whalers, whose trade took them into uncharted regions, chronometers soon became indispensable; but very few ordinary merchant ships carried them within the time-limits of this chapter. Even so, navigation became less and less a matter of mere guesswork, for an alternative method of finding the longitude, by lunar observations, was brought into something like general use by the Rev. Nevil Maskelyne, Astronomer Royal, from about 1767 onwards. It was very inferior in its results to the chronometer; but, especially as improved by the American Nathaniel Bowditch, whose *New American Practical Navigator* was published in 1802, it was a vast improvement on dead reckoning.

In hydrography, still greater advances were made. The British, French, and Dutch Governments were all active in subsidizing exploration, and the voyages of such men as Tasman, Dampier, Cook, Vancouver, and La Peyrouse, not only added Australia and New Zealand to the map, but added enormously to the certainty, and therefore to the safety, of navigation on more familiar trade routes. Officers of the British and French navies and of the Honourable the East India Company all did invaluable work in surveying and charting little-known waters, and no doubt many merchant ship-masters followed the example of our friend

Uring who, when cast ashore in the Gulf of Honduras through the combination of an incompetent local pilot and a very bad chart, spent part of his enforced leisure in making an accurate chart of that bit of the coast.

There was thus gradually accumulated that stock of knowledge concerning coasts, rocks, shoals, winds, and currents, without which commerce in the more distant seas must have been confined to occasional stray adventures. It might have been turned to still better advantage if there had been any provision at all for the education and examination in competency of officers in the mercantile marine; but there was none. Except in the East India Company's service, masters and mates were nearly all promoted from before the mast, and though their practical seamanship was often of a very high order, few of them were educated men, the chief exceptions being the owner-captains, who tended gradually to disappear. There were, of course, many exceptions. Kelly, the son of an Army officer who had come down in the world, and Uring, the son of a respectable tradesman, were men of parts and some reading, and there were plenty of runaways of good family and protegés of owners to be found in the merchant service, who were marked out from the first for promotion; but neither the character nor the rewards of the service were sufficient to attract a great number of educated men.

The life of the sailor was hard and the discipline often brutal. Conditions afloat, as regards food and accommodation, were pretty much what they had been in the seventeenth century, except that, as merchant ships came to rely less on their own armament, there was less overcrowding. The death roll from scurvy and yellow fever was still heavy;[1] slavers engaged in the unhealthy triangular voyage to Africa

[1] It is an extraordinary thing that the regular administration of lime-juice as a preventative of scurvy, adopted in the Navy in 1795, did not become compulsory in the merchant service till 1865.

and the West Indies often lost from one-quarter to one-third of their complement in a round voyage. The slave trade itself exercised a demoralizing influence on the many thousands of men engaged in it, and its bad traditions of recklessness and cruelty spread throughout the mercantile marine. Privateering with its usually lax discipline and its occasional hauls of quickly dissipated prize-money was, on the whole, a corrupting influence. In time of war there hung over every sailor the dread of impressment, and service in the Navy meant low wages, with interminable delays in their payment, and long commissions, with very few chances of shore leave.

Even in the merchant service wages were low, at any rate in time of peace. Sailing from the West Indies in 1712, in war time, Uring had to pay £4 a month, but on arrival at Lisbon he found that an armistice had been declared, whereupon he promptly paid off his crew and engaged others at 35s. Most of these, however, were discharged a month or two later at Leghorn, where more men were shipped "at cheaper wages."

In Kelly's time, 1782–1789, the Navy and the Packet Service paid 22s. 6d. a month, but in the packets married seamen could carry a small "adventure." The packets however, filled up largely with "able-bodied landsmen" at 16s. or 18s. The transport service paid better: 60s. per month for an A.B. and 40s. for an ordinary seaman.

The usual rate for an A.B. in the merchant service seems to have been 30s., which was about the pay of an agricultural labourer in receipt of board and lodging. At any rate, a conference of captains in the West India trade decided, in 1770, not to pay more than that amount.[1] The East India Company paid 35s.

In the coasting trade men were often paid "by the run." Kelly, as master of a coaster, received only 40s. a month.

[1] *Lloyd's Evening Post*, September, 21–24, 1770.

As a mate in the Philadelphia trade he had 60s., and as master £5 a month, out of which he had to keep himself on shore. "This," he feelingly remarks, "was a miserable income for the duty, anxiety, and responsibility of a ship-master." In all his time at sea, he only once cleared more than £75 in a year, in wages and perquisites combined.

When the seaman made more, he made it on the bye, and it is hard to blame him. A favourite trick was to sign on for a round voyage to the West Indies, desert the ship, and drive a bargain with a ship-master left shorthanded by desertion or yellow fever, to work the ship home for a lump sum payment. About 1742 the usual rate for "the run" was 17 to 20 guineas, with as many pounds of sugar and tobacco and as many gallons of rum as there were guineas in the run-money. Poor Kelly, earning hardly enough his £5 a month as master, had to pay each seaman for a run home in 1795, 45 guineas, about three times his own earnings.

In all the circumstances, it is not surprising that the standard of discipline was low and that desertions were frequent. Even a master like Kelly, who fed and treated his men well, had often to resort to something like kidnapping to complete his crews, and his experiences were probably a good deal better than those of rough, illiterate men such as the captain under whom he himself served, who spent much of his time gambling for coppers with members of the crew. Nor is it surprising that the great ports were scenes not only of brutal debauchery but of a vast and highly organized system of plunder and embezzlement, in which the officers and crews of the ships were too often participators.

It was at London, by far the greatest of British ports, that these depredations reached their height. Down almost to the very end of the century, the East India Company's dock at Blackwall was the only closed dock on the Thames; the warehouse accommodation was inadequate; valuable cargo lay for days and weeks in open craft or on open quays, and prior to the institution of the River Police in 1798, the annual loss by plunder and peculation was estimated at about £500,000, or about 8 per cent. of the total trade of the port.[1]

Neither the conditions of life afloat nor the conditions at the ports were creditable to a century which saw so great an expansion in British commerce, and even in the ships themselves the advance was smaller than we might expect. So late as 1788 there were only 105 vessels of 500 tons and upwards on the Register of the British Empire, practically the whole of these being in the East India trade, and even at the end of the century there were few trades in which a vessel of 150 tons would not be considered a fair-sized, and one of 350 tons an unusually large ship. In weatherliness and handiness there was some advance on the seventeenth century, and the introduction of copper sheathing, about 1780, added greatly to the life of ships; but the sailing qualities of most vessels were very poor by nineteenth-century standards. Combined with indifferent navigation, this led to very long passages, and even those made by skilful seamen seem very long to us to-day. As a sample we may take a few made by Kelly, who usually gives dates.

Liverpool–Philadelphia: 46,[2] 68, 63 days.
Philadelphia–Liverpool: 29,[2] 47, 47 days.
Sicily–Philadelphia, 89; Majorca–Philadelphia, 72.
Philadelphia–Barcelona, 67; Philadelphia–Malaga, 60.
Kingston (Jamaica)–London, 62.
Liverpool–Marseilles, 37.

His worst experience was a winter passage from Liverpool to New York, where he arrived 119 days out; but even this was a quick run compared with that made by one Captain

[1] See estimate in Colquhoun's *Commerce and Police of the River Thames*, 1800, p. 154.

[2] Estimated: dates not exact.

Higgins, who was forced, in 1741, to abandon his vessel for want of provisions, when 144 days out from Dublin for Philadelphia—a bid for the wooden spoon of the Atlantic well worthy of the immortality given to it by *Lloyd's List*.

Still, whatever their defects or limitations, the ships and seamen of the eighteenth century built up a great commerce for their country, and it is time to take a more general survey of British shipping and its employment at the close of the great struggle with France.

Pride of place would be claimed, as of right, by the fleet of the Honourable the East India Company. The trade with India and China could be carried on only by big and powerful vessels, for the voyage was long, accommodation had to be provided for troops and passengers, and it was necessary to carry strong armaments and strong crews in order to deal with the pirates who swarmed in the Eastern seas and with French cruisers in time of war. Hence the typical East Indiaman of the later eighteenth century was a solidly constructed vessel of from 500 to 1,400 tons, built and armed in very similar fashion to a man-of-war. Sailing in well-organized fleets, these aristocrats of the merchant service could easily be mistaken for King's ships, and the records of many hard-fought actions show that the resemblance was more than superficial.

The discipline on these ships was on naval lines. The pay, as already noted, was higher than in other merchant ships, and there was a pension fund for both officers and men. The officers were drawn from the same class as the officers of the Royal Navy, and the Company could offer inducements at least equal to those of the King's service, for the captain of an East Indiaman enjoyed trading privileges which held out a fair prospect of retirement on something more than a competency. Liberally treated, invested with a status little below that of the naval officer, and entrusted with cargoes worth £250,000 or £300,000, the gentlemen of the Company's service had some reason for regarding themselves as a class apart.

Until the very end of the eighteenth century, the clearances for Asia seldom exceeded 40 ships a year; but even this required a big fleet, for the ships for India mostly sailed one year and returned the next, and the round voyage to China might occupy the best part of three years. In 1801, when 77 ships cleared, the Company's fleet consisted of 122 vessels, averaging 870 tons, exclusive of India-built ships employed only in Asiatic waters. In no other trade did the ships average even half this size, and the monopoly of the East India traffic was one of the chief reasons for the towering supremacy of London above all other ports.

Of the trades open to free competition, by far the most important to the shipowner was that with the West Indies. The sugar, rum, molasses, coffee, cocoa, cotton, and dyewoods of the Caribbean were in ever-growing demand both for home consumption and for re-export, and the islands themselves were good markets for British manufacturers. Slaves, too, were needed in large numbers, and down to 1806, when the carriage of slaves in British ships was prohibited, many vessels trading to the West Indies cleared for the Guinea coast, to pick up a cargo of "black ivory." It was a vile trade, from which ship-masters of the better class, like Kelly, turned with loathing. Nothing in the oratory of the Anti-Slavery Society stamps it more firmly with its true character than the quiet provision in a Act of 1799, relating to marine insurance:

> No loss or Damage shall hereafter be recoverable on Account of the Mortality of Slaves by Natural Death, or ill Treatment, or against Loss by throwing overboard of Slaves on any Account whatsoever.

It was a profitable trade, none the less, and in 1771, there were said to be 190 English ships engaged in it.

Whether sailing on the triangular run or direct, few ships made more than one voyage to the West Indies a year, and the records of entrances and clearances show that, at the end of the Napoleonic wars, there must have been anything from 700 to 900 ships annually employed in the traffic. They ranged in size from about 150 to 350 tons, with an average of somewhere about 250 tons, and a West Indiaman and cargo might be insured for anything up to £60,000. The majority were slow-sailing vessels built with a single eye to maximum carrying capacity, and most of them by this time were unarmed, trusting to the convoy system for protection in time of war. Nevertheless, there were many owners who chafed against the restrictions of convoy, and were prepared to put money into fast, well-armed ships, which could obtain a license to sail independently, and pick up good freights from merchants anxious to forestall the market. Such a West India "runner," too, could always find good employment in other trades when West India freights were dull.

London, Liverpool, and Bristol were the chief ports in the West Indies trade. Liverpool owners were specially active in the slave traffic, as they were, in time of war, in privateering, and during the course of the eighteenth century Liverpool worked up from the forty-second to the second place among British ports in point of tonnage owned. It took second place, too, in point of the volume of foreign commerce, and was already prominent in the traffic with the United States. This trade tended more and more to fall into the hands of American shipowners, especially in time of war; but in peace it still gave employment to about 250 British vessels, with an average size of from 200 to 250 tons, bringing tobacco, rice, cotton, corn, timber, naval stores, etc., and carrying back British manufactures, and re-exports of Indian and foreign products. As a source of employment for British shipping, however, the trade with the United States was overshadowed by the rapidly increasing traffic with the British Colonies in North America which, by the end of the Napoleonic Wars, was rapidly overhauling the West India trade in respect of the number of ships cleared. Many of these were small vessels putting out from West Coast ports to fish on the Newfoundland Banks or supply the needs of the fishermen; but there were also many larger ships, such as those engaged in the timber trade, and the regular fur ships of the Hudson's Bay Company, whose homeward cargoes might be worth anything up to £200,000.

Many of the merchant ships in the Atlantic trades carried a few passengers in addition to their cargo. Our friend Kelly found the cabin of the *John* "fitted up with great elegance" for this purpose.

> The decorations were composed of plaster of paris and gilded. All the bed places had curtains of a blue running chintz pattern with white fringe, and the whole was extremely neat and clean which pleased me much.

Passengers provided their own sea-stores and struck a bargain with the master for their passage. Kelly tells us of one man who beat him down to £10, of which five guineas went to the owners, and the balance was the master's perquisite.

Most passengers, however, travelled by the Post Office packets—fast sailing vessels of about 200 tons, which carried the mails weekly to Spain, Portugal, and the West Indies, and at longer intervals to Halifax, New York, Brazil, Surinam, and Mediterranean ports. In 1808 there were 39 of these Falmouth Packets, and they carried, on all voyages, between 2,000 and 3,000 passengers a year. They were supplied under contract, in much the same way as the East Indiamen, and all passenger fares were the captain's perquisite. As the fare from Falmouth to Gibraltar was 35 guineas, the command of a packet was a profitable job.

It was often a job in both senses of the word; for the captain (the ships were run on naval lines) usually owed his berth to influence, and the sailing-master, promoted by merit, received only his wages of £4 a month.

Including packets and a number of little brigs employed in the wine trade with Madeira and the Canaries, some 500 or 600 vessels cleared annually for Spanish and Portuguese ports, and a substantially larger number, including many which had come from North America, entered therefrom. These figures, however, exaggerate the number of ships in the trade, as many regular traders must have made more than one voyage a year. They carried out manufactured goods, fish, and some re-exports, and brought back cargoes of wine, oil, fruit, cork, salt from Portugal, and fine wool from Spain. The average size of the ships in the trade was low, little over 120 tons, and some of the smaller western ports, such as Dartmouth and Plymouth, had a share in the traffic.

The Mediterranean trade, shorn of much of its former importance, accounted for about 250 clearances a year, and few of the ships seem to have exceeded 200 tons. About 70 ships a year sufficed for the direct trade with the Barbary States, the Guinea Coast, the Cape, and other parts of Africa. They brought home ivory, palm oil, gums, wine, and fruit, and it must be owned that, in addition to cheap textiles, they took out large quantities of liquor and gunpowder as a contribution to the spread of civilization among the blacks.

Last, but not least, in the list of long-distance trades, come the Greenland and South Sea whale fisheries. Whaling was still an extremely profitable industry, and from 100 to 150 ships sailed annually for the whaling-grounds from English and Scottish ports. As they were often away for two, three, or even four years, the total number of vessels employed must have been considerable. They had to be roomy, to carry stores for so long a voyage and bring back a paying cargo of oil, and the typical whaler was a sturdy, stocky, very deep ship of about 300 tons—a higher average tonnage than we find anywhere else outside the East India trade.

It is these long-distance trades that fill most of the space in histories of British shipping; but it is a very lop-sided picture which leaves out of account the huge block of tonnage employed in the more prosaic traffic of the Northern Seas. The combined exports of British manufactures and re-exports of foreign and colonial goods to Germany, Poland, Russia, and Scandinavia were greater than those absorbed by any other market. The imports of timber and shipbuilding materials, hemp, tallow, iron, potash, grain, yarns, and linen were valuable, indispensable, and bulky. The trade was largely carried in foreign bottoms, for even in peace the Navigation Laws permitted Danes, Swedes, and Lubeckers to carry their products to Great Britain in their own vessels; yet the number of British ships entered and cleared was far greater than in any of the long-distance trades. Even allowing for repeated voyages, there were probably at least as many British ships engaged in this traffic, before the outbreak of the Revolutionary War, as in the West Indies trade, and they were sizable vessels as big as or bigger than most of the Mediterranean traders.

The Short Sea Routes to Dutch, Flemish, and French ports carried, in times of peace, a very valuable trade, and gave employment to a large number of small vessels making several repeated voyages in the year; but the most important, to the shipowner, of the Short Sea Trades was what was sometimes described as "Foreign Coasting"—the traffic with Ireland, the Channel Isles, and the Isle of Man. Thanks to the care of English legislators, Ireland was still mainly dependent upon Great Britain for supplies of manufactured goods and colonial produce; the shipments of coal across the Irish Sea were large enough to give Whitehaven a place among the leading English ports; and Ireland could send, in return, linens, and large quantities of butter and salt provisions which became increasingly important with the growth of population in Great Britain. The repeated voyages of the small vessels (averaging 70 to 80 tons) which carried this extensive traffic ran into thousands a year, and the total clearances in the "Foreign Coasting Trade" accounted normally for at least half of the shipping movements recorded in the foreign trade of Great Britain. Statistics of shipping and losses during the French Wars are often vitiated by failure to distinguish this traffic from the "foreign trade" properly so-called. Its importance will be clearly seen in the table on p. 223, which gives a bird's-eye view of the employment of British shipping in the trade of Great Britain, immediately before and immediately after the last great struggle with France.

This, however, does not exhaust the activities of British shipping. The direct foreign trade of Ireland, though small, was not negligible; the clearances of British ships for ports outside Great Britain might amount to 500 in a year, of which rather less than two-fifths would be owned in Ireland itself. There were also many "cross-trades" of importance between ports abroad; notably the traffic between the West Indies and British North America, and the trade of Newfoundland with Spain and Portugal, who sent cargoes of wine and salt in return for supplies of salt fish. We have seen, too, from Kelly's and Uring's voyages, that there was a good deal of what we should now call tramp traffic between foreign ports. An analysis of the shipping losses recorded in *Lloyd's List* suggests that quite a substantial proportion of the tonnage under the British flag must have been normally engaged in these various cross-voyages.[1]

[1] The present writer had occasion to analyse the losses recorded in *Lloyd's List* for the months of March, June, September, and December

BRITISH SHIPS ENTERED AND CLEARED IN THE FOREIGN TRADE OF GREAT BRITAIN, 1792 AND 1816

1792			From or to	1816		
Number of Ships		Average Tonnage		Number of Ships		Average Tonnage
Entered	Cleared			Entered	Cleared	
2,746	1,367	186	Russia, Scandinavia, Baltic, and Germany	1,824	1,721	148
1,603	1,734	117	Holland and Flanders	1,148	1,070	99
1,413	1,317	73	France	1,522	1,442	70
975	615	126	Spain, Portugal, Atlantic Is., Gibraltar and Malta	806	545	120
138	215	143	Italy and Austria	175	230	143
38	48	224	Turkey, Levant, and Egypt	26	18	180
77	250	202	Africa (excluding Egypt)[1]	42	68	188
28	36	707	Asia[2]	116	164	657
219	383	147	British North America	783	772	220
202	223	221	United States	175	277	260
705	603	233	West Indies (British and Foreign)[3]	963	936	258
160	135	270	Whale Fisheries	175	164	320
8,304	6,926	151	Total, excluding "Foreign Coasting"	7,755	7,407	165
532	611	47	Channel Isles and Man	1,424	1,115	45
4,194	6,354	75	Ireland	7,575	8,861	82
13,030	13,891	117	Grand Total	16,754	17,383	116

[1] Ships cleared to Africa in 1792 include slavers ultimately bound to West Indies.

[2] Includes one or two ships for Australia. The great increase in 1816 shows the effect of the opening of Indian trade to private merchants in 1814.

[3] In 1816 includes some ships trading with South America.

To complete the picture, we must glance for a moment at the coasting trade which, in those times of no railways, and bad roads, was far more important relatively than it is to-day. Its most important branch, from the point of view of the shipowner, was the coal trade from Newcastle, Sunderland, and Blyth to London. Dating back at least to the time of Henry V, this trade greatly increased in importance after the Restoration, when coal began to supersede wood completely as a domestic fuel, and all through the eighteenth century it grew steadily with the growth of London. Although the colliers could make eight or nine round voyages a year, the trade employed, by the end of the century, some 500 vessels with an average size of over 200 tons; so that both in total and average tonnage it took rank with even the more important branches of foreign trade. It was highly valued not merely as a source of employment (the freights in 1797 averaged 10s. 6d. per London chaldron, say 14s. 10d. per ton), but as a school of navigation, for the "Geordie" skippers were as celebrated for their practical seamanship as for their lack of theoretical knowledge. If blown far out to sea they might have to rely on any chance-met deep-sea trader to give them their position; but they had a rare instinct for smelling their way among the shoals and sandbanks of the East Coast and the Thames Estuary. A voyage or two in a collier was a very usual form of apprenticeship to the sea. Uring served it, though "the bad provisions aboard, and their ill manner of dressing them" nearly choked him off a sea-life altogether.

in each of the years 1795, 1797, 1798, and 1799. Deducting transports, coasters, and vessels in "foreign coasting," the results were as follows:

		Per cent.
Foreign trade of Great Britain	396	72·0
Foreign trade of Ireland	52	9·5
Cross Trades	102	18·5
	550	100·0

So did a greater man, Captain Thomas Cook. Kelly did not, and as a consequence, was refused his rating as A.B. in the transport service.

There was, of course, a good deal of coal carried to other places than London, and, in addition, there was an immense general coasting traffic. In 1797, 100 vessels were regularly employed in the trade between London and Hull alone, and the total coasting traffic of London (exclusive of colliers) employed over 600 vessels, making about 6,500 round voyages in the year. They brought to London grain and flour, beer, cider, butter, cheese, fruit, provisions, and manufactures of all kinds from ports in England and Wales, and textiles, hosiery, fish, iron, and paving-stones from Scotland. They carried back East and West India produce, tobacco, rice, cotton, groceries, and all kinds of dry goods.

SOME BOOKS ON THE PERIOD

In addition to the light they throw on business methods, *The Voyages and Travels of Captain Nathaniel Uring*, ed. Captain Alfred Dewar, R.N., London, 1928, and *Samuel Kelly, An Eighteenth Century Seaman*, ed. Crosbie Garstin, London, 1925, give vivid pictures of life afloat and the risks and adventures incident to sea-trading in the eighteenth century. Hannay's *Sea Trader* is specially valuable for the East India Company, the slave trade, and impressment. For the East Indiamen see also *The Old East Indiamen*, by E. Keble Chatterton, London, 1914. His book, *The Mercantile Marine*, London, 1923, has also some useful details for this period. For the influence of the coffee-houses on business and the growth of marine insurance see *A History of Lloyd's*, by Charles Wright and C. Ernest Fayle, London, 1928. *The Maritime History of Massachusetts*, 1783–1860, by S. E. Morison, London, 1923, is full of valuable material as to shipowning and trading methods at the end of the eighteenth century. My statistics are mostly taken from *Chronological Records of the British Royal and Commercial Navy*, by César Moreau, London, 1827, a rare and most useful collection of tables.

CHAPTER IX

"WHITE WINGS" AND "TIN KETTLES"

THE CLIPPER SHIP ERA AND THE RISE OF STEAM

There's a fine full-rigged clipper just ready for sea,
Away-hay—blow the man down;
There's a fine full-rigged clipper just ready for sea,
Give us a chance to blow the man down.

SHANTY

"Oh, where are you going to, all you Big Steamers
With England's own coal, up and down the salt seas?"
"We are going to fetch you your bread and your butter,
Your beef, pork, and mutton, eggs, apples, and cheese."

KIPLING, *Big Steamers*

FROM the opening of the ocean routes by the Spaniards and Portuguese down to the close of the great eighteenth-century struggle for "Ships, Colonies, and Commerce," the history of the world's shipping industry had been one of continuous, steady development, undisturbed by revolutionary changes. Within some sixty years from the close of that struggle the character of the world's shipping and its contribution to the life of men were both in a fair way to be transformed by the transition from wood and sail to iron and steam. This transition was accompanied by an almost unprecedented increase in the efficiency of the sailing ship herself, and by a fierce maritime rivalry between Great Britain and the United States, in which the former ultimately triumphed at the cost, or by the aid, of a complete reversal of her traditional maritime policy. The evolution of the clipper ship, the rise of the steamer, the defeat of the American challenge, and the repeal of the Navigation Acts are so closely connected, by their own interactions and by their common origin in economic conditions, that an attempt must be made to weave them into a single story; leaving for a later chapter their effect, and that of two simultaneous developments—the electric telegraph and the limited company—upon the technique of shipowning.

The great French wars, like a more recent cataclysm, had left behind them an aftermath of economic dislocation. Falling prices, high taxation, recurrent financial crises, and widespread unemployment were among the fruits of victory in 1815 as in 1918. The workings of the Industrial Revolution which, at the time, aggravated the resultant distress, rendered ultimate recovery certain; but when that recovery first became clearly manifest, in the eighteen-thirties, capital and enterprise found their most profitable employment in the development of the country's internal resources, in the building and equipment of factories and the construction of railways, rather than in shipping and foreign trade.

These activities, however, were bound to affect, in the long run, the demand for tonnage. By about 1835 or 1840 the full effects of the industrial revolution were becoming apparent both at home and abroad. The growth of industry in all countries entailed a corresponding demand for bulky raw materials, and increased, at the same time, the purchasing power of the industrial nations. It was accompanied, especially in Great Britain, by a growth of population which rapidly outstripped the production of foodstuffs. Imports of grain, especially after a bad harvest, or in time of war, were no new thing; but the necessity for regular annual imports on a large scale was a new and most important factor in the world's freight markets. It gave, in particular, a new importance to the Black Sea trade.

On the other side of the Atlantic, the American people had begun to turn their attention to the exploitation of the vast unoccupied areas that lay behind the settled strip of coast land, and to welcome settlers from older and more densely peopled countries. During the ten years 1825 to 1834, an average of 32,000 emigrants left Europe annually for the United States, and during the following decade the average rose to 71,000. This was, in itself, an appreciable stimulus to the demand for tonnage, and still more important was its ultimate effect in increasing the exportable surplus and the import demands of the United States themselves.

The result of all these developments was a great expansion in the volume of world trade, in the benefits of which British shipping naturally shared. From the end of the French Wars until about 1835, the tonnage on the Register of the British Empire had remained stationary at round about 2,500,000 tons. At that point it took a sudden leap upwards, and by 1845 it had reached the figure of 3,700,000 tons.

Nevertheless, the supremacy of British shipping was now being effectively challenged. Left, at the end of the Napoleonic Wars, in a position of unquestioned predominance, British shipowners, like most people who are making money easily, seem to have assumed that their business would continue to go forward of its own momentum, without any need for special exertion on their part, and the automatic increase in tonnage between 1835 and 1845 served to cloak a real decline in comparative efficiency. On the other hand, the risks and profits of the neutral trade during the Napoleonic Wars had stimulated American owners and designers to the production of fast and handy vessels capable of showing a clean pair of heels to French or British cruisers, and on the return of peace they were quicker than their British rivals to realize the commercial advantages of speed in the carriage of passengers, mails, and certain classes of fine cargo. The speedy little Yankee brigs and schooners soon became prime favourites in the Mediterranean fruit trade, and the trans-Atlantic mail and passenger services fell almost entirely into American hands. It was in 1816 that the famous Black Ball Line of packets began a regular fortnightly service between New York and London. The Red Star Line, the Dramatic Line, and others followed in due course, and by the middle thirties there were services running regularly from American ports to London and Havre as well as to Liverpool.

It was not until 1838 that any serious attempt was made to dispute the monopoly of the Yankee Packets. When it did come, British competition took a novel and most significant form.

The first experiments in steam navigation go back well into the eighteenth century—Samuel Kelly saw a steamboat running on the Delaware in 1790—but the first steamer to be a real commercial success was Fulton's *Clermont*, which began a regular service between New York and Albany in 1807. In 1812 Bell's *Comet* began a regular service on the Clyde, and during the next ten years 151 steamers, ranging from 9 to 448 tons, with an average of 112 tons, were built in Great Britain. In the United States progress was still more rapid, for by 1822 there are said to have been 300 steamers employed on American lakes and rivers.

The utility of the steamer for river and canal navigation was obvious at once, and progressive British owners, such as the General Steam Navigation Company (founded in 1820), were ready to adopt it for coasting and short-sea passages; but it was some time before it was considered safe to trust the "tin kettle" far out of sight of land. The chief stimulus to development came from British and foreign Governments, who were quick to recognize the potential value of the steamer in war, and the benefits to be derived from its greater average speed, and, above all, from the regularity of its sailings, in the carriage of mails. These objects were held to justify the grant of State assistance, and in most countries the steamer was nursed through its experimental stage by lavish subsidies. The British Admiralty and the Honourable the East India Company, actually ran steam postal packets of their own, and, by 1837, they provided, in conjunction with a private enterprise, the Peninsular Steam Navigation Company, regular communication between Great Britain and India. This, however, was a matter of short and easy stages: London to Gibraltar, Gibraltar to Alexandria, thence overland to Suez, Suez to Bombay. The real test of the steamer's reliability for ocean voyages was generally recognized to be the conquest of the Atlantic. Although the American *Savannah*, fitted with lifting paddles, had made the passage in 1819, she was only under steam for 80 hours in a passage of 29½ days, and so late as 1835 a regular trans-Atlantic steamer service was pronounced to be as impossible as a voyage to the moon.

There was immense excitement, therefore, when in 1838, four British ships, the most notable of which was the *Great Western* of 1,340 tons, succeeded in crossing the Atlantic under steam. The *Great Western*, much the largest steamship yet built, reached New York 15 days out from Bristol and cut this time by a day on the return passage. This was a noteworthy demonstration of the value of steam, for the hard-driven Black Ball Packets had averaged 23 days from New York to Liverpool, during the first ten years of their running, and no fewer than 43 days on the westward run, against the prevailing winds and currents.

In the following year, Samuel Cunard, George Burns, and David McIver, having secured a contract for the carriage of the mails, formed the British and North American Royal Mail Steam Packet Company (famous to-day as the Cunard Line), and in 1840 they began a regular trans-Atlantic service with four paddle steamers of about 1,100 tons. From the first the Cunarders were a complete success, and although the American sailing packets continued for more than a decade to put up a gallant fight, it was soon clear that they were fighting a losing battle.

From 1840 onwards the development of "steam-packet"

companies grew apace; nevertheless it was many years before steamers began to take any substantial part in the carriage of the world's trade. The great defect of the early steamers was their extravagant consumption of coal. A typical modern tramp of about 4,300 tons can maintain a speed of 10 knots on a consumption of 26 tons a day. In 1848, the Collins Liner *America*, of only 1,400 tons, burned 60 tons a day to attain a speed of 10¼ knots. This put the steamer completely out of the running on the longest routes, for there were as yet very few ports where bunkers could be obtained, and even on the trans-Atlantic voyage the carriage of the necessary fuel left very little space for cargo. Steamer freights were high—the Cunarders were charging £7 10s. per ton before the competition of the American Collins Line brought them down to £4 10s.; but even at such rates it was impossible to carry sufficient cargo to offset the cost of bunkers. Outside the coasting and short-sea trades, the steamer could not compete with the sailing vessel as a cargo-carrier on equal terms, and for many years the participation of steamships in ocean trade was practically confined to a limited number of highly subsidized mail and passenger services, to which the carriage of a little fine cargo was merely incidental.

The sailing vessel was still the chief carrier of the world's commerce, and in the building and running of sailing vessels, British owners were being rapidly outclassed. Progress in ship design was hampered by an obsolete system of tonnage measurement which penalized breadth, and thus put a premium on the construction of deep, slab-sided, full-bottomed ships, capable of carrying a cargo much in excess of the registered burthen on which dues were paid, but slow and unwieldly. Both in equipment and manning, cheapness was more sought after than efficiency. There were many honourable exceptions; but the Report of a Board of Trade Commission appointed in 1847 showed clearly that

British shipping was being left behind by many of its rivals, as regards the design and fitting of the ships, the training, discipline, and treatment of the crews, and the professional education of the officers. Scamped workmanship, defective stores and equipment, professional incompetence, slackness, and excessive drinking, were all deplorably common. The fact was that British owners had learned to look more to the lead obtained during the Revolutionary Wars and to the protection provided by the Navigation Laws than to their own exertions.

Yet these laws had already been substantially modified. The fact that the West Indies were economically dependent on the North American Continent, and the importance of American trade to British shipping, had made it practically impossible, from the start, to enforce them consistently against American ships. British Governments were far too firmly wedded to the principles of the Navigation Acts to give immediate legal recognition to economic realities; but after half a century of futile and irritating diplomatic squabbles and measures of legislative retaliation, a definite agreement was at last reached in 1830, which allowed American ships to carry American produce direct to any British possession, and to carry exports from any British possession to any foreign country. They were even admitted to the trade between the United Kingdom and India.

By this time the whole system of the Navigation Acts was crumbling. The Napoleonic Wars were followed by the revolt of the Spanish and Portuguese colonies in South America, and this made it necessary to admit the products of the newborn Republics in their own ships. Further, the opening-up of direct trade with South America led to such severe competition with the products of the West Indies that it was thought politic to compensate the planters for the loss of their advantages in the British market by partially removing the restrictions on their choice of shipping, and allowing them to import European, American, or African goods under the flag of the producing country, and to export goods under the flag of the purchaser.

Several European countries too, as they recovered from the exhaustion of war, began to chafe against the restrictions imposed upon their ships in British trade, and their Governments showed the same regrettable tendency to impose "like penal laws" as had troubled Elizabethan statesmen. As British shipping had now far outgrown the capacity of the reserved trades to provide it with employment, the threat of retaliation was at once effective, and it was met by the negotiation of a series of Reciprocity Treaties with various Powers, beginning with Prussia and Denmark in 1824, by which equality of treatment was mutually conceded.

The result of all this was that when the Navigation Laws were solemnly revised and consolidated in 1845, it was estimated that about half the total trade was governed by the exceptions to the rules rather than by the rules themselves. It was an absurd position. The law was so complicated and inconsistent that merchants could hardly make a shipment without turning up the textbooks, and they often suffered grave inconvenience from being unable to charter a suitable and readily available vessel. On the other hand the protection given to British shipping was fully effective only in a comparatively few trades; yet the owners continued to regard the Acts as their sole guarantee of prosperity.

A rude awakening was in store for them. The prospects of a settled peace, the need for expanding markets, the need for raw materials, and the growing dependence of the country on imported foodstuffs had given a new turn to British commercial policy. The idea was gaining ground that commercial prosperity was more likely to be attained by encouraging freedom of exchange than by attempting to restrict the progress of other nations, and the experience gained since the negotiation of the Reciprocity treaties suggested that British shipping had more to gain from a general increase in the volume of world trade than to lose by the abolition of its special privileges. The decisive step was taken in 1849, when the entire body of the Navigation Laws was finally repealed, with the exception of the clauses relating to the coasting trade. In 1854 the coasting trade itself was thrown open to foreign ships.

With one or two far-sighted exceptions, such as W. S. Lindsay, the historian of merchant shipping, the shipowners had fought tooth and nail against repeal, and when British shipping was at last left to compete on its merits in every branch of commerce, a wail of despair went up from almost the entire industry. It was not long, however, before the keen spur of American competition roused the owners to take a manlier line.

The discovery of gold in California in 1847 gave an extraordinary stimulus to shipbuilding in the United States. There was then no trans-Continental railroad, and in their haste to the diggings people were ready to pay high for a quick passage round Cape Horn. They went in large numbers too—in 1849 no fewer than 90,000 people sailed for 'Frisco from the Atlantic ports—so that large as well as fast ships became a paying proposition.

In response to this demand Donald Mackay (a Nova Scotian by birth) and other great American shipbuilders produced a new and very remarkable type of sailing vessel, the California clippers. They were very big ships for their day. Few British merchantmen of 1848 exceeded 1,000 tons; but Donald Mackay's *Flying Cloud*, which set up the record of 98 days, New York to 'Frisco, was 1,783 tons by American measurement, and his *Sovereign of the Seas* measured 2,421 tons. Fine lines and a tremendous spread of canvas gave them a wonderful turn of speed, and, built as they were for the stormy passage round Cape Horn, there was nothing afloat that could live with them in strong winds. All sorts of gadgets were introduced to facilitate their working, and they were mercilessly driven by men who "carried sail" to the verge of recklessness. In beauty, power, and performance they were a revelation to the world.

As there was little except gold-dust to bring home from San Francisco, most of the clippers, after landing their passengers, crossed to China to pick up a cargo for New York or Boston, and when the repeal of the Navigation Acts threw open the trade between China and the United Kingdom, the astute American shipowners seized eagerly upon the chance. The China tea trade was one in which speed could be made to pay, for the first of the new season's teas to be placed on the London market realized the best prices. In August 1850, the American clipper *Oriental* arrived at Hong Kong and was promptly chartered to load 1,600 tons of tea for London at £6 per ton of 40 cubic feet, while British ships were finding it difficult to fill their holds at £3 10s. per ton of 50 cubic feet. On December 3rd she arrived in London, after a record passage of 97 days from Hong Kong, to be stared at as a wonder of shipbuilding and a portent of coming doom for British shipping.

There were men, however, to whom the cold blast of free competition came as a tonic. "We, the British shipowners," said sturdy Richard Green, "have at last sat down to play a fair and square game with the Americans and by God we will trump them." Yet when the discovery of gold in Victoria in 1851 drew a rush of emigrants to Australia, a large proportion of the emigrants were carried, and most of the best passages were made, by American-built ships, chartered, bought, or ordered by the big Liverpool shipowners, notably James Baines. It was for him that Mackay built the *Lightning* whose homeward passage of 63 days from Melbourne was never equalled under sail, and the *James*

Baines, of 2,275 tons English measurement, which was, perhaps, the great builder's absolute masterpiece.

Not only were American ships bigger and better than British in 1850; ton for ton they were cheaper, being built of soft woods, of which the Americans had an inexhaustible supply; while the oak used in British construction was becoming scarce and dear, and teak, a still more durable substitute, was even more costly. The softwood ships, however, had serious defects. After a voyage or two their hulls became waterlogged, and their sailing qualities deteriorated; nor could they be trusted to deliver a delicate cargo, such as tea, in perfect condition. The more costly hardwood ship was the more economical in the long run, and it was not long before British owners and designers, aided by new and more rational rules for tonnage measurement in the Merchant Shipping Act of 1854, proved fully equal to their rivals. Builders such as Hall of Aberdeen, Steele of Greenock, and Pile of Sunderland, turned out a series of lovely little ships for the China trade which ran the Americans clean out of the business. These China clippers such as *Sir Lancelot*, holder of the 89 days record from Foochow, or *Ariel* and *Serica*, the joint winners of the great tea race of 1866, were smaller than Mackay's products and less powerful in strong winds, but they were skilfully designed to take advantage of every puff of wind in the light and baffling airs of the Eastern seas.

In the Indian and Australian trades bigger ships were used. The finest of them, for many years, were to be found among the "Blackwall Frigates" owned by Richard Green, Money Wigram, Joseph Soames, and Duncan Dunbar, the representatives of firms that had once built ships for the Honourable the East India Company, and still retained something of the Company's traditions in the build and running of their ships. The ships were handsome vessels, solidly built, long-lived, and good passage makers, if not exceptionally fast. The crews were well fed and well treated, and signed on for voyage after voyage. The officer came from the same class as those of the Company's service, and were trained in the owners' own ships. Even as apprentices they wore uniform and were honoured with the title of "midshipmen."

The Blackwallers were the aristocrats of the Merchant Service, but the general conditions afloat were at last beginning to show a much-needed improvement. Down to 1849 the State had been more concerned with the protection of British shipping from competition than with the promotion of its efficiency or of the safety of life and property. The Registration of shipping had been made compulsory in 1787; the influence of the underwriters was strong enough to procure some check on the grosser forms of fraud in relation to marine insurance; from 1793 onwards something had been done to regulate food and conditions in the passenger trade; and that was about all. When, however, British shipping was exposed for the first time to unrestricted competition in every sea, it was felt that the state of things disclosed by the Board of Trade Report of 1847 could no longer be regarded with indifference, and in 1850, the year after the repeal of the Navigation Laws, an Act was passed, "For improving the Conditions of Masters, Mates, and Seamen, and Maintaining Discipline in the Merchant Service." By this Act the Board of Trade was given for the first time a definite responsibility for the welfare of those employed in shipping or entrusting their goods or persons to British ships. Provision was made, for the first time, for the examination of Masters and Mates and the issue of certificates of competency; the keeping of an Official Log was rendered obligatory; regulations were laid down for the discipline of mercantile crews; a definite scale of accommodation, food, and medical supplies was established; and local Marine Boards were constituted at the principal ports, to supervise the engagement of seamen and the administration of the Act.

This belated acceptance by the State of its most elementary obligations towards the merchant service was followed in 1854 by the first Merchant Shipping Act, which greatly extended the powers and responsibilities of the Board of Trade, notably in respect of the supervision of ship construction and equipment. From this time onward, the responsibility of the State for the social welfare of the shipping industry, and for enforcing the performance of its duties towards the public was definitely recognized.

To many shipowners this "grandmotherly" legislation seemed a poor exchange for the protection which they had lost; but its beneficial effects were soon shown in a revival of efficiency, to which the bracing effects of competition also contributed. Nevertheless, the American challenge was not immediately staved off. By 1860, the tonnage on the Register of the British Empire had increased to 5,800,000 tons; but American tonnage registered for foreign trade had grown from about 1,000,000 in 1835 to 2,500,000 tons—a still greater proportional advance—and the total tonnage under the American flag, including coasting, lake, and river craft, was only half a million tons short of the Empire total, and exceeded by more than half a million the tonnage on United Kingdom Register. Twenty years later, American tonnage had diminished by nearly one-half, while British tonnage had increased in almost the same ratio.

One cause of this extraordinary decline in American shipping was, undoubtedly, that most often alleged—the ravages of the Confederate cruisers during the Civil War of 1861–1865, which caused a transfer of something like half a million tons of American shipping to the British flag; but the ground lost in the Civil War would soon have been recovered had not more fundamental causes been at work. One of these was the immense development of the West and Middle West which followed the War of Secession. Apart from a few of the New England States the faces of the American people had always been set Westwards, and when the political quarrels arising from the question of slavery had been disposed of, capital and enterprise found a far better return from the exploitation of the vast undeveloped resources of the Western States than they could obtain from investment in shipping. Yet the swing-over from sea to land would probably have been much less marked had not American shipowning been rendered unprofitable by the greatest of nineteenth-century developments in the shipping industry itself—the change from wood and sails to iron and steam

We have seen that the great expansion in American shipping depended on the abundant supplies of soft wood available. British owners, partly of choice, and partly of necessity, stuck to the more costly, but more durable hard woods, and as the readily available timber supplies were running short, they began to consider the use of a material more durable still. Most of the later clippers were of composite construction, with iron frames and wooden planking; but long before their day experiments in iron shipbuilding had been made, and during the sixties iron came rapidly into favour for the building both of steamers and sailing vessels.

Commercially, iron had two great advantages as a shipbuilding material. In the first place, although iron is heavier than wood, its greater strength permitted so large a reduction in thickness that an iron ship weighed about a quarter less than a wooden ship of the same dimensions; so that she could carry considerably more cargo, without diminishing her buoyancy. This was important both in sail and in steam; but to the steamship owner, who had to provide for the carriage of bunkers, a still greater advantage was that iron permitted the construction of much larger vessels.

Whereas the structural limit of length of a wooden ship was about 300 feet, there was practically no limitation on the size of an iron ship other than the capacity of her owners to fill and of the ports to handle her. In practice, the growth in size of sailing ships was restricted by the difficulty of handling spars and sails of abnormal dimensions. In the very last days of sail a few big five-masted barques and schooners of about 5,000 tons were turned out by German and American yards, but right down to the end of the nineteenth century any sailing vessel much over 2,000 tons was something exceptional. The steamer knew no such restrictions and the marine engineering shops proved capable of keeping pace with any increase in size. So early as 1858, the *Great Eastern*, designed by the great engineer Brunel to solve the problem of combining carrying power with bunker capacity on long voyages, reached the unparalleled dimensions of 680 feet in length and 18,914 tons gross register. She proved a white elephant commercially, but she was a portent in ship construction. It was not till the last decade of the century that any ship was built which even approached the tonnage of the *Great Eastern*, but by 1875 steamers of from 3,000 to 5,000 tons had already proved themselves a paying proposition.

Even this increase in size would not have enabled the steamer to compete successfully for cargo had it not been accompanied by a great reduction in running expenses; but the problem which Brunel had attempted to solve by the "monster ship" had been solved in more practical ways by improvements in marine engineering; by the general substitution of the screw for paddles as motive power, and above all by the introduction of the compound engine, which reduced by about one-half the coal consumption required to generate a given horse-power, with the double result of reducing bunker costs and increasing freight-earning capacity. Its effects can best be illustrated from a table prepared by the Cunard line in 1876 to illustrate the development of their fleet. Four ships may be taken as illustrating the main stages of development:

1840. *Britannia.* Wood built. Paddle. Simple Side Lever Engines.
1855. *Persia.* Iron. Paddle. Simple Side Lever Engines.
1865. *Java.* Iron. Screw. Simple Inverted Engines.
1874. *Bothnia.* Iron. Screw. Compound Engines.

Name	Tons Gross	I.H.P.	Average Speed Knots	Coal per day Tons	Bunker Capacity Tons	Cargo Capacity Tons	Cabin Passengers.
Britannia	1,139	740	8·3	38	640	225	90
Persia ..	3,300	3,600	12·9	150	1,640	1,100	180
Java ..	2,697	2,440	12·8	85	1,100	1,100	160
Bothnia ..	4,556	2,780	13·0	63	940	3,000	340 [1]

[1] The *Bothnia* could carry also 800 third class passengers.

For each horse-power generated, the *Britannia* burned per hour, 4·7 lb. of coal, the *Persia* 3·3, and the *Bothnia* 2·2; and it will be observed that the *Bothnia* obtained a speed equal to or greater than that of her fastest predecessors with a much smaller ratio of horse-power to tonnage.

The crucial date in the struggle between steam and sail is usually given as 1869, when the opening of the Suez Canal gave the steamer a shorter route to the East, studded with bunker stations at convenient intervals. More truly, perhaps, it may be given as 1865, when the original Holt liners astonished the world, and revealed the possibilities opened up by the compound engine, by making a non-stop run of 8,500 miles from Liverpool to Mauritius. From that date the ultimate triumph of steam in the cargo as well as the passenger trade was only a question of time.

Both in the development of the ocean-going steamer and in the use of iron for shipbuilding, Great Britain took the lead. Her iron industry was already well developed, and both the coalfields and the chief centres of metallurgical and engineering activity were within easy access of the ports. By 1870 the steam tonnage on the Register of the United Kingdom already amounted to 1,100,000 tons, and of the tonnage under construction in that year three-quarters consisted of steamers and nearly five-sixths of iron ships. Of the other European countries, France alone, with 154,000 tons of steamships had so much as one-tenth of the British total. The United States, too, was falling behind. The American metallurgical industries could not produce shipbuilding material at a price which would enable American owners to compete successfully, and a high tariff on imports prevented them from supplying themselves with British plates. Small wooden steamers continued to be built for inland and coastal navigation, but for ocean voyages big iron vessels were needed, and although over a million tons of steam shipping flew the American flag in 1870, only just under 200,000 tons was registered for foreign trade. Twenty years later, the figure remained the same.

Even the American softwood sailing vessels of the seventies and eighties were at a big disadvantage in competition with their British rivals, and this, too, was a serious matter, for the rivalry between steam and sail was still far from ended. It was only very gradually that the effect of the reduction in the steamer's operating costs and increase in freight-earning capacity made itself felt in the carrying trade, and the iron sailing vessel of this period—with a bigger cargo capacity than the extreme clipper and a more economical sail-plan—was a formidable competitor in all trades where speed was not the main consideration.

By about 1875 the steamer had already obtained a practical monopoly of the carriage of mails, passengers, and fine cargo on all routes except the Australasian. The Cunard, White Star, Anchor, P. & O., Royal Mail,

Hamburg-Amerika Norddeutscher Lloyd, Messageries Maritimes, and other lines which are household words to-day, together with some that have passed away or have been merged in existing services, were already flourishing institutions, by which the chief European countries were linked up with those of North and South America, with India, and with the Far East. The British India Company's services provided regular communications between the ports of India and Burmah, Malaya, the Persian Gulf, and the East Coast of Africa. The West Indian services of the Royal Mail and of the West India and Pacific Navigation Company were linked up by the railway across the isthmus of Panama with the coastal and trans-Pacific services of the American Pacific Mail and the South American West Coast service of the Pacific Steam Navigation Company. Nearer home, the Austrian Lloyd and Messageries Maritimes covered the Mediterranean with their services, and a number of lines, among which that of Messrs. Frederick Leyland & Company was conspicuous, connected the Mediterranean and Black Sea ports with Great Britain.

The newest ships on most of the services had a cargo capacity little if at all inferior to that of a big sailing vessel, and some steamers were now being built with a single eye to freights and without regard to passage monies. It was a sign of the times that two of the P. & O. steamers were described as "Cargo vessels" pure and simple, and there were some very fine ships of this class in the Mediterranean trade. The Leyland liner *Bavarian*, for instance, could carry 4,800 tons of cargo, exclusive of bunkers, on a gross tonnage of 3,052. In the coasting and short-sea trades, the bulk of the cargo as well as the passenger traffic was now carried in steamers; in particular, steam colliers had already replaced the greater number of the "Geordie brigs."

Turning casually over the last volume, published in 1876, of W. S. Lindsay's *History of Merchant Shipping*, from which the details above are taken, it would be easy to get the impression that the triumph of steam was already complete when he wrote; but a more careful reading, supplemented by other sources, will soon dispel the illusion. Lindsay himself tells us that sailing vessels still carried "by far the largest proportion of the goods traffic" in the Indian and Australian trade. Tea cargoes could bear high freights, and by 1875 the China clippers were already suffering severely from the competition of steam; about 1880 most of then went off into other trades. Much of the Indian produce, however, was cargo of lower grade such as rice and jute, which could not afford to pay steamer freights swollen by Suez Canal dues, and to quote Lindsay, "steam-boats, even though largely subsidized, especially to India by way of the Cape, have found it impossible to compete successfully with the sailing ships of Messrs. Green of Blackwall, Messrs. T. and W. Smith, and other private shipowners long engaged in the trade." Even the services of the P. & O. Company were only maintained by the aid of sail; for although the steam-collier was a paying proposition on the short run from the Tyne or Wear to London, it would have been a desperately expensive business to supply the Mediterranean, Indian, and Far Eastern bunker stations by this means, and the company employed annually no fewer than 170 sailing vessels in this service.

On the Australian run the steamer was at a still greater disadvantage. The few voyages of full-powered steamers to Australia prior to 1875 were of merely historical interest, and an attempt to solve the problem by combining sail and steam power, in vessels with auxiliary engines, had proved a disastrous failure. The P. & O. ran a steamer service between Colombo and Sydney to which mails were transferred from the trunk-line ships; but a large proportion of the mails, most of the passengers, and practically the whole of the goods traffic was carried in sailing vessels. In 1877, the Orient Line initiated a direct, regular steam service, going out by the Cape and returning *via* Suez; but all through the eighties the big passenger sailing vessels were well filled. (Incidentally this book might never have been written if "the wonderful *Torrens*" had not still been carrying a few passengers, mainly convalescents, in 1900.)

In the goods traffic the sailing vessel held her own for a still longer period. The big iron wool clippers, accompanied by two or three of the later ships built for the China tea trade, such as *Thermopylae* and *Cutty Sark*, continued to race home from Sydney, Melbourne, Adelaide, Geelong, and Newcastle until well into the nineties. It was a big and for a long time a paying trade. So late as 1891 there were 77 sailing vessels in Sydney alone loading wool for the London market, and a clipper like *Mermerus* of 1,651 tons could screw 10,000 bales into her holds, representing the fleeces of a million sheep and worth anything up to £130,000; while in 1874 her general cargo on the outward voyage brought her owners £5,000 in freight money. It was a sailing vessel too, the New Zealand Shipping Company's *Mataura*, which brought to England, in 1882, the first cargo of frozen meat.

Another very big trade which was long almost the monopoly of sail was the shipment of grain to Europe from the west coast of North America. It reached its climax after the bumper harvest of 1882, when no fewer than 550 sailing vessels, mostly British or American, cleared from the Californian and Oregon ports, with cargoes amounting to about a million and a quarter tons of wheat and barley.

Indeed, right down to the opening years of the twentieth century, there were still trades in which the sailing vessel could successfully compete, especially in the carriage of low-grade cargoes on long voyages, and in the service of ports at which the processes of loading and discharge were lengthy and uncertain. Many a once famous member of the tea fleet or the wool fleet ended her days in carrying wheat from Australia or round the Horn from 'Frisco, nitrate from Chile, timber from Quebec, or coal from Newcastle, N.S.W., to South America.

Rapid as was the development of the steamship from about 1840 onwards, it was not until about 1880 that the total sailing tonnage of the world began to decline; not until the nineties that it was overhauled by that of the world's steamships. Taking one ton steam as roughly equivalent during the period of transition to three tons sail, it was not until the eighties that steamships comprised even one-half of the world's available carrying power. The following tables will give a bird's-eye view of the gradual process of displacement; but it should be remembered that in the first of them, the multiplication of steam tonnage by three may exaggerate a little its actual cargo-lifting power in at least the first two decades, and that the ratio of steam tonnage entered to the total, as shown in the second table, was undoubtedly higher at British than at most foreign ports.

TOTAL TONNAGE ON REGISTER (1,000 TONS NET)

Year	British Empire			Other Chief Maritime Countries[1]		
	Sail	Steam	Steam as Sail	Sail	Steam	Steam as Sail
1860	5,301	500	1,500	Statistics not complete		
1870	5,947	1,202	3,606	6,295	554	1,662
1880	5,498	2,949	8,847	6,380	1,037	3,111
1890	4,274	5,414	16,242	4,865	2,293	6,879
1900	3,011	7,740	23,220	3,732	4,199	12,597

[1] U.S.A. (shipping registered for foreign trade only), France, Germany, Norway, Sweden, Denmark, Italy, and Austria-Hungary. Statistics for other leading countries (e.g. Spain and Greece) are not complete for the whole period.

Year	Total Chief Maritime Countries				
	Sail	Steam	Steam as Sail	Steam Percentage of	
				Total Tonnage	Carrying Power
1870	12,242	1,756	5,268	12·5	30·0
1880	11,878	3,986	11,958	25·1	50·2
1890	9,139	7,707	23,121	45·7	71·7
1900	6,743	11,939	35,817	63·9	84·1

Percentage of Steam Tonnage to Total Tonnage Entered and Cleared in the Foreign Trade, with Cargoes and in Ballast, at Ports in the United Kingdom.

	1860	1870	1880	1890	1900
All Ships	20·1	41·1	63·4	83·0	91·7
British Ships only ..	30·1	53·2	74·9	90·8	94·7
Foreign Ships only ..	7·2	15·0	35·9	62·3	83·8

With the gradual replacement of wood and sail by iron and steam, we have come to the transition between past and present in the story of the world's shipping industry. Since the adoption of the compound engine first enabled the steamer to compete successfully with the sailing vessel in the general cargo trade, there have been many developments of great importance in shipbuilding and marine engineering; the substitution of steel for iron, which made rapid headway during the eighteen-eighties; the adoption, during the same decade, of twin screws, and the consequent abandonment of the sails which most steamers had hitherto carried, at first as an auxiliary, and later as a precaution against the breaking of a propeller shaft; the successive introduction of the triple and quadruple expansion engines and of the marine turbine; the challenge of oil to coal and the appearance of the motor-ship. With every decade, the rate of progress has accelerated. The typical passenger liner of to-day is larger, faster, and more luxurious than her counterpart of 1890 or even 1900; the typical cargo boat is better equipped with loading and discharging gear and more likely to be built with special reference to the requirements of a particular trade. All these developments have contributed to make the carriage of goods and passengers by sea quicker, safer, and cheaper. Each of them would require detailed attention in a book devoted to the history of the ship itself, or in one which traced the progress of the shipping industry by stages rather than by epochs. Their effect, however, has been merely to accelerate and emphasize tendencies which were already in operation. They have not, even in combination, brought about any such fundamental change in the character and functions of the shipping industry as was brought about by the substitution of the steamer for the sailing vessel as the general carrier of the world's trade. If Mr. W. S. Lindsay, who completed his *History of Merchant Shipping* in 1876 could read Mr. Clement Jones's account of *British Merchant Shipping*, published in 1922, he would find many terms that were new to him; while rejoicing in the fulfilment of many of his prophecies, he would be startled by the size, speed, and capacity of the vessels described; but he would have little difficulty in following the general drift of the analysis, either of shipping services or of business methods. On the other hand, Lindsay's own description, in his fourth volume, of the liner services of his own day would have been unintelligible gibberish to an eighteenth-century shipowner.

There remains, therefore, from our present point of view, only the task of endeavouring to sum up the effect of this transition on the life of the world. It has not, perhaps, been all gain. It is almost impossible to write of the passing of the sailing vessel without a sigh of regret. There are very few who, having known both, would deny that the white-winged clipper possessed not merely a beauty, but a life and personality denied to her successful rival. The steamer's capacity is determined, before her launch, in the designing-loft and the engineering yard, and between her best and her worst performance there is little variation. The sailing vessel's performance depended on luck and skill. Each ship had her own peculiarities; there were certain conditions and certain methods of handling in which and by which she would give of her best, and the men who learned to know her ways and spent themselves to get the last knot out of her, learned to love her in the process. It was not purely the innate conservatism of the seafarer that made old-timers talk of "giving up the sea and going into steam."

That is for other pens. We are concerned here with what the world has gained in material welfare from the replacement of sail by steam; not with those less tangible values that it has lost.

The difference which the steamer has made to the world depends mainly on that certainty of performance which has robbed sea-life of so much of its adventurous thrill. The clipper ship at her best could log 15 knots or more in the hour. The average cargo boat to-day can do no more than ten or twelve; but she can do it all the time, whereas the clipper might spend day after day almost motionless in the Doldrums, or lie for a fortnight, wind-bound, at the entrance to the Channel. The steamer can make a direct course between port and port; the sailing vessel was tacking all the time and might have to prolong her voyage by a thousand miles in order to take advantage of prevailing winds. The Australian clippers would sight St. Paul's Rocks, off the Brazilian coast, before "running their easting down." The steamer's outward and homeward passages are practically the same; the Black Ball Packets, as we have seen, averaged nearly twice as long on the westward as on the eastward run. As soon as the steamer has discharged her cargo and loaded another, she is ready for another voyage, and within narrow limits of fluctuation, she can repeat her record performance time after time. The sailing vessel must sail at certain seasons of the year to make her best speed, and even then her passage depended on her luck. In 1866, *Serica* came home from Foochow in 99 days; in the following year she took 120 days.

The result of all this is the power to make a greatly increased number of round voyages in the year. The steamer's advantage is greatest on the shortest tracks; but, taking an average of all trades, the annual carrying-power of a modern cargo boat is probably at least four times that of a sailing vessel of the same cargo capacity, and, owing to the great increase in the size of ships which steam has made possible, her cargo capacity is, in fact, likely to be three, four, or five times as great as that of her forerunner. A steamer of 10,000 tons dead-weight, making eight round voyages a year in the North Atlantic trade, will do in a year the work of at least ten or a dozen sailing vessels of the largest type formerly employed in that trade.

Thus the net effect of the substitution of steam for sail is that an enormously greater volume of trade can be carried without any corresponding increase in the number of ships employed; that this trade can be brought forward in a steady regular stream, instead of in seasonal rushes, and that arrangements for its reception and disposal can be made in advance, with absolute confidence in the arrival of cargoes at the time expected. Even with modern facilities for the distribution of cargoes from the ports, it would be hopelessly impossible to handle the present volume of the world's trade if it had to be carried under the conditions of the days of sail.

It was in the mail and passenger traffic that steam first made its mark, and both the increased speed and regularity of postal communication, and the increased attractiveness of travel by sea, have contributed to a multiplication of personal and business contacts between people living in distant lands which has done much for the enlargement and diffusion of ideas, and something towards the breaking down of national prejudices. Steam, too, has played an immensely important part in accelerating the peopling of the world's undeveloped territories, and thus speeding-up the development of its resources. In the ten years 1825–1834, as we have seen, an average of 32,000 emigrants left Europe annually for the United States. For the ten years immediately preceding the Great War, the average was over a million a year.

When all is said, however, it is the cargo boat, rather than the passenger liner, that has influenced most profoundly the life of the world. The increase of carrying power due to the introduction of steam has raised the standard of life in all countries. That standard is not nearly so high as we should like to see it; but we are apt to forget that discontent is a sign of progress, and that many common articles of comfort and convenience of whose high price we sometimes complain to-day were either wholly unknown a hundred years ago, or were the luxuries of a very small wealthy class. That is the work of the steamship; but the influence of steam goes deeper than that. It has converted foreign commerce from a means for the enrichment and adornment of life into a necessity of life itself. There have been many communities in the past whose power and wealth depended upon foreign trade and a very few, such as Imperial Rome, to whom sea-borne supplies were a vital necessity; but steam alone could have permitted the growth in every industrial country of vast aggregations of urban population, dependent alike for their daily bread and for the materials of the craft whereby they earn it, upon the regular delivery, week by week, of supplies running into millions of tons in the course of every year. We may or may not like all the features of the complicated industrial civilization which is fast transforming the whole world into one economic unit. One thing is certain: for good or evil it is the child of the steamship.

SOME BOOKS ON THE PERIOD

An almost bewildering number of books have been written on the last great days of sail. The author has made special use of *The Clipper Ship Era*, by Captain A. H. Clark, London and New York, 1910, and the writings of Mr. Basil Lubbock: *The China Clippers*, Glasgow, 1914, *The Colonial Clippers*, 1921, *The Blackwall Frigates*, 1922, *The Western Ocean Packets*, 1925, and *The Down Easters*, 1929. The story of the rise of steam and its development down to 1875 is fully told by Lindsay in Vol. IV of his *History of Merchant Shipping*; and more briefly by A. W. Kirkaldy in *British Shipping: its History, Organisation, and Importance*, London, 1914. For later developments see the book last named and *The British Merchant Service*, by R. J. Cornwall Jones, London, 1898. Lindsay's third volume gives a full account of the repeal of the Navigation Acts and the beginning of the Merchant Shipping Acts. For statistics see Cd. 7033, *Tables showing the Progress of Merchant Shipping*, 1913.

CHAPTER X

LINERS AND TRAMPS

THE EVOLUTION OF THE MODERN SHIPPING INDUSTRY

The British Shipping industry has come into being, not by decree, but as a result of the cumulative independent activities of men and groups of men engaged in their own concerns.

JOHN HILTON, in *Edinburgh Review*, April 1918

THE culmination of the sailing vessel in the Clipper Ship, the rise of steam, and the great expansion of the world's maritime commerce which accompanied these developments, partly as cause and partly as effect, were accompanied also by very important changes in the methods by which the ships were owned and operated. Indeed, one of the most significant of these changes, the replacement of the "constant trader" of the eighteenth century by regular liner services, had already made substantial headway before the competition of steam had become generally effective in the world's carrying trade.

The term "liner" had better be defined; for it is not always understood—partly because many owners both of steamers and of sailing vessels have called their vessels the "Such or such Line" as a mere badge of common ownership, without reference to the kind of trade in which the ships were employed. Strictly speaking, a liner service implies to-day a fleet of ships, under common ownership or management, which provide a fixed service, at regular intervals, between named ports, and offer themselves as common carriers of any goods or passengers requiring shipment between those ports and ready for transit by their sailing dates. A fixed itinerary, inclusion in a regular service, and the obligation to accept cargo from all comers and to sail, whether filled or not, on the date fixed by a published schedule; these, and not the size and speed of the ships nor the number of vessels in the fleet, are what distinguished the "liner" from the "tramp," "seeker," or "general trader"—the ship which can be hired as a whole, by the voyage or the month, to load such cargo and to carry it between such ports as the charterer may require.

It will be observed that neither the East Indiamen nor the "constant traders" of the eighteenth century were liners in the true sense of the word. The East Indiamen sailed in groups, not at regular intervals, and they were not common carriers. The "constant trader" was simply an individual ship which usually, but not necessarily always, traded between the same ports. The volume of oversea trade was not, in fact, sufficient to make the running of regular, periodical services worth while.

Obviously, the absolute regularity and certainty of the modern liner service was always impossible under sail; but as the volume of trade expanded, it began to occur to some big shipowners that, especially on routes where there were mail contracts to be obtained and a considerable passenger traffic to be carried, it would pay them to maintain in their chosen trade fleets large enough to permit of vessels being despatched at regular intervals, at any rate on the outward passage. The Black Ballers and other Yankee Packets in the first half of the nineteenth century were true ancestors of the trans-Atlantic liners of to-day.

During the last great days of sail, most of the crack ships were either liners or at least regular traders, and a large proportion of them belonged to substantial fleets. The China Tea Clippers were mostly owned in twos and threes, for the total tonnage in the trade was never very large; but the pick of the Indian trade was carried in the big fleets of the great Blackwall firms. It was in the Australian trade, however, where the flow of emigration had been quickened by the gold rush of 1851, that the development of the true liner service reached the farthest point it ever attained under sail. James Baines's Black Ball Line (not to be confused with the American packets of the same name), the White Star Line founded by Messrs. Pilkington and Wilson, George Thompson's Aberdeen White Star Line (pioneers of the wool traffic), and Bethel, Gwyn and Company's London Line of Australian Packets, were among the more important of many services, each of which provided monthly sailings from Great Britain to Australian ports. Even in the eighties and nineties, after the steamers had wrested from the clippers the bulk of the passenger traffic and it no longer paid sailing-ship owners to arrange regular monthly sailings, the bulk of the wool clippers were regular traders, belonging to big fleets whose house-flags were as familiar in Sydney Harbour or Hobson's Bay as in the Thames or Mersey.

A regular monthly service to Australia implied a fleet of at least a dozen ships, and as a Colonial Clipper might cost anything up to £30,000 or £40,000 there were very few firms who could provide such a service entirely from their own resources. Some owners chartered vessels to fill the gaps in their sailing list. Others, like James Baines, were ship brokers as well as shipowners, and could easily arrange for vessels entrusted to them for loading to carry their house-flag and fill the vacant dates. Some managing owners of lines, like Bethel, Gwyn and Company, were ship brokers first and foremost, and most of the ships which carried their flag were privately owned. Messrs. Devitt and Moore, who carried much of the Blackwall tradition into the Australian passenger trade, started as ship brokers, loading on commission, but later acquired an interest in, or bought outright, many of the ships on their list.

In these long-distance trades, even the splendid clippers of the sixties and seventies had to be content with one round voyage in the year; but their sailing powers often gave them a substantial margin, and in order not to let their freight-earning capacity lie idle, they would fill in time with an intermediate voyage. A favourite programme for the China clippers was to leave London in October or November with a general cargo for Hong Kong or Shanghai, and, after delivering it, drop down to Saigon or Bangkok to load rice either for China or Japan. Two such intermediate rice voyages were often made before putting in to Foochow or Whampoa in time to load the new season's teas, which began to arrive in May. Most of the ships in the Australian trade sailed straight out and home; but there were exceptions, such as the little Tasmanian built barque *Harriet McGregor*, whose regular round in the seventies was: Hobart to London with wool and sperm oil (sailing always on Christmas Day); London to Hobart with general cargo; Hobart to Mauritius with coal, and back to Hobart with sugar in time to load for London again by Christmas. There were, too, a good many ships, outside the regular wool fleet, which, after carrying passengers and general cargo to Melbourne or Sydney, usually put across to an Indian port, often with walers as remounts for the cavalry, and loaded jute at Calcutta or rice at Rangoon.

The collection of cargo, whether by the ships of the big clipper fleets or by their humbler sisters who knocked about the Seven Seas unhonoured and unrecorded, but doing a very large proportion of the world's carrying trade, was now a much easier matter than it had been in the eighteenth century. At the home ports there were well-established firms of ship brokers, ready to act as intermediaries between shipowner and shipper. At most of the leading foreign and colonial ports there were brokers and agents through whom cargo could be booked, or big firms of regular shippers to whom the vessel could be consigned. Thus the presence of a supercargo became less and less necessary, and the captain himself had generally little to do with the engagement of freight. His chief concern was rather with the stowage of the cargo, for the trim of a clipper ship had a great effect upon her speed, and in later days, when the sailing vessel was fighting desperately against the competition of steam, stowage became even more important from the point of view of carrying capacity. It was by minute attention to the screwing of wool cargoes into her holds that Captain Woodget of *Cutty Sark* gradually increased her cargoes from 4,289 to 5,304 bales.

In truth, the responsibilities of the masters of the clipper ships were greater, in some respects, than any men of their profession have had to carry. A very rudimentary knowledge of navigation had sufficed for the leisurely voyages of the eighteenth century. The modern liner captain has under his hand an instrument whose exact powers are ascertainable and ascertained. For the master of a Yankee Packet or California Clipper, or of a racing ship in the tea or wool trade, time was of the essence of the contract—a reputation as a quick passage maker might mean thousands of pounds to his owners and the assurance of continuous employment to himself—but a quick passage depended largely on his own exertions and abilities. It took an iron nerve to "carry sail" as Bully Waterman carried it, or to take short cuts as Robinson of *Sir Lancelot* used to take them, through the reefs and islets of the treacherous Eastern Seas. It required the nicest judgment to bring out a ship's "ghosting" qualities in light winds.

Not only consummate seamanship, but nerve and vigilance of another kind were required in the Australian emigrant trade. *Lightning's* passenger list of just over 400, or the 700 carried by the *James Baines* in 1854, may look small beside the human freight of nearly 5,000 for which the *Aquitania* was built in 1914; but then the *Aquitania* has about twenty times the tonnage of the Black Ball Liners. To keep 400 passengers, largely emigrants of the rougher class, healthy, orderly, and contented, when cooped up for two or three months in a ship measuring 244 feet long by 44 feet broad and 23 feet deep, called for no common qualities of tact and firmness, especially when a combination of hard driving and heavy weather necessitated long periods of confinement below. Captain Enright, under whom the *Lightning* attained her greatest popularity, was well worth the £1,000 a year which he astonished her owners by demanding, not only for his skill as a passage maker, but for the rare combination of authority and good humour with which he ruled the motley crowd he carried, and his constant ingenuity in devising games, concerts, dances, debates, and "rags" of all kinds for their amusement. Incidentally he was assisted by the thoughtfulness of Messrs. James Baines and Company in placing, even at this early date, a printing press on board each of their ships, for the production of a ship's newspaper.

While the performances and the commercial success of the later sailing vessels depended very much on their captains, they depended also on the technical knowledge as well as the business ability of the owners. Some of the fleets were big—the great Duncan Dunbar owned 40,000 tons of shipping, representing probably about fifty ships—but there were many owners, even of substantial fleets, who made a point of giving personal attention to the equipment, storing, and sometimes the loading of their ships. There were owners who were also merchants; the firm of Dunbar had a liquor export trade; and some of the crack China clippers were built to the order of great tea-importing firms like Jardine, Matheson and Company. A large proportion, however, were men bred to a practical knowledge of sea affairs. Some as we have seen were brokers. Others, such as Green and Money Wigram and Company, started as shipbuilders. Many of the most successful owners were retired ship-masters. Old John Willis, owner of *The Tweed*, *Lammermuir*, and other famous ships, and the hero, according to Captain Shewan, of the well-known chanty "Stormalong,"[1] had worked his way up from before the mast. His son, John Willis the younger, owner of *Cutty Sark*, had served as a master in his father's ships.

Many owners of this type, whether actually bred to the sea or not, lived as near to the docks as their wives and families would let them, and supervised personally everything that went on aboard their ships in port. It is said that old John Willis could hardly be forced away from any ship of his which was in dock, and Mr. T. B. Walker, a Chairman of Lloyd's Register, and the owner of a fleet of speedy little barques in the Tasmanian and Queensland trade, used to arrive punctually at 9.30 every morning for a tour of inspection. In the spring when most of his vessels were home, one of the recognized sights of the docks was "Mr. T. B. Walker and his Satellites"—the procession in which his captains used to escort him to West India Dock Station, to proceed to his day's work in the city.

Sometimes the members of a firm would share the work between them; each taking that part which he could do best. The Loch Line of Glasgow, for whom a score of splendid iron wool clippers were built between 1867 and 1885, was founded by two young men who had worked together in a shipowner's office. One, William Aitken, made a daily round of exporters' offices—"cruising the City for cargo" as Kelly would have said. The other, James Lilburn, personally supervised the loading and despatching of the ships.

For big business, however, money is as necessary as skill, and while it was largely by the ability and enterprise of owners who were themselves shipping experts that the extraordinary prosperity of British shipping was built up during the middle years of the nineteenth century, there were not enough of them to provide the capital required

[1] *The Great Days of Sail*, p. 45.

by the industry as a whole. With the great increase both in the number of ships required to carry the world's trade and in the size and cost of the individual ship, it had become necessary to broaden the basis of ownership, and attract into the industry the money of sleeping partners.

By the Merchant Shipping Act of 1854, the interest in every British ship was divided into sixty-four parts, and every owner of such a part was registered as a part owner of the vessel. These parts could not be subdivided, but any number of parts, from one to sixty-four, could be registered in a single name. By taking advantage of this law a group of people, many of whom might have no other connection with the sea, could arrange for the purchase or building of a ship without any one of them putting down more than a few hundred pounds, and entrust her for management to one of their number who had experience of shipping business and received a salary or a commission on freights in return for his services.

Although the owners of sixty-fourths were very often investors pure and simple, the chief members of the group were frequently men who had some connection with various aspects of the shipping business. A shipbuilder, a ship broker, a merchant with occasional shipments to send abroad, a dealer in marine stores, and a provisioning contractor, might agree together to build and operate a vessel for their joint benefit. The ship broker would probably be appointed managing owner. Each of the others would do his best for the vessel in the matter of construction, equipment, or repairs, the supply of stores or the provision of cargo, and would receive the benefit of a stimulus to his ordinary business in addition to his share of the profits on each voyage, If they did not care to put down between them the whole cost of the vessel, they could dispose of a certain number of sixty-fourths among their families, friends, and business associates.

This system applied to steamers as well as to sailing vessels; but, as we have seen, the majority of the early steamers belonged to the fleets employed in regular liner services, and these were mostly owned either by very wealthy capitalist firms or by joint-stock companies incorporated under Royal Charter. The application of the joint-stock system to shipping was a great step in advance, for it extended the field of ownership to the whole investing public. So long, however, as the liability of shareholders was unlimited, industrial investment was a very risky business, and although there was not nearly so much money lost in shipping companies, during the first half of the nineteenth century, as in railway and insurance bubbles, the risks were sufficient to restrict in practice the circle from whom capital could be drawn.

It was the passing of the Companies (Limited Liability) Act of 1862 that made the modern development of shipping possible. From that time the man with money to invest could take shares in a shipping company with the knowledge that, at the very worst, he could lose only the amount he had decided to risk; that its creditors could not come down upon any of his other assets. The circle from which the great lines could draw capital for the building up of their fleets was no longer confined to the comparatively small class of wealthy men, but embraced every man and woman in the country who had saved or inherited money, whether in large or small amounts. It would have been impossible to draw from any smaller circle the share capital, sometimes running into seven figures, of the great lines of to-day.

It is not, however, only by the great lines that the modern shipping industry has been built up. The reduction in operating costs and increase of freight-earning capacity, which followed the introduction of the compound engine, brought the steamer into competition not only with the sailing packets and the big fleets of regular traders, but with the crowd of undistinguished ships that did the dirty work of the Seven Seas.

By this time the volume of foreign commerce had entered upon a period of very rapid expansion. The great increase in the world's gold supply through the discoveries in California and Australia had given the usual stimulus to enterprise. Industry and population grew apace and the older countries required every year larger and larger supplies of foodstuffs and raw material from oversea; year by year they sent out hundreds of thousands of emigrants to assist in building up their sources of supply and the markets for their manufactures.

This affected the growth of steam shipping in two ways. In the first place, the volume of regular cargo traffic on the routes came to rival the passenger and mail traffic in importance, and during the last twenty years of the nineteenth century this was increasingly reflected in the differentiation of the liner fleets. There were the "Passenger Liners"—big, fast, and luxurious ships, of very moderate cargo capacity in proportion to their size, and only profitable to their owners by reason of the receipts from passage monies and mail contracts. There were the "Intermediate Liners" of lower speed, but greater cargo capacity, in the running of which the carriage of passengers was, at most, an important secondary consideration. Finally, there were the "Cargo Liners," built with a single eye to the carriage of goods. Some of them might carry half a dozen or a dozen passengers as a sideline, but there were already many for which no Board of Trade Passenger Certificate had been obtained, but which carried large mixed cargoes on services as regular as those of the mail boats.

The world's trade, however, was not all of a regular character. There were seasonal products, like wheat and cotton, with the rush of which the liners could not cope during the shipping season. There were ports without sufficient trade to induce owners to provide a regular service, yet where paying cargoes could often be picked up. There were rough, bulky cargoes like iron ore, coal, and timber, which were usually bought and shipped in consignments large enough to fill a fair-sized vessel, and could not be carried conveniently as part of a mixed liner cargo.

These "odd jobs" made up between them a very large proportion of the world's commerce. Some of them continued for many years to be performed by sailing vessels, but from about 1880 the sailing vessel had a very formidable rival in the tramp steamer. The superiority of steam was not, at first, so marked as in the regular services; but as soon as bunker depots had been established at all the principal ports, the steamer began to gain ground. She could make more voyages in the year; she was independent of wind and weather conditions, and the comparative certainty with which the length of her passage could be calculated made it much easier to fix charters in advance. All this gave her operations a greater elasticity and ease of adaptation to the requirements of commerce; but the full advantage of this elasticity could never have been reaped but for the linking up of the world's ports by the electric cable during the eighteen-fifties and sixties.

The invention of the submarine cable is of hardly less importance in the history of the shipping industry than the invention of the steamship. It was steam that made possible the enormous expansion in the volume of modern commerce; but the whole vast and complicated machinery by which that commerce is carried on and arrangements made for the purchase, transport, insurance, reception, and distribution of the goods, depends on the electric cable and its child, wireless. The carrying power available to us to-day would be robbed of half its value if we had to revert to conditions in which the despatch of orders, enquiries, or instructions, and the receipt of an answer took as many weeks as it now takes hours.

Apart from its general effect in facilitating the growth of commerce, the introduction of the submarine telegraph cable had a very great effect upon the technique of ship-owning. Before the days of cables, an owner was obliged to entrust the task of arranging for a return cargo or "embracing an eligible freight" for some alternative port either to the master or supercargo, as his representative, or to an agent or correspondent at the port of discharge. Unless the ship was running in a regular trade in which cargo would be automatically forthcoming, he had to leave a wide discretion to the man on the spot; for there would be little or no chance of communicating with his agent or representative before the ship was fixed. This discretion, too, could be exercised only in the light of immediate local conditions. If the ship was loaded for a direct run home, she might find the freight markets stagnant on her arrival; if a charter was accepted for an intermediate voyage, it would be matter of chance whether she could pick up at her destination a cargo for her home port. In these circumstances most ships were naturally sent out with overriding instructions which would bring them back within a limited period to their owners' immediate control.

The introduction of the electric cable brought about a complete and startling change. Henceforward an owner in London or Liverpool could keep in daily touch with the demand for shipping in every trade and in every port, and could reach the master with instructions at every port at which his vessel touched. She might be employed for years at a stretch in trading between port and port abroad, and yet remain during the whole of that period under his control.

Let us take an imaginary, but quite probable itinerary for a modern tramp. The owner has chartered her to carry rails from Middlesbrough to Calcutta. Long before she arrives he or his brokers have fixed up by cable the terms of a charter to load gunny-bags required by the Australian farmers for bagging their harvest. At Sydney, the master finds cabled instructions awaiting him, to proceed in ballast to Newcastle, N.S.W., and there load coal for Iquiqui, with the expectation of picking up a nitrate cargo at that port. The nitrate ports, however, prove to be well supplied with tonnage, and an exchange of cables brings him instructions to proceed in ballast to the River Plate, where the maize harvest will soon be coming forward and the demand is likely to be brisk. In due course the ship arrives at Buenos Aires; but freights are low, for many coal-laden ships have recently come out from Great Britain and are now ready to load a return cargo of grain, so that the supply of tonnage exceeds the demand. The ship is kept lying idle for a week or two while the owner is waiting for freights to harden; but eventually they go up a point or two and a charter is arranged, of which the master is duly advised. The charterer, however, is a trader in maize, not a consumer, and he does not yet know where he can dispose of the cargo to the best advantage; so the charter contains a clause giving him the option of ordering the ship to London, Rotterdam, or Genoa, for each of which the appropriate freight is specified. It contains also a provision that the ship will call "for orders" at St. Vincent in the Cape Verde Isles, where she will also replenish her bunkers. At St. Vincent, the master learns that the maize has been sold to Dutch importers and is to be delivered at Rotterdam. Arrived at Rotterdam he finds a charter awaiting him to load Ruhr coal (brought down the Rhine) for Genoa; and from Genoa, still in obedience to instructions received, he may cross to Algeria and load a cargo of iron ore with which, after an absence of many months, he returns at last to the Tees.

To complete the picture, it may be added that there are two other ways in which a tramp-owner can employ his ship. He may lease her out for a period of three, six, or twelve months, to a Time Charterer, who can use her during this period (subject to any special restrictions in the Charter-party) in such trades as he may think fit. Or, more rarely, a tramp may be "placed on the berth" for a particular port; that is to say she is advertised as sailing for that port on a specified date, and open in the same way as a liner to receive offers of cargo from shippers or their agents.

It will be seen that the ownership of tramp shipping is a very different matter from the running of a liner service. The maintenance of a regular service requires a fleet of some size. It requires also the services of big shore staffs; for in obtaining a quick turn round for ships carrying large mixed cargoes, the work done in the office and the docks is as important as the ships themselves. Further, the liner is not filled like the tramp by the goods of a single charterer, but by "parcels" received from hundreds of different shippers, and in order to keep their vessels fully employed the big lines have had to build up branch offices or agencies at every foreign port at which their ships touch, and even at inland centres where passengers or cargo can be booked. All this involves a very heavy outlay, and although some of the great lines, like the Cunard itself, started as private concerns, they have grown inevitably into huge companies with a capital of which a great part, at least, has been subscribed by the investing public.

The tramp-owner is in a very different position. Every voyage is a separate adventure; every tramp steamer is a self-contained competitive unit. No elaborate organization is required to run her. All that is needed is access to the offices of the cable companies and to the freight markets, such as the Baltic Exchange in St. Mary Axe, the world's chief centre both for the chartering of tramp tonnage and for the sale of bulk cargoes.[1] The qualities required for success are practical knowledge of shipping, iniatitive, readiness to take risks, and a watchful eye on working expenses, rather than the financial acumen and power of organization required in liner management. Hence while many general traders are owned in big fleets by companies with large subscribed capital, it is perfectly possible, when times are good, for a retired ship-master, or a small ship broker with a few thousands saved, to purchase a single second-hand vessel, and go into the business with a fair chance of making money.

In the early days of the steam cargo-boat most tramps were owned either by individuals or private firms, or by small syndicates formed on the sixty-fourth system; but as the cost of shipping rose, with the steady increase in the average size and speed of ships and the complexity of the gear required for competitive efficiency, it became more and more common for even single vessels to be owned by small limited companies, whose capital was often provided mainly by the associates or townsfolk of the promoters. These promoters were usually the Managing Owners of the vessels. Although it had become necessary to broaden the basis of investment, skill and experience were as much as ever required in the running of the ships, and a firm which had proved successful in the operation of its own vessels, might find itself, in due course, the Managing Owner for the ships belonging to half a dozen small companies, each of which owned a single ship or a little group of tramps. As under the sixty-fourth system, the Managing Owners were usually remunerated by a commission either on gross freights or on net profits, and they usually

[1] The Baltic Shipping Exchange was opened in 1883; but its functions had long been performed, in a less highly organized form, by the Baltic Coffee House.

held office under a contract which made them practically irremovable.

Although the development of the tramp steamer was much later than that of the liner services, it was by the tramp rather than by the liner that the sailing vessel was finally ousted from her position as the carrier of the great bulk cargoes, and by the end of the nineteenth century, the volume of tramp tonnage had outstripped that of the liner fleets. There were already signs, however, of a swing back of the pendulum. Many trades originally opened up by the occasional voyages of tramps or sailing vessels had increased to a point at which it became profitable to put on a regular, periodical service. With the steady increase in the world's demand for foodstuffs and raw materials, and the growth of storage facilities at the ports of shipment, the liners began to take a larger share in the carriage of seasonal products. Some companies found it worth their while to augment their fleets by chartering tramp tonnage during the rush season; others maintained larger permanent fleets, and during the quieter months placed their unemployed vessels on the freight markets to seek a charter in any trade where demand was brisk.

Yet even with the greater elasticity given by these methods to the regular services, no purely liner organization could serve the needs of modern commerce. The trade of ports specializing in the shipment of one heavy bulk product such as ore, coal, nitrate, or timber, and doing little general traffic, is always unsuitable for liner services, more especially if the imports are also restricted in character, as at the great coal ports in this country, where ore and pit-props comprise the bulk of the inwards cargoes. In order to adjust the supply of bulky imports of universal consumption, such as grain, to local demands, occasional deliveries must be made to ports which are not the home port of any regular line. The world's seasonal products do not all come forward at the same time; even in a single commodity such as wheat, there are wide divergencies between the dates of the harvests in the chief producing countries. Again, the exportable surplus of wheat, or maize, or sugar available at the chief shipping centres varies from year to year according to the yield of the crop; the demands of importing countries for foodstuffs and raw materials vary according to their own production and the state of trade. A bumper crop or a bad harvest in Canada or Argentina; a good or bad cereal year in Continental Europe; a boom or a slump in the iron and steel industries of Great Britain and Germany, may mean a difference of millions of tons in the trade to be carried on a particular route.

In order that the available carrying power may be adjusted, quickly, easily, and economically, to these wide fluctuations both in the aggregate annual demand and in its distribution between route and route, it is essential that the regular services should be supplemented by the existence of a world-pool of tonnage, composed of ships tied to no particular trade and no particular route, and upon which all countries can freely draw to meet the requirements of the moment.

This world-pool of tonnage is composed of ships of all nationalities, but always a large proportion of them have been British; for under the British flag the proportion of tramps has always been high. It is estimated that in 1914 they comprised about two-thirds of the ocean-going steamers on United Kingdom Register and about 60 per cent. of the tonnage. Of the total tonnage about 40 per cent. was engaged in trading between ports abroad, and in this trade the proportion of tramp tonnage rose to 75 per cent.

The vessels so engaged have sometimes been spoken of as "lost to British trade." This is a very silly delusion. Apart from their value as a sort of floating reserve of tonnage which can be called back into United Kingdom trade to meet any emergency of war or peace, their services have been as valuable, economically, to Great Britain as to the world in general. The typical tramp whose imaginary itinerary we sketched a few pages back was not directly engaged in "British trade" when she was carrying maize from the Plate to Rotterdam; but she was helping to swell that net balance of freights which is among the leading credit items in our trade balance; she was helping to build up one of our chief sources of supply and one of the leading markets for British products, and she was helping to earn dividends for the British investors in Argentine railways, whose leading source of revenue is the carriage of grain to the ports. To a nation of traders and investors, no services can be reckoned as "lost" which are helping to develop the world's resources, to expand its purchasing power, and to facilitate the exchange of products.

SOME BOOKS ON THE PERIOD

There are a great many valuable details about sailing-ship ownership and management scattered about Basil Lubbock's books cited in the note to Chapter IX. *The Great Days of Sail*, by Captain Andrew Shewan, London, 1927, may be mentioned for its picture of old John Willis and his methods, and its account of the China tea trade by one who had actually commanded a clipper ship. Kirkcaldy's *British Shipping* gives perhaps the best short summary of developments in ownership and management covering the whole period. See also the Note to Chapter XI.

CHAPTER XI

COMPETITION AND COMBINATION

THE ORGANIZATION OF MODERN SHIPPING

Flaunt out, O sea, your separate flags of nations!
WALT WHITMAN

THE evolution of the modern shipping industry has been described, in the last two chapters, mainly from the point of view of British shipping. This involves no treachery to our title; for the predominance acquired by British shipping towards the close of the eighteenth century, and regained or confirmed at the time of the transition from sail to steam has, on the whole, been retained, and what has happened under the Red Ensign may fairly be taken as typical of what was happening under other flags.

It was inevitable, nevertheless, that as conditions in Europe became more stable, and the Continental countries began to make up the leeway in the development of their resources, they should gain ground also in the carrying trade, and by the beginning of the present century, international competition at sea had become desperately keen. This was no new thing; but whereas, in the eighteenth century, international rivalry had mostly taken the form of legislative restrictions on the carrying trade, and armed conflicts for the possession of trades and markets which could be brought under such regulation, the maritime rivalries of the later nineteenth century were carried on by peaceful means and in an open field. They took the form of competition in efficiency, which was all to the good, and of rate-cutting competition, the effects of which were sometimes very bad.

In the tramp trades, the Scandinavians, especially the

Norwegians, were formidable competitors. The Norwegians are born shipowners, and have developed the shipping industry for its own sake to a degree rare among Continental peoples; that is to say, they have long maintained a fleet much larger than is required for the purposes of their own commerce, and a large proportion of their ships are always busily seeking charters in the world's general carrying trade—a fact which proved of first-rate importance to ourselves and our Allies during the Great War. They were rather late in "going into steam"—Norway is almost the only country whose sailing tonnage continued steadily to increase down to 1890, and many fine British clippers ended their days under the Norwegian flag—but when they did make the change, they showed themselves to be peculiarly enterprising and successful in the operation of tramp steamers. The Greeks, too, running cheaply acquired second-hand tonnage on cheap lines, were often able to undercut the owners of British tramps in the Mediterranean freight markets.

German, French, Italian, Dutch, and American owners turned their attention mainly to the liner trades, although the Italians have a good many of their own tramps employed in carrying their imports of coal and cereals, and in France there was a rather remarkable recrudescence of the big sailing vessel during the early years of the twentieth century.[1]

In the liner as well as in the tramp trades, competition was keen; for the big lines, with their numerous ports of call, and their widespread agency organization, collected cargo and passengers from many countries. The great German lines, in particular, efficient, well organized, and working in close association with each other, with the banks, and with the State Railways, made their com-

[1] After diminishing rapidly from 918,000 tons net in 1870 to 444,000 tons in 1890, French sailing tonnage actually rose to 676,000 in 1905.

petition felt by British liner companies in every sea. It is an illustration both of their tendency to form big units, and of their aggressive methods, that ten lines which owned, just before the war, over 60 per cent. of the tonnage under the German flag, were members of a single association, with a joint reserve or pool of tonnage, on which any member of the group could call for the purposes of rate-wars.

Thus both in the tramp and the liner trades, British shipping was called upon to fight hard in order to maintain its supremacy, and it must be added that much of the competition to which it was subjected was lavishly aided by foreign Governments. Although the general principle of the Navigation Acts had broken down abroad as well as in Great Britain, many countries reserved their coasting trade to their own ships, and some of them, notably France, Russia, and the United States, extended the definition of "coasting trade" to include traffic with distant possessions, so that a voyage from Odessa to Vladivostok, from Marseilles to Saigon, or from New York to Honolulu would be covered by the reservation. Apart from this, direct encouragement to national shipping was given in all sorts of ways; such as shipbuilding bounties on tonnage constructed, navigation bounties on mileage run, repayment of Suez Canal dues, the imposition of differential dues on goods carried in foreign ships, and the grant of special rates on State Railways for goods to be shipped in national vessels.

It is extremely doubtful whether all the millions so lavished by foreign Governments were well spent. Navigation bounties were a peculiarly questionable investment, as tending to keep old and inefficient tonnage on the Register long after it should have been broken up. It is an unquestionable fact, and it may be a significant one, that some of the most highly subsidized liner services were notoriously inefficient, and were unable, even with a high subsidy, to pay respectable dividends to their shareholders. On the other hand, the highly subsidized Japanese lines made profits so large that they could have distributed a handsome dividend even without the subsidy, which thus became a sheer gift from the nation to the shipowners.

In the main, it was not in the countries where shipping received the most aid from the State that it gave the best returns to investors, nor was it the ships in receipt of large direct subsidies that proved the most formidable competitors of British shipping. Dutch and Danish shipowners, who received little assistance from the State, were exceptionally prosperous, and the mail subventions received by the big German lines were mere payment for services rendered. The practices of which British owners chiefly complained were measures not of direct subsidy but of flag discrimination; differential dues in some foreign ports, the differential rates granted by the German State Railways, and the abuse of the Emigrant Control Stations on the German frontier to compel emigrants to travel by German lines, as a condition of the right of passage through Germany.

In Great Britain, with very rare exceptions, the State gave no financial assistance whatever to the shipowners. Tramp shipping had never been subsidized by the British Government, and the postal subventions granted to the mail lines had long ceased to be anything more than fair payment for the work done. Down to 1902, a comparatively small number of fast liners were in receipt of Admiralty subventions to cover the cost of compliance with the regulations for ships capable of serving in war as Armed Merchant Cruisers, but a Parliamentary Inquiry in that year showed that the majority of the larger and faster liners complied, irrespective of subsidy, with the Admiralty's requirements, and the practice was generally discontinued. By 1914 the only ships receiving any kind of assistance from the British Government were the Cunard cracks, *Mauretania* and *Lusitania*, and Messrs. Elders and Fyffes's West Indian fruit-ships, to whom a subsidy had been granted in 1897, in the hope of relieving the distress caused by the collapse of the market for cane-sugar.

In so far, therefore, as it held its own, British shipping did so strictly on its merits, backed by the natural advantages of its position. The central situation of Great Britain, rendering its ports natural entrepôts for the world's trade; an indented coast-line bringing the great centres of production within easy reach of the ports; abundant coal supplies to furnish the motive power of industry and provide shipping itself with cheap bunkers, and with outward cargoes for the tramps; the demands of a dense and rapidly growing population for foodstuffs and raw materials; the accumulation of capital in a small country and the employment of the surplus in shipping, in commerce, and in foreign investment —all these things, and the aptitudes derived from them, counted for much more in maintaining the status of the British Mercantile Marine than any subsidy system could have done. In June 1914, British tonnage (including ships registered in the Dominions and Colonies) accounted for 45·2 per cent. of the world's steam tonnage.[1] What is even more significant, it is estimated that it carried one-half of the total volume of the world's sea-borne trade. By values, its total share was 52 per cent.; it carried 92 per cent. of the trade between the various countries of the Empire; 63 per cent. of the trade between the Empire and foreign countries, and 30 per cent. of the trade between countries outside the Empire.

Of the other Powers, Germany had shot up into second place, and while her steam tonnage was still only a quarter of that under the Red Ensign, it was more than two and a half times as great as that of any other country with the exception of the United States, whose position as third on the list was mainly due to the very large volume of shipping

[1] For the United Kingdom alone, the figure was 41·6 per cent.

employed in the Great Lakes and coasting trade. If the Great Lakes shipping be excluded, the United States would fall into an intermediate group, comprising Norway, France, Japan (whose meteoric rise to prominence was a feature of the opening years of the twentieth century), Holland, and Italy. These were followed at an appreciable distance by Austria-Hungary, Sweden, Spain, Greece, and Denmark. The fleets of the remaining Powers were of comparatively small importance.[1]

If international competition had failed to deprive British shipping of its predominant position in world trade, it had, nevertheless, had a very marked effect on the prosperity of the industry, and an equally marked indirect effect on methods of operation, by intensifying the competitive element which is always strong in the carrying trade. The extreme elasticity of tramp shipping, the ease with which new-comers can establish themselves, and the very wide fluctuations of demand, make the ownership of tramp steamers one of the most speculative of all forms of legitimate business. A boom in trade or a demand for shipping for military transport (as during the South African War) would quickly produce a disproportion between supply and demand; sending freights soaring upwards. In the hope of sharing the profits of the boom, owners hastened to increase

[1] Disregarding American and Canadian ships on the Great Lakes, and also (as obsolescent and inefficient) wooden and composite steamers, the percentages of the world's gross steam tonnage owned by the various Powers in July 1914 may be grouped as follows:

A. British Empire, 47·7 (United Kingdom, 44·4).
B. Germany, 12·0.
C. Norway, 4·5; France, 4·5; U.S.A., 4·3; Japan, 3·9; Holland, 3·5; Italy, 3·4.
D. Austria-Hungary, 2·5; Sweden, 2·3; Spain, 2·1; Greece, 1·9; Denmark, 1·8.
E. All othei Powers, 5·6.

See *Brassey's Naval and Shipping Annual*, 1924, pp. 207–209.

their fleets and new owners came into the business. The world's tonnage was rapidly increased to a figure beyond its normal requirements, and the short-lived boom was usually followed by a prolonged slump. During the thirty years preceding the Great War, *Fairplay's* Index Figure of homeward freights varied between the extremes of 125 and 58, and outward freights between 119 and 50. Between 1898 and 1913, inclusive, the price of a new ready cargo-steamer of 7,500 tons dead-weight, varied from a maximum of over £60,000 to a minimum of £36,000. A great deal of money was made during the good years by tramp ship-owners; but during the bad years a great deal was lost, especially by companies who were sufficiently imprudent to forget that shipping is a wasting asset, and continued to distribute dividends out of earnings that should have been devoted to writing off the depreciation of their fleets.

The liner trades were somewhat less affected by variations of demand, and liner rates, which are fixed for a definite period in advance, were not subject to so feverish a fluctuation as tramp freights; but they were, perhaps, even more affected by international competition. In the North Atlantic passenger trade, the competition for "The Blue Riband of the Atlantic" proved a very costly form of advertisement, and this competition in speed was accompanied on the one hand by an almost insane increase in the luxury of the accommodation provided for first-class passengers, and on the other by a process of rate-cutting in the emigrant traffic which left little if any profit on the average voyage.

While it was in the tramp trade that freights and profits fluctuated most widely, the liner companies were especially sensitive to rate-cutting competition. Their whole existence depended on the goodwill derived from the regularity of their services. Whether laden down to their marks or half-empty, the ships must sail on the appointed dates; they could not be held back for a rising market; they could not be diverted at will from unprofitable to profitable routes; only a small proportion could be laid up to wait for better times—for at least a skeleton of the regular services must always be maintained. In good times or bad the heavy overhead charges of the companies' organization at home or abroad must be provided for.

Thus, to the liner companies, an assured minimum revenue was an absolute necessity, and their effort to secure it led to two very notable developments in the technique of shipowning. The first of these was the process of bringing many lines "under one umbrella," either by direct purchase—the absorption of one line in another; by the formation of great combines, in which each line retained its separate directorate, house-flag, and services, while the financial results of the year's operations were pooled; or by the exchange of large blocks of shares between lines, each of which thus obtained an interest in the prosperity of the other. These various forms of merger, partial, or complete, all had the same objects—the reduction of competition, economy in services and in administration, and the spreading of risks by giving a single ownership an interest in more than one trade. The outstanding example of this process, in British shipping just before the war, was the great combine headed by the Royal Mail, which united in one group most of the lines in the South American, West Indian, and African trades.

The other method adopted to reduce rate-cutting competition was the formation of the Liner Conferences. The Liner Conference is simply an association of lines engaged in a particular trade for the purpose of regulating freights in that trade. The lines remain quite independent; there is no financial merger, and the grouping is by trades, not by ownership. The lines comprised in a big combine may each be members of a separate Conference; a single Conference may comprise lines belonging to several combines, and owned in several countries. The only tie between them is an agreement to charge the same freights for the carriage of each class of goods between the ports they jointly serve. Sometimes, though not always, they agree also as to a demarcation of interests; that is to say, they agree as to the ports to be served, or the number of sailings to be announced by each line, or the maximum percentage of the total trade for which each may compete; but an agreed schedule of rates is the essential link.

The most questionable feature of the Conferences, adopted almost from the start, was the system of "deferred rebates" used to tie shippers to the Conference lines. By this system, a shipper who had shipped his goods exclusively by the Conference lines during a fixed period, say six months, would be credited with a refund of 5 or 10 per cent. on the freights paid; but this refund would not be payable until the conclusion of the following half-year, and would be forfeited if, in the meantime, he had shipped even a single consignment by a vessel belonging to an owner outside the Conference.

The obvious objection to the Conference system was that it tended to give the Conference lines, especially when their position was strengthened by use of the rebate weapon, a monopoly of the trade concerned, which might be used to extort freights in excess of the economic value of their services. On the other hand, the companies argued that it would be impossible to provide the regular, adequate, and efficient services demanded by shippers, unless the lines were assured of a sufficient volume of traffic to render the services profitable; and that it was better for trade that freights should be fixed and held at a reasonably remunerative level, than that they should be subject to the sudden, violent fluctuations characteristic of rate wars.

The monopoly, of course, could never be complete. It was limited, theoretically if not always practically, by the possibility of new lines breaking into the trade; and so far as all bulk cargoes were concerned, it was limited by the actual or potential competition of the tramp. Mainly as the result of tramp competition, a large proportion of the homewards trades were always free from Conference regulation. In the outward trades, Conference agreements covered the greater part of the shipments to South America, Africa, India, Australasia, and the Far East, with the exception, of course, of coal and some other rough, bulky exports which were handled by tramp shipping. The North Atlantic Conference was concerned only with the regulation of the outwards passenger traffic.

On a general view of the evidence, often highly contradictory, put forward by shipowners and shippers, it seems reasonable to accept the conclusion of the Royal Commission on Shipping Rings, 1909, that while the monopolistic tendencies of the Conference system required to be carefully watched by the State, there was little or no evidence of the system having been used, in practice, to lay unfair burdens on commerce. Its general effect was to keep liner rates a little above tramp freights when times were bad, and a little below them when times were good.[1]

The tendency towards more elaborate organization of the shipping industry which produced the big combines and the Liner Conferences, and gave the tramp trades the Baltic Exchange as the chief headquarters for the world's chartering, was reflected also by the establishment of the Liverpool Steam Ship Owners' Association in 1858, and the development, from the General Shipowners' Society, of the Chamber of Shipping of the United Kingdom in 1878. To the latter were affiliated a large number of Local Shipowners' Associations and of Protection and Indemnity

[1] It is a curious instance of the general lack of knowledge of shipping affairs that the great rise in freights during the war was often attributed to the action of "shipping rings," although regulated freights rose, in fact, much less than open market freights.

Clubs, formed to give insurance on a mutual basis against third-party risks and legal expenses. By 1914 almost every important shipowner in the country, other than those who had joined the Liverpool Association was a member, direct or through his local association, of the Chamber of Shipping, and the heads of these two great bodies were thus able to speak for and pledge the industry as a whole in all negotiations with the State or with the representatives of other industries; a fact which greatly facilitated the control of shipping during the Great War. With regard to all matters of legislation they acted jointly through the Shipowners' Parliamentary Committee, on which both were represented.

Something more will be said of these two great Associations in the final chapter of this book; but for the moment they must give place to two other Societies which, while primarily concerned with the allied business of marine insurance rather than with shipping, have exercised a very strong influence on the development of the industry. We have already said something of the origin of Lloyd's. The story of how this association of underwriters became, during the Revolutionary and Napoleonic Wars, the chief channel by which shipping intelligence reached the Admiralty, and by consequence, the chief spokesman of the shipping interest in its relations with the Government; of its incorporation in 1870, and of all its multifarious activities, has been told in the *History of Lloyd's*, and there is no space here even to summarize it. We are concerned only with the influence of Lloyd's on the shipping industry, considered in its broadest aspects.

Lloyd's, as an institution, has no ostensible functions other than the provision of facilities for underwriting and the regulation of the underwriters' business with a view to establishing the credit of the whole body of underwriters by ensuring the maximum security to the assured; but in discharging these functions it has created for itself and cheerfully accepted responsibilities of national and international importance. The provision of cheap, prompt, and above all safe insurance for ships and cargoes is, in itself, an essential part of the mechanism by which the vast commerce of to-day is carried on, and while the market is now shared by the great marine insurance companies (all of them subscribers to Lloyd's) it may fairly be claimed that it was Lloyd's who led the way and set the standard. This, however, is not all. For the convenience of its members Lloyd's maintains some 1,500 Agents and Sub-Agents all over the world, whose primary function is to protect the interests of underwriters in cases of casualty or salvage, but whose services have always been freely placed at the disposal of British ship-masters in foreign ports. From these Agents also, and from about 150 Signal Stations on prominent headlands at home and abroad, Lloyd's receives by cable or wireless, daily and almost hourly news of the arrivals, departures, and movements of shipping in all ports and seas, as well as of casualties and salvages; this information being made available to the general public through the medium of *Lloyd's List*. The importance to underwriters of this unique system of shipping intelligence needs no emphasis, and it has contributed very largely to the position of London as the world's chief marine insurance centre. It has been of equal importance in the defence and control of shipping in time of war, and in the conduct of the shipowners' business in times of peace.

There is something more. The underwriter's main interest in shipping is that the number of disasters to ships and cargoes should be reduced to a minimum. Many causes have combined in modern times to reduce progressively the risks of maritime adventure—the progress of shipbuilding and engineering science; the regulations as to construction, equipment, manning, and stowage, laid down under the British Merchant Shipping Acts and corresponding legislation abroad; the survey and charting of all seas by the British and foreign Admiralties; better lighting and buoying of the coasts, and more stringent regulations as to pilotage. In most of these movements Lloyd's have co-operated by assistance or advice, and in matters more strictly within their own sphere they have had much to do with amendments of the marine insurance laws, which have gradually stamped out the fraudulent casting away of ships and cargoes which was rampant at the beginning of the nineteenth century and not unknown in later times; but their biggest contribution to the safety of life and property afloat was, undoubtedly, their share in the founding of Lloyd's Register in 1834, as a direct descendant of the society of underwriters who had published a Register Book in the mid-eighteenth century.

The Society of Lloyd's Register, though a wholly independent institution, is thus an offshoot of Lloyd's, which is strongly represented on its Committee, in common with other bodies representative of marine insurance, shipbuilding and marine engineering, shipping, and commerce. Its sole function is to assist the underwriter in his assessment of risks by publishing annually a Register Book containing a description of all sea-going vessels, British or foreign, and by assigning to those ships whose owners desire it, a "class" symbol indicating their efficiency. Here again, however, the service of the underwriters' interests has become a service to the world at large. In order to obtain cheap and ready insurance it is practically essential that a ship should be classed either by Lloyd's Register, by its only British rival, The British Corporation for the Survey and Registry of Shipping, founded at Glasgow in 1890, or by one of the corresponding Classification Societies abroad, such as the Bureau Veritas. In order to obtain classification, the ship must be built and equipped under the supervision and to the satisfaction of the Society's surveyors, from materials which they have tested, and in accordance with regulations which the Society has laid down. In order to retain its class, the ship must be periodically surveyed, for the purpose of ascertaining that the condition of hull and equipment is satisfactory.

In addition to this self-assumed responsibility for securing a high standard of construction and equipment, Lloyd's Register, the British Corporation, and the British Committee of the Bureau Veritas were entrusted by the Board of Trade, in 1890, with the task of assigning loadlines to British ships. We have seen traces of this principle in the Venetian Statutes of the Middle Ages, but the fierce national rivalries and hard commercialism of the seventeenth and eighteenth centuries, and the earlier part of the nineteenth, had blinded men's eyes to considerations of safety and humanity. States were more concerned with promoting, often by mistaken means, the interests of shipowners, than with enforcing their obligations to the public they served and the men who served them. Unfortunately there were some owners whose greed for freights or for more dubious forms of gain stood in sore need of restraint. The great shipping boom in the middle years of the nineteenth century offered opportunities to such men which they were quick to seize, and drew others into the business, and it was widely alleged that many ships were sent to sea ill-found, grossly overloaded, and sometimes overinsured, so that their total loss would represent a profit to the owners. The chief mover in this agitation against "coffin-ships" was Mr. Samuel Plimsoll, M.P. for Derby, and it was mainly as a result of his efforts that a Royal Commission on Unseaworthy Ships was appointed in 1874. On the recommendation of this Committee an Act was passed in 1876, by which shipowners were required to place, on each side of their vessels, a conspicuous mark—popularly known as "the Plimsoll Mark"—to indicate the greatest depth to which the ship could safely be loaded, and the Board of Trade were authorized to detain any vessel loaded below her marks. The responsibility of fixing the load-line was fixed upon the shipowner; for no formula of general application could be devised at the time; but the publication by Lloyd's Register, in 1882, of a series of reserve buoyancy tables assisted to put the matter on a scientific basis, and by 1890, as we have seen, it became possible for the Board of Trade to assume a responsibility which they promptly delegated to the great Classification Societies.

It is not creditable to the shipowners of the eighteen-seventies that Mr. Plimsoll's name was for many years a byword in shipping circles, though it must be admitted that he injured his own cause by his undiscriminating attacks upon shipowners as a whole. That there were some who could appreciate the value of his work, even before its final triumph, was shown in 1873, when the crack new wool clipper of the Aberdeen White Star Line was christened by the name of the great agitator, whose frock-coated and top-hatted effigy she bore as her figurehead. He did much for the British seaman; he left much to be done, as for instance, in eliminating the danger caused by excessive deck-loads—a problem which had found legal occupation, for Demosthenes, and with which the Board of Trade were still wrestling in the early years of the twentieth century.

In their efforts to raise both the standard of safety and the standard of working conditions afloat, the Board of Trade frequently found themselves, during the last quarter of the nineteenth century, at loggerheads with the shipowners. They were accused of cramping the development of the industry by laying down hard-and-fast rules which, in effect, punished the whole industry for the sins of a small minority, and of hampering British shipping in international competition, by imposing restrictions from which foreign ships were free, even in British ports. There was force in these complaints, and they were ultimately met by the Merchant Shipping Act of 1906, which swept away many obsolete rules, and applied the bulk of the British safety regulations to foreign vessels using ports in the United Kingdom. The creation, at the same time, of the Merchant Shipping Advisory Committee, on which shipowners, seamen, and shipbuilders were represented, provided a permanent link between the Board and the industry which went far to ensure better relations in the future.

On the whole, the British Mercantile Marine had, at the moment when it was called upon to face the supreme test of the Great War, much of which to be proud, and little of which it need be ashamed, so far as commercial efficiency and safety of life and property were concerned. It had less reason for complacency as regards the treatment of the men who manned the ships. Since the *régime* of the Navigation Acts had been succeeded by that of the Merchant Shipping Acts, a great deal had been done to ensure the sailor fair conditions of engagement, protection from crimps and sharks, facilities for saving, and proper medical attention; but his quarters, especially on tramps and sailing vessels, were too often miserably rough, and grossly inadequate as regards floor and air space and sanitation. The standard of diet, as laid down by the later Merchant Shipping Acts, was a vast improvement on anything the sailor had previously received; but even when the regulations were strictly adhered to and the food was of good quality, it was apt to be spoiled by rough-and-ready cooking. One of the most needed reforms introduced by the great Merchant Shipping Act of 1906, was the provision for the carriage of certificated cooks on all ocean-going vessels; but it took, of course, some years before the supply of trained cooks was equal to the demand.

The seamen's life, especially on small ships, has inevitable elements of hardness, and landsmen's criticisms of conditions afloat are sometimes vitiated by ignorance as well as by sentimentality; but the repeated protests made by the Medical and Sanitary officers at the ports, and other first-hand witnesses, leave no doubt that the general conditions of employment afloat down to 1914 were often unworthy of a great and expanding industry. Unfortunately, it must be added that, while the average conditions under some foreign flags were much worse than under the Red Ensign, British ships did not in this, as in other respects, take pride of place amongst the world's mercantile fleets. The grim records of the *Return of Deaths of Seamen and Fishermen* show that, during a period of eleven years from 1901–1902 to 1911–1912, inclusive, the death-rate by disease (excluding shipwreck and accident) among the crews of British trading vessels varied from a worst record of 1 in 207 in 1905–1906, to a best record of 1 in 269 in 1909–1910. This high death-rate was no doubt due in part to the exposure incident to the sailors' calling (though it is noteworthy that in almost every year the mortality was, comparatively, heavier on board steamers than among the crews of sailing vessels); but bad food, cramped, damp, and dirty quarters, and the careless living bred of bad conditions must bear a large share of the blame.

Wages were low in comparison with other occupations, even when the food, accommodation, and medical attendance provided are taken into account. Moreover, the actual cash wages varied not merely between trade and trade but as between one home port and another. The most commonly prevailing rates per month for A.B.'s on foreign-going vessels (neglecting figures which are exceptionally high or exceptionally low for the year) were as stated in the table on p. 288.

Firemen's wages in 1914 varied from 105s. to 120s. In a typical 4,000-ton cargo boat, the Master would receive £22, the Chief Engineer £20, and the Chief Mate £12 10s. per month. In the coasting trade, the usual rate for an A.B. was about 35s. a week, the men finding their own food.

	1880	1890	1900	1910	1914
In sailing vessels ..	50s. to 55s.	60s. to 70s.	60s. to 65s.	60s.	—
In steamships ..	55s. to 70s.	80s. to 95s.	70s. to 90s.	70s. to 90s.	100s. to 110s.

It will be noted that in 1914 the seamen's wages, thanks perhaps to the efforts of the National Sailors and Firemen's Union and the great seamen's strike of 1911, were appreciably higher than at the opening of the twentieth century. Moreover, working conditions were distinctly on the upgrade, thanks to the provisions of successive Merchant Shipping Acts; thanks also to the fine example set by many owners, who needed no prodding to keep them up to their duties, and went, of their own free will, well beyond their legal obligations. One noteworthy result of this improvement in pay and conditions was an increasing proportion of British seamen among the crews.

There had always been many foreigners among the crews of British ships. Even under the Navigation Laws a fourth of the crew might be of foreign origin, and this proportion was often exceeded in time of war. Indeed, the seafaring community is inevitably cosmopolitan, for many crews are discharged or engaged in foreign ports, where it would be difficult or impossible to pick up a purely national complement. The comparative conditions of life ashore and afloat are another big factor. The American clippers were manned mainly by British and Europeans, because native Americans, during the forties and fifties, could make more money and make it more easily in other occupations. So, too, during the last few years of the nineteenth century there was a decline in the proportion of British seamen in British ships, because the pay and conditions attracted good and steady men more readily from countries with a lower standard of life. This increase in the foreign element reached its height in 1903, when, excluding Lascars and other Asiatics employed in ships trading in or to Eastern waters, there were very nearly 23 foreigners employed in British ships for every 100 British. From this date, owing to the improvements already recorded it showed a substantial decline. The following figures will trace its rise and fall sufficiently:

Year	Number of British Employed	Number of Foreigners Employed	Proportion of Foreigners to 100 British	Number of Lascars Employed	Grand Total
1880	169,692	23,280	13·72	?	—
1890	186,147	27,227	14·63	22,734	236,108
1895	180,074	32,335	17·96	28,077	240,486
1903	176,520	40,396	22·88	41,021	257,937
1907	194,848	37,694	19·35	44,604	277,146
1912	208,635	30,960	14·84	47,211	286,806

Despite the improvements in pay and conditions the relations between employers and employed in the merchant service were not happy in 1914. The employers were grouped together in the Shipping Federation (1891) and the Liverpool Employers' Association (corresponding respectively to the Chamber of Shipping and the Liverpool Steam Ship Owners' Association). The Imperial Merchant Service Guild and other bodies represented the deck officers. The Marine Engineers had an association of their own; but many of them were members of the Amalgamated Society of Engineers. The catering department was represented by the National Union of Ships' Cooks, Stewards, Butchers, and Bakers, but also contributed members to the National

Sailors and Firemen's Union (1889) which, since the strike of 1911, had absorbed or crushed out most of the small local unions which previously existed at the ports, and now claimed to represent 90 per cent. of the organized lower-deck ratings, though there was also a large amount of non-Union labour, mainly foreigners and Asiatics.

The Officers' Associations stood, as a rule, equally aloof from those representing the employers, and from the lower-deck Unions. Both of these were essentially fighting bodies. At Liverpool there was a Seafarers' Joint Committee which provided machinery for conciliation, but the Shipping Federation and the National Sailors and Firemen's Union were uncompromisingly hostile to each other. The strike of 1911 had left a legacy of bitter bad blood on both sides, and it was matter of common knowledge that both sides were building up their resources and improving their organization with a view to a fight to the finish.

SOME BOOKS ON THE PERIOD

For a general account of the Shipping Industry just before the Great War, see Kirkcaldy's *British Shipping* (especially for ownership, regulation, organization, and the economic side of the industry); *Ocean Trade and Shipping*, by Sir Douglas Owen, Cambridge, 1914 (very full on chartering, ship's papers, and marine insurance), and *Ocean Traffic and Trade*, by B. Olney ✓ Hough, London and Chicago, 1914. *British Merchant Shipping*, by Clement Jones, London, 1922, gives an invaluable and very readable description of the shipping industry from within, and is probably the best account, for the general reader, of shipping as a business. For the Plimsoll agitation, see Lindsay, Vol. III. For shipping statistics and wages see Cd. 7033. Other Parliamentary Papers freely used in these chapters are H.C. 385 *of* 1902, *Report from the Select Committee on Steamship Subsidies*, Cd. 4668, *Report of the Royal Commission on Shipping Rings*, 1909,

Cd. 6629, *Return of the Deaths of Seamen and Firemen*, 1913, and Cd. 6899, *Report on Bounties and Subsidies in respect of Shipping and Navigation in Foreign Countries*, 1913. For Subsidies, see also Grosvenor S. Jones, *Government Aid to Merchant Shipping, Special Agents' Series, No.* 119, Department of Commerce, Washington, 1916.

CHAPTER XII

THE WORLD'S KEY INDUSTRY

For as much as we are not by ourselves sufficient to furnish ourselves with competent store of things needful for such a life as our nature doth desire, a life fit for the dignity of men, therefore to supply these defects and imperfections which are in us living single and solely by ourselves, we are naturally induced to seek communion and fellowship with others.

BISHOP HOOKER

WE have brought our story down to the verge of the Great War and there, on the whole, we must leave it. It would be merely impertinent to attempt to summarize in a few pages the maritime events of that great struggle, or to do justice to the quiet heroism of those hundreds of thousands of non-combatants of many nations who faced, day by day, the perils of mine and torpedo, in order that the peoples of the Allied countries might somehow be fed, and their armed forces provided with the means of continued resistance. It would be absurd to attempt to sum up, in the little space left to us, the contribution of carrying power to the victory of the Allies, or to discuss the merits and defects of that complicated mechanism of national and international control by which it was sought to adjust the flow of supplies to the demands and exigencies of the war.

It would be absurd, and it would also be irrelevant; for in the history of the world's shipping industry even the Great War was but an episode. We are concerned only with its ultimate effects upon the industry, and of these no adequate account can yet be given, because they are still taking shape. Only when the political and economic structure of society, so badly shaken by the war, shall have settled into some sort of equilibrium, shall we be able to distinguish clearly between the temporary and the permanent effects of the great upheaval and say in what the new order differs from the old.

Yet there are some tendencies set in motion or reinforced by the war of which a word must be said here; not merely because of their intrinsic importance, but because they are so closely connected by the chain of cause and effect with the developments of the past, that the record of those developments would be incomplete without them.

We must say something, in the first place, of the war's effects in intensifying international competition in the business of shipowning, and of the change which it has brought about in the relative position of the world's fleets. We may confine our examination to steam and motor tonnage; for although the war undoubtedly hastened the disappearance of the sailing vessel from the ocean trade routes, the part played by sailing vessels in the carriage of the world's commerce was already insignificant in 1914.

Despite the appalling destruction of shipping during the war (amounting, including sailing vessels, to between 12,000,000 and 13,000,000 tons gross), the world's total tonnage in June 1919 was actually greater, and by June 1920, much greater than in 1914. The main factor in this rapid recovery from war losses was the enormous shipbuilding programme embarked upon by the United States after their entry into the war; partly in response to the frantic appeal of the Allies for assistance and partly in the hope of regaining their old position in the carrying trade. There were, however, other causes at work. In the endeavour to bring replacements up to the level of losses, British shipyards had been largely extended, with Government assistance, during the last two years of the war, and the shipbuilding facilities in many other countries had also been enlarged. The expansion of the Japanese shipyards had been stimulated both by orders from the British Government, and by the enterprise of Japanese shipowners, who found in war conditions an excellent opportunity of extending their activities in the Eastern and Pacific trades. In Europe, many neutral countries had suffered heavy losses, and being unable as in normal times to place orders with British builders or to purchase ships second-hand, they naturally turned to the development of their own shipyards.

In all, it has been calculated that the shipbuilding capacity of the world was multiplied about two and a half times as the result of the war, and for some years this capacity was very freely used. The war had impressed on all peoples the national importance of carrying power, and, especially in countries which had been hard hit by the withdrawal of British shipping during the war from trade between foreign ports, shipowners received every encouragement from public opinion and from their Governments, not merely to replace their losses but to increase their fleets. A short-lived boom in freights during 1919–1920 had the usual result of stimulating construction, and the transfer of enemy tonnage to the Allies under the Reparations scheme acted as a further stimulus; for while the German ships continued to run under other flags, the German companies hastened to build up their fleets anew.

The results were really rather ridiculous. By June 1920, the effective ocean-going tonnage at the disposal of traders had increased by about 14 per cent., while the volume of trade to be carried had greatly diminished, owing to the economic dislocation caused by the war. The natural result was that the *post-bellum* boom in freights was followed, in the summer of 1920, by the beginning of the worst and longest continued slump in the history of shipping. Year after year, private shipping companies passed their dividends or paid them only out of accumulated reserves. Year after year, the taxpayers of the United States, Australia, and Canada, had to make good the colossal losses incurred by the lines acquired by their Governments at inflated prices during and immediately after the war. In many other countries, only the support given by the State, in the form of subsidies and bounties, enabled the shipowners to balance their accounts.

Even this did not stop the increase in the world's tonnage. It is an amazing paradox that years in which more voyages were run at a loss than at a profit, and in which millions of tons of shipping were laid up for lack of employment should have seen a steady growth in fleets.

In one trade, and in one only, the explanation may be found in a genuine demand. The enormous increase in the world's consumption of petroleum since the war has afforded a real economic justification for the increase of the world's tanker fleets from about a million and a quarter to about nine million tons; for the tanker is the only ship which can carry oil in bulk, and as she can carry (with a few exceptions such as whale oil and molasses) no other form of cargo, she does not come into competition with ordinary traders.

As regards liners and cargo boats of ordinary type, the increase in tonnage may be partially accounted for in two ways. Under conditions of exceptionally severe international competition, only new and efficient ships can hope to earn profits; hence owners have been compelled to build. At the same time, they have been reluctant to scrap ships built or acquired at inflated prices during the war, and this reluctance has kept on the registers much laid-up tonnage composed of obsolescent vessels, or of American ships hastily and badly constructed under the Emergency Programme, none of which are ever likely to take the sea again. When all is said, however, the main cause of the growth in tonnage has been the doctrines of that revived economic nationalism which regards it as better to lose money in doing a thing uneconomically for yourself, than to pay someone else a fair price to do it for you, while you get on with your own job.

British shipowners may fairly claim that they have little share of responsibility for this unwarranted expansion. The tonnage under the British flag has increased only by a small percentage, and the increase is almost wholly accounted for by the growth of the tanker fleets. British owners, at least, have not hesitated to scrap obsolescent tonnage, and while the percentage of ships under ten years old is higher under the British flag than for the world at large, the British percentage of tonnage over 25 years old is only 8·3 per cent. as against a world average of 17·0 per cent. The result has been, as shown in the table on p. 297, to diminish substantially the British percentage of the world's shipping, but it is certain that neither the British percentage of ships employed and employable, nor the share of British ships in the carriage of the world's trade has diminished to the same extent.

Postponing for the moment any further consideration of the problem of surplus tonnage in its broader aspects, we may turn to the effects of the war on the composition of the British Mercantile Marine. Heavy as were the losses among all classes of ships, they were particularly heavy in the tramp fleets; comparatively slow ships, of which a large proportion were engaged in specially dangerous trades, such as the Mediterranean coal and ore traffic. On the other hand, the liner companies, having their fixed services to maintain, were under a special compulsion to make good their losses. Many tramp steamers were purchased during the war, to be run as cargo liners, and after the war it was the liner companies, with their more definite commitments and larger accumulated resources, who were the quicker to renew their fleets by purchase and new construction.

The prolonged slump which began in the summer of 1920 tilted the balance still further in favour of the lines; for the regular services were able to take care of a large proportion of the diminished volume of cargoes on offer. The decline in coal exports from Great Britain hit tramp-owners particularly hard, since it was mainly to the coal shipments from the Tyne and Bristol Channel that the tramps looked for their outward cargoes.

GROSS TONNAGE OF STEAM AND MOTOR SHIPS RECORDED IN LLOYD'S REGISTER BOOK

	1,000 Tons		Percentage of Total	
	1914	1931	1914	1931
United Kingdom ..	18,892	20,194	41·6	29·4
British Dominions ..	1,632	2,933	3·6	4·3
Total British ..	20,524	23,127	45·2	33·7*
U.S.A. Sea	2,027	10,356	4·4	15·1
U.S.A. Great Lakes and Philippines ..	2,303	2,536	5·1	3·7
Total American ..	4,330	12,892	9·5	18·8
German	5,135	4,226	11·3	6·1
Norwegian	1,957	4,062	4·3	5·9
French	1,922	3,513	4·3	5·1
Japanese	1,708	4,276	3·8	6·2
Italian	1,430	3,274	3·1	4·8
Dutch	1,472	3,111	3·2	4·5
Other Flags	6,926	10,242	15·3	14·9
Grand Total ..	45,404	68,723	100·0	100·0
Tankers, included above				
British	683	2,945	—	—
Others	562	6,079	—	—

* In 1931 the British percentage excluding tonnage on the Great Lakes was 34·5 per cent. (United Kingdom 30·6 per cent.). In tonnage of ships under ten years old the Empire percentage was 44·8 per cent.; in tonnage of ships of 8,000 tons gross and over 42·1 per cent.; in number of ships of 12 knots and upwards 46·1 per cent.

As the slump progressed, many liners, as well as tramps, found their way to the long rows of laid-up ships which furnished concrete and melancholy evidence of the severity of the depression; but in those dreary queues of the unemployed the tramps predominated. In 1930 the tonnage, other than tankers, on U.K. Register was probably divided about fifty-fifty between tramps and liners; but in the tonnage actually employed in trade the liner percentage was almost certainly higher.

In the liner trades themselves, the war had accentuated the tendency to combination already noticed. When fleets had been seriously depleted by war losses or by the requisitioning of vessels for war purposes, the merger of two lines in the same trade or the absorption of an independent line by one of the big combines was often the most effective means of enabling a regular service to be maintained, and economizing on the heavy overhead charges of the branch and agency organization. Many well-known flags disappeared finally from the seas; other lines, maintaining their identity and separate management, passed under the financial control of one or other of the leading groups. The depression in the shipping industry after the war and the pronounced general tendency to the formation of big industrial units have favoured a continuance of this policy of consolidation, and while it would involve heavy research work to trace all the ramifications of interlocking interests between lines nominally independent, it would probably be safe to say that about a quarter of the tonnage on the Register of the United Kingdom has been controlled more or less directly, since the war, by one or other of the "Big Five"—the P. & O., Royal Mail, Cunard, Ellerman, and Furness Withy Groups.

How far this tendency will prove permanent, it is impossible to say. Many of the mergers effected at inflated values, during and immediately after the war, left the controlling companies saddled with a heavily watered capital which has handicapped them severely during the subsequent depression; and apart from this, there are those that believe that the big combines, built up by men who had learned their business in a school of unrestricted competition, will prove too big and unwieldy for their successors, and may ultimately split up into smaller, though still substantial units.

Another tendency which the war strongly reinforced was that towards closer organization of the shipping industry as a whole. Opinions differ as to the merits and defects of the elaborate machinery of State Control erected during the war; there can be very little dispute as to the advantage which the Government, the Admiralty, and the Shipping Controller derived from the co-operation of the Liner Conferences, and of the great representative bodies through whom they could negotiate with the whole body of shipowners, and from whom they could receive advice based on the pooled experience of the industry. One of the results of the war has been to establish a much closer contact between the Chamber of Shipping and the Liverpool Steam Ship Owners' Association. To-day, a proposed change in load-line regulations, a suggested alteration in the form of shipping documents, or an allegation that trade is being hampered by excessive port charges in the United Kingdom entails, almost automatically, the appointment of a joint Committee of the Chamber and the Liverpool Association, and on broad questions of shipping policy their united influence is generally decisive.

In this, as in many other respects, the war merely quickened and strengthened tendencies already at work; but in the relations between the organized employers and employed it brought about a revolutionary change. To the seamen, the war brought, in its immediate or ultimate consequences, a very much higher standard of accommodation on all new ships, inclusion in the Unemployment

Insurance Scheme, a general improvement of working conditions, and at least the beginnings of a pension fund. These improvements were in part the result of a quickened public interest in the Merchant Navy, brought about by a sudden realization of the national dependence on those who "do their business in the Great Waters." A still bigger factor was the birth of a better spirit in the industry itself. There were times when relations between the two sides were very severely strained, for to the various bones of contention existing in 1914, there were added new grievances arising from the difficult conditions of the war itself. Fortunately, the seamen's representatives, led by Mr. Havelock Wilson, were resolved that "the nation's extremity should not be the seamen's opportunity," and their patriotic moderation was met by a corresponding spirit in their old opponents. On every question that arose with regard to the manning of the ships, representatives of the Shipping Federation and the National Sailors and Firemen's Union found themselves meeting in friendly conference, and the pressure of a common peril drew together in close co-operation the great bulk of those engaged in the industry—owners, officers, and men. The ultimate upshot was the creation, in 1917, of the National Maritime Board, reorganized on a permanent basis in 1919, as a governing body for the whole industry.

The National Maritime Board is composed of representatives of the two great shipowners' organizations and of all the various bodies representing the deck officers, engineers, and crews, with the exception of the Seafarers' Union, a minority organization of somewhat extremist tendencies. The functions of the Board embrace the prevention and adjustment of disputes, the fixing of standard wages and conditions for the whole industry (thus eliminating the old discrepancies between port and port), and the supervision of engagements; the supply of seamen and firemen being jointly controlled by the Shipping Federation and the National Union. On questions relating to any particular department of the service, the representatives of the officers or men concerned meet a shipowners' panel of equal numbers, and a system of District Boards and Port Consultants, also representative of both sides, provides for the carrying out of the Board's decisions and the settlement of local disputes.

Wages in shipping, as in other industries, soared during the war. They reached their peak in the autumn of 1918 when the A.B.'s wages stood at 290s. including war bonus, and they were maintained at this figure, as a consolidated wage, until the spring of 1921. The "real wage," allowing for the change in the purchasing power of money, was at its highest in the spring of 1919, when 290s. represented a wage of about 141s. 6d. at the old values. Unfortunately, the prolonged slump has deprived the seamen, in this respect, of all that he had gained; but it may be put to the credit of the National Maritime Board that the whole process of inflation and deflation has been accomplished without the disastrous conflicts and embittered sense of injustice which have proved so ruinous in other industries. It must be added that wages were maintained at a boom level long after the slump had set in, and that in 1924, when the outlook brightened for a moment, they were temporarily increased in anticipation of better times.

Improved working conditions, recognition of the Union, the right to a national standard wage, and the establishment of permanent machinery for conciliation and consultation represent to the seaman the lasting gains of the war. The officers have gained less in proportion, though the authorization of a standard uniform, and the appointment of H.R.H. the Prince of Wales as Master of the Merchant Navy imply a welcome advance in status. Behind all these things there lies an intangible, but not therefore less important, change in outlook and attitude which has found expression for example, in the co-operation of educational authorities, of many leading shipowners, and of the National Union in the work of the Seafarers' Education Service—an organization formed in 1919 for the purpose of providing libraries on board merchant ships, available both to the officers and the men, and of encouraging and directing reading and study afloat. The work of the Service is still in its infancy, but it has already proved an unqualified success in relieving the tedium of long voyages, in providing opportunities for self-advancement, and in developing a spirit of self-respect. It finds its place in this history because nothing could show better the change in the general status of the seaman. Before the war few people would have thought of offering "Merchant Jack" anything better than pornography or tracts. To-day, in many ships, he has ample opportunities to make acquaintance with science, history, poetry, and first-class fiction, and he avails himself of them with enthusiasm and discrimination.

For a recovery in wage rates and a further improvement in conditions, the seaman must look mainly to international developments. The revival of prosperity in the shipping industry depends upon a revival of world trade, and the industry itself is so largely international in its operations that there are very definite limits to what any one country can do either in facilitating the conduct of the business or in raising its social standards.

In shipping policy, as elsewhere, the war has given birth to two violently conflicting tendencies—the revival of economic nationalism and the growth of a movement towards international co-operation. The future of the shipping industry in this and in all countries will depend upon which of these forces ultimately triumphs.

It was the spirit of nationalism rather than socialistic theories which inspired the acquisition during the war by the American, Australian, and Canadian Governments, of State-owned merchant ships. They have now got rid or are fast getting rid of them, and the Soviet Government alone, consistently with its principles, is definitely pledged to the State ownership of merchant shipping.

It would be unfair to draw a general moral as to the efficiency of State trading from the failure of these experiments. The United States Shipping Board and the Commonwealth Government came into the business when costs of construction were so extravagantly high that it required a continuance of abnormal freights to earn profits or even to cover the depreciation of the fleets. Most private companies formed at or about the same time went into liquidation during the early years of the great slump. Yet it may fairly be said that shipping is an industry to which the rigidity and departmentalism which seem to be inseparable from State ownership are peculiarly unsuited. It may be added that in no other industry is State ownership likely to give rise to so many occasions of international friction. A rate war between two lines, or the arrest of a ship in a foreign port, either in the course of legal proceedings or for failure to comply with local regulations, will inevitably attract much more attention and arouse much stronger resentment when public vessels are concerned.

The main objection to State ownership, however, lies in the ever-present temptation to run services at uneconomic rates and cast the resultant loss upon the national exchequer; either for political reasons or in response to the clamour of mercantile interests for low freights. The competition of such ships is grossly unfair to shipowners who are competing solely on the intrinsic merits of their services, and in the long run it is definitely injurious to world trade. It destroys, in large measure, the incentive to efficiency in the shipping services themselves, and it tends inevitably to burden the world's resources with the cost of maintaining and operating surplus and obsolescent tonnage, for the existence of which there is no real economic justification.

The same objection applies, in only slightly lesser degree, to all forms of general subsidy. There may be particular cases in which grants in aid are justified, for the purpose of encouraging experiment or providing adequate communications for the development of a backward territory; but every ship which is built, as a result of subsidies, in excess of the world's actual tonnage requirements, assists to depress the general level of earnings, and becomes ultimately a burden on the world's commerce.

Still stronger is the objection to measures of flag discrimination. An agitation which sprang up, after the war, for the revival, in some form, of the British Navigation Acts, was happily defeated; largely through the opposition of the shipowners themselves, who realized that any such step must invite reprisals which would be disastrous to an industry which could only prosper so long as its activities were world-wide. The objection to flag discrimination, however, goes deeper than the interests of shipowners in any particular country. We have already seen that the supply of tonnage is adjusted to the seasonal and annual fluctuations of demand as between route and route, by the existence of a world pool of tonnage, composed of ships under all flags, and upon which shippers of all nations can draw. If the working of this tonnage pool is to be interfered with by reservation of trades to the national flag, quotas, differential dues, and all the other paraphernalia of discrimination, one (or both) of two results must follow. Either shippers will be continually handicapped by the absence of ready available and suitable tonnage of the only flag under which shipments may legitimately be made, or each State will be compelled to build up a reserve of tonnage in excess of its own normal needs, and unemployable except during a rush season. In either event ballast voyages will be multiplied and freights will rise to cover their cost.

It is sometimes proposed to apply the principles of the Navigation Acts to imports alone. That is a game at which both sides can play. Its logical outcome is a state of things in which every ship would sail empty on her outward passage.

Flag discrimination, in whatever form and however carefully applied, inevitably involves a waste of carrying power and a burden on the world's commerce. It involves also endless occasions of international strife. It is perfectly legitimate no doubt—whether it is wise is another question—for Governments to prevent their subjects from trading with foreigners by tariffs, quotas, or import and export prohibitions; but in so far as international trade is permitted at all, it must be admitted for what it is. A shipment of coal from Cardiff to Bordeaux is just as much "British Trade" as "French"; a shipment of pit-props from Bordeaux to Cardiff is just as much "French Trade" as "British." In either case buyer and seller are equally interested in the question of transportation, and neither the Government of the buyer nor the Government of the seller has any right to dictate the terms of transport. The ultimate objection to flag discrimination is that it is an attempt to assert national jurisdiction over an international traffic, and as such is bound, in the words of the Booth Committee on Shipping and Shipbuilding After the War, not merely "to hamper the natural flow of trade," but to "lead to endless quarrels among the maritime nations of the world."[1] The policy of the Navigation Acts was the outcome of conditions in which "Ships, Colonies, and Commerce" were alike regarded as the prizes of successful war, and it tended to perpetuate those conditions.

The Great War, happily, gave birth not only to the

[1] Cd. 9092, p. 110.

revived economic nationalism which inspired the proposal to revive the Navigation Acts, and the abortive American Ship Subsidy Bill of 1921[1], but to a new sense of the interdependence of nations and the necessity for economic co-operation, and the League of Nations Convention on Flag Discrimination has gone a long way to give effect to the Booth Committee's slogan: "Freedom of the seas, in the sense of equal treatment of all flags in all ports." British shipowners, indeed, have been among the warmest supporters of the League; but it must be remembered that, on its economic side at least, the creators of the League were only giving tardy political recognition to practical necessities which had already forced themselves upon traders and shipowners.

Shipping, as we have said, is an international business, and the business of shipping can only be effectively organized and controlled on an international basis. It is all very well, for instance, for road traffic to keep to the left in Great Britain and to the right on the Continent; but the risks of travel by sea would be greatly increased if the good old rule:

> Green to green, or red to red
> Perfect safety, go ahead.

were followed by some ships and reversed by others. Again, it is inconvenient, to say the least of it, if a ship has to comply with one set of regulations as regards load-line, deck-load, and safety appliances before she can leave her port of shipment, and with a different and contradictory code before she is allowed to enter her port of discharge. It bears hardly, too, on the shipowners of the more progressive countries, if they are put to heavy expense in providing a high standard of safety and accommodation, and are then

[1] Objectionable less from its subsidy proposals than by reason of its discriminatory clauses.

subjected to rate-cutting competition by owners whose Governments have a less exacting conscience.

The same difficulties arise on the purely business side of the industry. All ports are served by ships under many flags, and a single ship may serve ports in many countries. The parties to each individual transaction—the shipowner, ship broker, shipper, and consignee, the banker who finances the deal, and the underwriters who insure ship and cargo—may belong to three or four different nationalities. It is clearly desirable therefore that common forms of Charter-party, Bill of Lading, and Marine Insurance Policy shall be agreed upon, and that laws relating to such matters as shipowners' liability, collision, and salvage shall be as nearly as possible the same in all countries; the more so, because a ship is liable to arrest, and detention pending legal proceedings, in the ports of any country where an action may lie against her owners.

We have seen that, during the Middle Ages, the inconveniences arising from conflicting laws and jurisdictions were overcome, to a great extent, by the growth of a large body of widely accepted customary law, and its incorporation in local codes. The fierce nationalism of the seventeenth and eighteenth centuries obliterated most of these customary codes, and the nineteenth century was surprisingly slow to put anything in their place. It is somewhat of a shock to find that it was not until 1857 that an International Code of Signals was adopted, and not until 1862 that the nations were able to agree on an International Rule of the Road for shipping. For even the draft of a Convention on Safety of Life at Sea the world had to wait until 1914.

During the thirty years or so which immediately preceded the war, shipowners, underwriters, and business men had done a good deal to straighten out the tangle. In many trades a common form of shipping documents had been hammered out by negotiation between organizations representing the shipowners and traders of the various countries concerned. Some progress had been made—thanks very largely to the efforts of the International Maritime Committee—in the unification of laws relating to maritime contracts. In particular, codes relating to collision and salvage had been adopted by all or nearly all the leading shipowning countries. In other instances, international codes for which no legislative sanction was sought or obtained, had been voluntarily accepted by the interests concerned, and embodied, by reference, in the standard forms of contract. An early and very important example of this process was the adoption in the eighteen-seventies of the York–Antwerp Rules for the Adjustment of General Average Claims.

This tendency towards international regulation of the shipping industry has become much stronger since the war International Conventions have been concluded dealing with safety regulations and appliances, load-lines, helm orders, and the carriage of goods by sea. Other codes relating to such matters as shipowners' liability, and maritime mortgages and liens, have been drafted by the International Maritime Committee. The International Labour (Seamen's) Conference, held at Genoa in 1920, came to agreement with regard to the minimum age for employment afloat (fixed at 14 years), unemployment insurance, compensation to shipwrecked seamen, and other matters of social welfare. The value of the work done by the League of Nations in its Conventions on Freedom of Transit and Maritime Ports has already been emphasized.

There is still a great deal to be done, and there has been much bitter criticism by British shipowners of the long delays in ratifying and giving legislative effect to the Conventions already signed. There can be little doubt, however, that this tendency to international co-operation in the regulation of shipping represents the line of future progress;

for it springs from the conditions and the necessities of the industry itself. Its strength has been shown not only by the conclusion of formal international conventions, but by such developments as the closer co-operation between the great Classification Societies, and the formation of Branch Committees of Lloyd's Register in some of the principal maritime countries abroad. It has been shown, above all, by the work of the International Shipping Conference, comprising representatives of all important associations of shipowners throughout the world. The Conference was originally called together, in 1921, on the initiative of the Chamber of Shipping and the Liverpool Steam Ship Owners' Association. Its discussions proved so fruitful that a permanent organization was set up to prepare the ground for future meetings, and to the Conference and its Committees much of the success recently attained in the international regulation of shipping must, in fairness, be ascribed.

The dream of an international wage scale, which was discussed in some quarters during the years immediately after the war, is likely to remain a dream so long as standards of life and shore wages remain so widely different in the leading maritime countries. There are greater immediate possibilities in the improvement, by international agreement, of general working conditions; but it is doubtful whether much advance can be made until some measure of prosperity shall have been restored to the industry as a whole. That, as has been said, can come in full measure only from a revival of world trade; but the restoration of prosperity might be hastened and the burden of the present slump might be more easily borne, if some agreement could be arrived at as to the scrapping of surplus tonnage, the removal of such restrictions as still exist on the employment of the most convenient ship irrespective of her flag, and the removal or limitation of artificial stimulants to new construction or the retention of obsolescent vessels. There are many obstacles to the carrying out of such a programme: not merely in national policies and prejudices but in the intensely competitive character of the industry itself, and its strongly individualistic traditions. Yet it is easier, perhaps, to conceive of such a programme to-day then it would have been to conceive of an International Shipping Conference fifty years ago.

It is fitting that this brief record should close on a note of international co-operation; for it has been the task of the shipping industry, all through its long history, to act as the chief factor in the unification of the world. The lure of conquest, the greed of plunder, and the mere restless impulse to make trial of the unknown, all played their part in the development of the ship; but the shipping industry proper owes its birth to the discovery that an adequate supply of those oversea products which added to the convenience, comfort, and enjoyment of life, could be better assured by trade than by robbery—and trade implies giving as well as taking.

With every step forward in material civilization there came a corresponding increase in the number of things esteemed "needful," in Bishop Hooker's words, "for such a life as our nature doth desire, a life fit for the dignity of man"; and in the search for these needful things the sea-traders were driven to push out further and further into unknown seas, establishing trading relations between peoples sundered by impassable land barriers or by hundreds of miles of tossing waters, and opening the way to an exchange of ideas—political, social, and religious—as well as an exchange of products. The new contacts thus formed gave plentiful occasions for the display of human perversity, and trade and battle too often went hand in hand; but at least the contacts were established. To fight your neighbour is one step nearer to loving him than not to know of his existence.

Thus every seafarer who carried his own goods or another's to a foreign country and brought back a cargo in exchange, was doing something to build up the prosperity and the culture of his own land and of the land he visited; but almost from the first there were nations with special facilities or special aptitudes for the building and operation of ships, who found their profit in the service of the world at large. The Phoenicians in ancient times, the Venetians and Hanseatics in the Middle Ages, the Dutch in the seventeenth century, and the English in the eighteenth were very far from being altruists; they sought only their own profit; they were ready to fight and intrigue without scruple in order to force as much as possible of the world's trade through their own ports, and preserve for themselves a monopoly in its carriage; but they could not help contributing, half unwillingly, and half unconsciously, to the growth in wealth and civilization of all the countries between whom they carried goods.

Their services to the world remain; their monopolies vanished one by one, broken down, mostly, by rivals whom their own services as general carriers had helped on the path to full national development. The last to survive—the partial monopoly conferred by the British Navigation Acts—was voluntarily relinquished when it became clear that it could no longer be maintained in a world to which the utmost freedom of sea transport had become not merely desirable but necessary.

In fulfilling the needs of men, shipping has helped to multiply them, and its work to-day is not merely to provide a more plentiful supply of "things needful for such a life as nature doth desire," but to assure to hundreds of millions of people the necessities of bare existence. The growing tendency to international organization of the shipping industry itself is but a reflection of the part which it has played in bringing about those conditions of economic interdependence which are slowly teaching the nations that they must co-operate or perish.

If too little has been said in this book about the seamy side of shipping—the horrors of the slave trade, the foul conditions of the early emigrant traffic, the callous indifference too often shown to the welfare of the men who manned the ships—it is not from any deliberate desire to ignore these things, or to minimize them. The shipping industry, like other industries, has many things in its past of which to be ashamed, and some things which it has still to put right. Yet in painting on so small a canvas, it is perhaps the truest perspective which keeps our eyes fixed mainly on that astonishing record of enterprise and achievement, of restless feeling-out after new forms of activity, and of constant adaptation and adjustment to ever-increasing needs, by which the World's Key Industry has played its part in the progress of mankind.

SOME BOOKS ON THE PERIOD

Those who wish to know what merchant seamen achieved and suffered in the war will find the story in *The Merchant Navy*, by Sir Archibald Hurd, 3 vols., London, 1921–1929. *Merchantmen-at-Arms*, by David W. Bone, new ed. London, 1929, tells, very vividly, how the war looked to a ship-master. *National Service of British Seamen*, 1914–1919, by Father Hopkins, London, 1920, should be consulted for wages, conditions, and the setting up of the National Maritime Board. Of two books by the present writer, *Seaborne Trade*, 3 vols., London, 1920–1924, is concerned with shipping during the war from the point of view of the Allied supply system; *The War and the Shipping Industry*, London, 1927, is concerned with the effect of the war on the industry itself, and carries the tale down to the beginnings of the great slump in 1920. The *Report of the Committee on Shipping and Shipbuilding after the War*, Cd. 9092, 1918, is invaluable to students, especially on questions of shipping policy.

INDEX

NOTE.—All references to individual ships are grouped under "Ships, names of," and to individual lines under "Lines, Shipping." For Dutch Shipping, French Shipping, etc., see under names of countries. Names of places only incidentally mentioned and covered by such general headings as "Hansa," "Ports," "Trade Routes," are not separately indexed.

Index

For Product Safety Concerns and Information please contact our EU representative GPSR@taylorandfrancis.com Taylor & Francis Verlag GmbH, Kaufingerstraße 24, 80331 München, Germany